TALES OF
THE FOREIGN SETTLEMENTS
IN
JAPAN

By the same author:

SHADES OF THE PAST or INDISCREET
TALES OF JAPAN

FOREIGNERS IN MIKADOLAND

Tales of the
FOREIGN SETTLEMENTS
in
JAPAN

by

HAROLD S. WILLIAMS

Decorations by

JEAN WILLIAMS

CHARLES E. TUTTLE COMPANY
Rutland, Vermont & Tokyo, Japan

Representatives
Continental Europe: BOXERBOOKS, INC., *Zurich*
British Isles: PRENTICE-HALL INTERNATIONAL, INC., *London*
Australasia: PAUL FLESCH & CO., PTY. LTD., *Melbourne*
Canada: M. G. HURTIG LTD., *Edmonton*

Published by the Charles E. Tuttle Company, Inc.
of Rutland, Vermont & Tokyo, Japan
with editorial offices at
Suido 1-chome, 2-6, Bunkyo-ku, Tokyo, Japan

© *1958 by Charles E. Tuttle Co., Inc.*

Library of Congress Catalog Card No. 58-11101

International Standard Book No. 0-8048-1051-6

First edition, 1958
First paperback edition, 1972

0221-000294-4615
PRINTED IN JAPAN

*Affectionately
dedicated
to
my wife and children
but for whose frequent absences from home
this book
could not have been written*

"They are more warlike and valiant than the Chinese; ...the Countrie men are strong and valiant and for much labour."

Antonio de Herrera, 1601

"The people of this Iland of Japan are good of nature, courteous above measure and valiant in warre."

Will Adams, 1611

"And have an especial care not to trust any man with Companies goods without making ready payment, for I am informed these country people are not to be trusted."

Richard Cocks, 1613

"The people are generally courteous, affable and full of compliments... They feed not much upon varietie..."

Rev. Arthur Hatch, 1625

"...always excepting the officials and our servants...the behaviour of the Japanese from the meanest countryman up to the greatest prince or lord is such that the whole empire might be called a school of civility and good manners."

Dr. Engelbert Kaempfer, 1693

"There is a certain Antipathy between them and the Chinese, they cannot bear with one another."

Christopher Fryke, 1700

"There is a mighty difference between this England, talking about liberty, or cherishing free trade, and Dai Nippon, in which not a soul does as he pleases..."

Charles Dickens *"Household Words,"* 1851

"Of all heathen nations I have ever heard described, I think this is the most lewd."

Rev. Samuel Wells Williams,
Chief Interpreter with Perry, 1854

"We were all much pleased with the appearance and manners of the Japanese. I repeat they are superior to any people east of the Cape of Good Hope."

Townsend Harris' Diary, 1856

"The Japanese are the least interesting people in all the world— about on a level with the Feejees of the South Seas or the Esquimaux of the northern continent."

American Whig Review, XV, (1858)

PREFACE

Most of the articles in this book originally appeared in *The Mainichi* newspaper during the years 1953 to 1957 in a series entitled *Shades of the Past*. Since then they have been expanded and largely re-written.

With the exception of some phantasy and imagination which may have entered into some of the stories in the second portion of the book, all are considered to be historically accurate in every detail.

Japanese names are customarily written with the family name (corresponding to our surname) followed by the given name (corresponding to our Christian name). This is the order that I have attempted to maintain, but in some cases I have reversed the names and followed the order by which the person is generally known to Westerners.

For obvious reasons Japanese words have been reproduced in the form familiar to most Westerners —the rational Romanised form known as the Hepburn System—such as, for example, *Fuji-San* (Mount Fuji) rather than the Japanese official but eccentric form where the same word is reproduced as *Huzi-San*, which travellers are expected to recognise and pronounce as *Fuji-San*, but never do. Indeed many English-reading Japanese cannot recognise *Huzi-San* as being their beloved mountain. In a few exceptional cases, alternative or Anglicised forms have been used, for example—ricksha or rickshaw for *rikisha,* which is the contraction of the greater mouthful, *jinrikisha.*

Although Japanese nouns have no plural form, I have for the convenience of non-Japanese readers and for clarity of meaning, in some instances such as *Shogun* and *Tokugawa,* treated them as subject to English laws of grammar, and used a plural form of *Shoguns* and *Tokugawas.* In doing so, I hope I shall be forgiven by the purists.

If my use of capitals appears excessive and irritating to some readers, I can only plead that long residence in Japan may have caused me to fall into the custom of using capitals when mentioning various institutions and personages that might elsewhere pass in small letters. Indeed in pre-war days one risked the charge of lese majesty to write the name of anyone connected with the Imperial Household without capitals.

Grateful acknowledgements are made to my wife for the decorations, to Mr. Paul C. Blum for making available from his collection of Japanese prints a rare picture for reproduction on the jacket of this book and to Mr. F.D. Burrows and Mr. J.T. Helm for furnishing photographs.

H. S. WILLIAMS

SHIOYA, JAPAN

CONTENTS

THE FOREIGN SETTLEMENTS IN JAPAN

Contents

STRANGE TALES

ILLUSTRATIONS

(Following page 176)

13

Illustrations

PLATE VII.   Premises of International Club (later to be known as Kobe Club) at 79 Kyo-machi, Kobe, until about 1875, when the club moved into premises near Recreation Ground. In 1879 the Club Concordia (German Club) occupied the premises at 79 Kyo-machi. (Courtesy of J.T. Helm, Esq.)

PLATE VIII.   The Foreign Concession, Kawaguchi, Osaka, during the Meiji era, from an old woodblock print.

14

THE FOREIGN SETTLEMENTS
IN
JAPAN

THE
FIRST
BRITISH
CONSUL

Then there came forth from the crowd a man of about fifty years of age, who wept, and hopped about like a sparrow, and, sending forth a loud voice cried 'Yapanisu,' 'Yapanisu,' meaning men of Nippon.

Japanese account of reception at Dover, 1862

There are not many foreign women who can claim that their portrait has been pirated by the Japanese and used on the labels of *sake* bottles. Certainly the first who could make claim to that doubtful honour was Mrs. C. Pemberton Hodgson, wife of the first British Consul in Nagasaki.

According to the consul *"the portrait is hideous and as much like the original as a butterfly to a salamander."*

* * * * * * * *

On 18 June, 1859, H.M.S. "Sampson," carrying Queen Victoria's first consular representatives to Japan, arrived at Nagasaki for the purpose of disembarking Consul Hodgson. The vessel then proceeded to Yokohama with Consul-General Alcock, the same who, unable to approve of the financial dealings of many of the early foreign merchants in Yokohama, was banned from the Yokohama Club for having dubbed the foreign community *"the scum of the earth."*

Concerning Nagasaki, however, Consul Hodgson was the first British Consul to open a consulate in Japan and so he achieved the distinction of hoisting the first Union Jack over a consulate in Japan.

It may be recalled that over two hundred years earlier Will Adams had unofficially and without authority, as others have done since, flown his country's flag in Japan, but in those days the Union Jack had not yet come into being, and it was the Cross of St. George that Will Adams unfurled.

Mrs. Hodgson, who arrived with her husband, was in all probability the first British woman to come to Japan. The Governor of Nagasaki very kindly sent a gift of welcome, comprising a little fat round pig, a basket of *daikon,* a basket of garlic, and four hundred eggs. The unpacking of such articles upon the spotlessly clean quarter-deck of one of Her Majesty's ships created quite a sensation. The midshipmen sniggered in the background, but the deck-officer nearly had a fit.

Mrs. Hodgson was the first British female resident in Japan, and until she and her Chinese cook had mastered the difficulties of foreign housekeeping in what was then a very strange country, the family had to live mainly on omelettes.

The consulate was located in a Buddhist temple, and the first despatch which the Consul addressed to his superiors was to ask that *"a few chairs, two tables and a large cupboard in which to deposit the consular papers and books"* be provided. There is some reason therefore, to believe that the first consular business was transacted on the floor with the consular records reposing on the *tatami*.

His second despatch served to acknowledge due receipt of some consular stationery and an iron safe.

The third despatch acknowledged receipt of five boxes of treasure containing 4800 clean Mexican dollars which were promptly placed in the iron safe. The dollars were referred to as "clean" because in those days some people used to buy, at cheap prices, chipped, light-weight, or inferior Mexican dollars, which they then endeavoured to palm off on the unwary. That, in fact, was one of the many rackets in which the Chinese compradores made a steady profit.

His fourth despatch, only three lines, makes dull reading because it merely acknowledges receipt of official correspondence from his superiors. But thereafter there are items of interest in most of his despatches during the few months he was stationed in Nagasaki.

Such well-known names as Dent & Co., Jardine & Co., and Keswick dotted his letters. There is mention of Frazer's Store, probably the first foreign-owned retail store in Japan, outside of Chinese establishments.

Much of the Consul's time, during the three months he was at Nagasaki, was devoted to the problem of selecting a suitable site for the future Foreign Settlement, a subject on which he wrote no less than twenty-five letters to the Governor, receiving in return only two satisfactory replies, *"the remainder being equivocal and unsatisfactory."*

19

The First British Consul

In those days in Nagasaki, as in other large cities of Japan, there were a number of barrier gates, which in the event of crimes or disturbances could be closed, thus isolating one section of the city from another. There were several such gates before the approach to the Governor's residence and finally an entrance similar to that of better class Japanese residences to-day, comprising a large door and a smaller door at the side. The large door was thrown open for the Governor or other Japanese of rank, whilst lesser folk, and the foreign consuls, were required to enter with a stoop through the smaller door, at least that was so until a Russian or an American officer (history is uncertain as to which) kicked at the main door until it was opened! Thereafter the main door was thrown open for consuls. Consul Hodgson had a great regard for the dignity of the Japanese officials, but he rightly stood firm when any lack of respect was shown to the dignity of his own office. One night when returning home, he met the Vice-Governor proceeding in the opposite direction with a numerous suite of armed men, who demanded that he give up the whole street to His Excellency. During the ensuing discussion the consul offered to give up one half of the road but no more. The Vice-Governor accepted the proposition, although his suite of two-sworded samurai looked very fierce and displeased with the arrangement.

Japanese official visitors to the Consulate were frequent and were liable to descend upon the Consul at inconvenient hours—

...*coming in at all times, disturbing us at break-*

The First British Consul

*fast and dinner, even remaining until ten o'clock
at night....*

*Pipes or cigars, tea, sherry and cakes were always
offered our visitors, until it became so expensive,
that tea alone was offered, unless to the governor
or vice-governor.*

When Hodgson arrived in Nagasaki he found
fifteen square-rigged foreign vessels already in the
harbour waiting to pick up cargoes as soon as the
port was opened for trade. He commiserated with
the Japanese officials at being suddenly called upon
to handle export trade on such a scale, and he spoke
with thinly veiled contempt for the methods of many
of the first foreign merchants, whom he referred to
as *"greedy vultures"* and *"unscrupulous specimens of
all nations."*

The treaties specified that the Japanese should exchange foreign currency for Japanese currency on
the basis of weight for weight, but they made no
mention of the amount. The Japanese authorities,
fearful of the consequences of opening the country
to foreign trade, sought to restrict trade with the
newcomers by fixing the maximum amount to be exchanged.

Language was a constant difficulty in most
negotiations, but when it came to discussions as to
the interpretation of the treaties or discovering
loopholes, the Consul found that the Japanese could
argue their case by reference to either the Japanese,
Dutch or English versions with equal ease!

On 1st July, 1859, the day that Nagasaki was
opened to international trade, Consul Hodgson sought

21

to obtain some Japanese currency in order to be able to make some local purchases:

I therefore went with some silver to the Treasury and as a great favour obtained change for twenty whole dollars. The representative of Jardine's was with me and he was favoured with five dollars worth of Japanese currency to trade with. In vain boxes of 1,000, 2,000, 3,000 and 4,000 dollars of the best Mexican silver were opened before the eyes of the Treasury officers, the Japanese government was poor, was willing, but could only exchange a certain limited amount daily, or its supply would speedily be exhausted.

Later the merchants were required to make application for the amount of Japanese currency that they required, which applications were granted to very limited amounts. It then became the practice for some foreigners to lodge applications for large amounts in the hope that they might at least receive a goodly portion. Some then lodged several applications often for fantastic amounts, using all manner of fictitious names, polite and otherwise.

Just as Consul-General Alcock was critical in Yokohama of the methods of some of the early foreign merchants, so also was Consul Hodgson. Said he:

Merchants, or men calling themselves so, owning only some thousand dollars, put down applications (to the Japanese Treasury) for millions under the gentlemanly names of 'Nonsense,' 'Snooks,' 'Jack Ketch,' 'Walker,' 'Brown,' 'Jones' and 'Robinson.' ...They asked from the treasury of Kanagawa, on the 2nd Nov., 1859, only four months after the

opening of the port, exchange for 1,200,666,778,244,
601,066,953 dollars!!!

During Hodgson's short stay in Nagasaki, one of
the most exciting news topics was that of a Frenchman who arrived as a round trip passenger on one
of Dent & Co.'s schooners. When the Frenchman left
he had in his cabin a number of souvenirs which had
attracted his fancy, including a Japanese mistress (a
professional, of course). It was not until the schooner
had departed that the secret leaked out. Then, instead
of all derisively bidding her "Hail and farewell," as
did the Japanese Press when one of her modern
counterparts left Japan, there was a great hullabaloo.

Actually the Frenchman's mistress had broken one
of the most rigid laws of Japan—a law which had
been in force for more than two hundred years. In
those days no Japanese was permitted to leave Japan
—not even if he had paid his income taxes—and if
any were so rash as to do so, the penalty was death.

The Governor arrested the girl's parents and put
them in prison to be kept there until the girl returned
to take her punishment. Rather than that they
should be left to die in prison, the Frenchman decided
to give up his butterfly, and an attempt was then
made to smuggle her back into Japan on the same
schooner. According to Sir Thomas Sutherland, later
Chairman of the P. & O. S. N. Co., who happened to
be travelling as a passenger on that vessel, much
secrecy surrounded the attempt but the girl nevertheless was captured.

Whilst it had not been possible to prevent foreigners
from coming into Japan, and while the Japanese

authorities were glad to see them depart again, no Japanese was then permitted to go abroad.

After a crowded three months in Nagasaki, Consul Hodgson was transferred to Hakodate where, except on the occasional visits of British ships, there were only two other British subjects, namely his wife and his young daughter. The demands on their time were few because, according to Hodgson, *"Hakodate, although nominally opened, was as hermetically sealed as in the days of the Portuguese,"* and the three thus had the time to travel extensively throughout the island of Hokkaido. And so it was that ninety-seven years ago, an Englishman, his wife, and young daughter, travelling mostly on horseback, visited many places in far-off Hokkaido, where foreigners occasionally go these days blandly imagining they are the first foreigners to visit such places.

Upon arrival at Hakodate, Consul Hodgson found *"the welcome much warmer than that experienced at Nagasaki."* The kindly Governor of Hakodate laid out the Japanese equivalent of a red carpet—a pathway of sand—upon which the Consul trod when walking from his horse to the hotel.

Despite the ill will which murderous *ronin* bore towards foreigners in those days, the Consul went unarmed, except for his court-sword, which badge of office would have been useless in attack or defence. The Governor, however, provided three guards, but wrote Hodgson:

I was soon obliged to part with them, as I discovered that they not only levied blackmail on all things introduced for sale, but were also faithful reporters of everything that occurred, however trifling, within the precints of the Consulate.

Hodgson returned to England in 1861 where he did his utmost to publicize the new found and little known country of Japan. But his wife's portrait continued to adorn the *sake* bottles for some years, until the Japanese brewers were able to discover another picture which they thought would prove even more inspiring to the tipplers of Nagasaki.

When the Embassy which the Tokugawa Government sent to Europe in 1862 arrived at Dover, the enthusiastic Mr. Hodgson was there to organize a great welcome and a "hip-hip-hooray" for them, and thereby, quite unwittingly, he was responsible for a rather bad impression which was created in the minds of the visiting Japanese dignitaries.

In those days the lords and nobles in Japan moved about at a dignified and slow measured tread in an abyssmal silence.

"Shita-ni-iro, Shita-ni iro" was the raucous order to all below the rank of samurai to kneel on the ground and to bend low when the Great Ones passed.

(The order *"Shita-ni-iro"* was largely forgotten until it became the prerogative of all members of the Japanese Army to bark at their adversaries.

It is in fact the memory of that order, which was barked so often, by so many, in so many places to the Australian prisoners-of-war, that is still holding apart the two countries.)

However, to return to Dover on that spring day in 1862, the following is a description by one of the Japanese visitors of the welcome:

The First British Consul

Then there came forth from the crowd a man of about fifty years of age, who wept, and hopped about like a sparrow, and, sending forth a loud voice cried 'Yapanisu,' 'Yapanisu,' meaning men of Nippon. This person came formerly as Consul to Hakodate and dwelt there; he is an Englishman; and now stepping forth from the crowd to congratulate our countrymen on their safe arrival, took off his hat, and holding it up in his hands, shouted in a loud voice 'Peyapeppe hore'—the meaning is not clear but it appears to be a congratulatory expression. Upon this, all united in the same sound with one voice. Thus they welcomed us, without ceasing, by shouting in a loud voice in a most unpleasant manner.

And so I close this chapter with the picture of an elderly Englishman excitedly rushing forward with hand outstretched to greet the first Japanese Embassy to Europe—an enthusiastic welcome from the first British Consul in Japan.

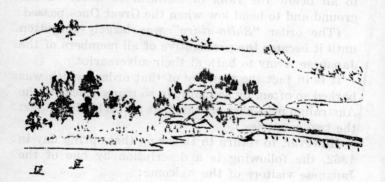

NAGASAKI DAYS

It is the opinion of merchants in Nagasaki that Yokohama is in many respects much better situated.... and will benefit accordingly until the opening of the port of Hyogo (Kobe) which will doubtless become the principal port of foreign trade.

British Consular report from Nagasaki, 1859

Before Yokohama was opened to trade on 1st July, 1859, it was just a small village of fishing huts, lying across the bay from the old post-town of Kanagawa. Similarly before Kobe was opened on 1st January, 1868, it was just a sandy waste with a few fishermen's huts nestling under the pine trees that lined the shore. Across the bay was the old town of Hyogo.

Nagasaki was opened on the same day as Yokohama, but the opening was a very different affair. Nagasaki had been a thriving centre of international trade for centuries. In the early years of the 17th century, at the heyday of its glory, there were at times ten or more foreign vessels tied up in the harbour and several hundred seamen on spree ashore. Then Japan closed her doors to all the outside world and expelled all the foreign merchants with the exception of the Dutch, who were confined to the island of Deshima in Nagasaki harbour, and the Chinese who were restricted to a compound on the edge of the harbour, where for over two hundred years they shared the same type of humiliation and restrictions as the Dutch. The Japanese officials extorted from the Dutch and the Chinese in presents and penalties the maximum amounts possible, whilst the latter both exercised their ingenuity in levelling the score by indulging in discreet private smuggling.

On 1st July, 1859, when Nagasaki was opened to trade, the Dutch and the Chinese were at liberty once more to conduct their trade as free merchants. No longer were the Dutch confined as prisoners within the fan-shaped island of Deshima—about two hundred and fifty yards in length and about three acres in area. However with the opening of the port, although the Dutch recovered their liberty and their pride, they lost their valuable monopoly of trade. The host of Japanese officials, through whom that trade had passed, were likewise faced with the loss of valuable concessions without any compensating advantages, and accordingly did everything possible to hinder the change-over.

Whilst the officials who controlled the trading operations at Nagasaki of the Dutch and the Chinese, viewed the opening of the port to foreign trade as a personal disaster, great benefits lay ahead for the mass of the people who were then living in much the same primitive conditions of more than a century earlier, the same primitive conditions as were described in the musty pages of Kaempfer. Most of the imports which had been brought in by the Dutch and the Chinese found their way into the palaces of the *shoguns* and the *daimyo*, or were utilised for the benefit of the privileged classes. Few of the imports brought in by the Dutch or the Chinese improved the lot of the common people, with perhaps the single exception of the highly prized but also highly priced Dutch vermifuge. That drug was then in great demand by the highest and the lowest in the land. It is of interest to recall that during the Pacific War when the doors of Japan were kept closed by Allied submarines, supplies of vermifuges could only enter Japan in a trickle. Consequently in 1945 when the Occupation opened the doors, one of the greatest demands was for santonin and other vermifuges, just as it had been in Nagasaki about eighty-six years earlier at the opening of that port to world trade.

The Chinese Trading Guild's share of the trade in Nagasaki had been considerable. They had acquired a monopoly in certain lines, and naturally they were not readily disposed to part with any of it to the foreign merchants who began to pour into Nagasaki, and so they threw in their lot with the Japanese officials in placing all manner of hindrances in the way of the newcomers crashing into their business.

In the face of all this it was not possible to open up international trade within a few days, as was done at Yokohama. For months, indeed for years, the consuls were busy writing blistering notes of protest to the Japanese authorities at the difficulties which were being placed in the way of trade. In the opening weeks there were fifteen ships in Nagasaki harbour waiting in vain to pick up return cargoes, which could not be obtained because of the efforts made by the officials to protect their concessions.

The Japanese merchants did not dare by-pass the officials by attempting to do business direct with the foreign merchants. Gradually, however, the transition came about, and thereafter Nagasaki was for many years a very important centre of Japan's overseas trade and also the principal coaling station in Japan for overseas vessels.

As in all the treaty ports, accommodation was the first problem that had to be solved.

The Dutch still had their quarters on Deshima, but the newly arrived merchants and traders were mostly lodged in small Japanese houses that had been temporarily adapted to European use and to serve as warehouses until a margin of the shallow sea-front had been reclaimed to form the site of the future foreign settlement.

The Dutch continued to rent Deshima until 1863, when they allowed the island to revert to the Japanese. Thereafter it was included in the new foreign settlement and various lots were sold under perpetual leases to individuals of all nationalities. Reclamation schemes eventually linked the tiny island to the shore. It became part of the mainland, and was known as Deshima-cho.

The British Consulate was located in a Japanese temple for five years until a suitable site on the sea front was available. For the first eighteen months all diplomatic correspondence was carried out with the Japanese in Dutch, that being the only European language sufficiently well-known to them.

During the first six months of trade, over fifty British trading vessels alone came into port, quite apart from a number of men-of-war. Nagasaki had also become a busy port during the winter months for whalers, mostly under the American flag, that came in to refit. At times there were as many as fifteen or more whalers in the harbour at one time.

When the whalers were in port, there was excitement ashore; the teahouses and saloons were busy, and the respective consuls were often very harassed men, rescuing their nationals from the clutches of the Japanese police, and protecting the Japanese public from the drink-crazed seamen.

In 1860, a year after the opening of the port, the population of Nagasaki was estimated at about 65,-000 of whom 100 were Europeans and about 450 Chinese. In January, 1861, the British community comprised 25 persons including merchants, shopkeepers, compradores, and one butcher. By 1864, there were over 200 British merchants in Nagasaki. Adding the other nationalities, the consular guards, and the men from the war-vessels in the harbour there were often as many as 7,000 foreigners on shore. Those were really the days when Nagasaki had a lucrative souvenir trade.

The imports at first were mainly cotton piece goods, manufactured goods and metals, whilst the exports were tea, silk, coal, vegetable wax, gall nuts, copper, gold coin, and various foodstuffs for the China market. Some raw cotton was also exported from Nagasaki, although Yokohama later took away most of that trade. In those days, as the population of Japan was only about 35 million, much of the land that is now necessary for the growing of rice and other foodstuffs was available for cotton fields. The surplus cotton was exported abroad, especially during the American Civil War when supplies from the Southern States were cut off. Indeed it was during that period that Japan actually exported raw cotton to the northern states of America.

Later as Japan became industrialised and the population increased, the cotton fields had to be converted to rice fields to produce food for the increased population, and raw cotton had then to be imported from the United States and other countries.

Every age seems to have its racket; and the racket then was tied up with the Chinese. The only persons who were permitted to land at the newly opened treaty ports were those nationals whose Governments had signed a treaty with Japan, except that servants were allowed in and remained under the protection of the consul of their employers. As China did not at that time have a treaty with Japan, the Chinese theoretically were barred from scrambling onto the bandwagon and participating in the great adventure of the opening of Japan. Many of the foreign adventurers who had come into Japan saw in this an easy opportunity of making a quick living. They rented houses in the Japanese quarter and made them available, for a substantial consideration, to Chinese posing as their servants. From those protected quarters the Chinese carried on all manner of clandestine gambling, trading and smuggling. The consuls found it extremely difficult to ascertain who were genuine servants and who were spurious. When the Settlement was eventually completed, the consuls

ordered those of their nationals who were living in
the Japanese town to take up residence within the
Settlement where they and their so-called servants
could be more effectively controlled. As was often
the case their orders were largely ignored, and it
required the threat of deportation to bring this state
of affairs to an end. That the lot of a consul in
Nagasaki in those days was not a happy one is amply
recorded by one consul, who, when appealing to the
British Minister in Yedo for an increase in salary,
wrote:—

> ....*some compensation more than bare subsist-*
> *ence is due, in consideration of an exile to the*
> *extremity of the earth, of banishment from society*
> *and from the relations of home, and exposure to*
> *discomforts and privations difficult to depict and*
> *cruel to endure. I say nothing of the climate, which*
> *is for some months in every year destructive to*
> *health, and even to property, or of the water we*
> *have to use, which at this port is so bad as to be*
> *almost poisonous. Neither do I dwell on the im-*
> *portant and harassing duties with which a Consul*
> *is entrusted.*

Considering the rather poor types of adventurers
among the earliest arrivals it is understandable that
the Consul found his duties harassing. Nor is it
surprising that many harsh things have been said
about the earliest foreign communities in Japan. The
Bishop of Hongkong was no exception, when, describing Nagasaki in 1860, he wrote that the first arrivals
were largely comprised of

> *the disorderly elements of California adventurers,*

33

Portuguese desperadoes, runaway sailors, piratical outlaws, and the moral refuse of European nations. In time many of those early arrivals drank themselves to death or otherwise departed from the scene. Some, with the passing of years, assumed a measure of respectability, but it was the presence of so many undesirables among the first arrivals that gave rise to the slur that was attached to the letters BIJ (born in Japan), a slur that some of the snobs in later and more respectable days were prone to throw around.

Costs of living were cheap and a person with a salary of 250 yen per month lived in a state of luxury. The chief amusement appears to have been horse-riding, walking, bowling, and drinking. The Nagasaki Club was formed about 1860. In 1862, the first church was erected, and a foreign jail a few years later, although the British Consulate did purchase a pair of handcuffs as early as September, 1859. The entry in the Consular cashbook simply reads *"$10 for a pair of handcuffs—much needed,"* but considering some of the types that the harassed consuls had to deal with, it is reasonable to assume that the entry was intended to read an *extra* pair of handcuffs! Owing to the ritual of drinking, business proceeded in slow motion time, but in any case there was no great hurry, except on mail days, because the nearest telegraph office was in Colombo.

When completed, the foreign settlement was found to be hot in summer because it missed the sea breezes, and so in later years the more important merchants in the Settlement built attractive residential bungalows on the hillside overlooking the harbour.

Nagasaki Days

The Nagasaki Foreign Settlement was at first controlled by a foreign municipal council, based on the system in force in Shanghai, but later with the number of foreign residents dwindling the responsibility had to be handed over to the Japanese Government. In Yokohama the system failed from the beginning because of the complete inability of the foreign consuls to agree with their nationals, or vice-versa. Only in Kobe was the foreign municipal council completely successful, and Kobe thus came to be known in the Far East as the Model Settlement.

At one time Japan's overseas trade was divided equally between Nagasaki and Yokohama, but when Kobe was opened in 1868, Nagasaki's eventual fate was sealed, and thereafter as trade grew, Yokohama at first, and later Kobe, forged ahead.

After the Russo-Japanese War, the prosperity of Nagasaki dipped sharply. Prior to that time it was a rendezvous for ships of the Russian Asiatic Squadron, and the wives and families of the Russian naval officers used to spend the winters there to escape the rigors of the Siberian climate. The Russians in those days lived high, spent freely, and added much to the gaiety and prosperity of Nagasaki.

The naval vessels of other Powers often used to remain in Nagasaki for three or four months at a time, refitting. And we know from Pierre Loti what that led to!

Certainly Pierre Loti, and later Luther Long and David Belasco when writing the libretto of *Madame Butterfly*, gave Nagasaki a boost, but it did not bring more trade or dollars, because those who came to

Japan to find *musume* of the calibre of Mesdames Chrysanthemum or Butterfly were able to find them just as readily in the other treaty ports.

* * * * * * * *

About three hundred and forty years ago the Tokugawa Shogunate decided to extirpate the Christian religion from Japan, and tradition relates that thousands of Japanese Christians, who preferred to die rather than to renounce their religion, threw themselves down the precipitous sides of the island of Papenberg, known to the Japanese as Takabokoshima. Churches were sacked, Christian emblems destroyed, and even the Christian cemeteries were destroyed *"and the bones scatterred to the windes."* In 1945, the atom bomb was dropped on Nagasaki, and once again the churches and the cemeteries were destroyed. Again there was great suffering and loss in Nagasaki, and little now remains to remind us of the early Settlement days.

However, somebody recently had the rare foresight to discover the "actual" house in which Lieut. Pinkerton, U.S.N., resided with his common-law wife, Madame Butterfly, and so the optimistic city fathers now hope that the tourist traffic will flood to Nagasaki, just as it does to Stratford-on-Avon!

THE EARLY YEARS OF YOKOHAMA

"I observe, Harris," said the Consul, "that they are erecting houses on the Yokohama flat opposite to Kanagawa. I suppose the Japanese Government intend this for a second Deshima, but of course we cannot accept that sort of thing." "Certainly not," replied the Minister.

JOSEPH HECO's diary,
1st July, 1859

Yokohama came into being despite international treaties. The treaty which Townsend Harris, the first U.S. Minister to Japan, signed with the Japanese specified Kanagawa as the port to be opened for foreigners and fixed the opening date as 1st July, 1859. That treaty formed the basis of other treaties concluded by the other powers with the Tokugawa Government.

Kanagawa was then, and had been for hundreds of years, a thriving post town and a flourishing port, but it was on one of the regular routes to Yedo and a place through which the *daimyo* processions passed on their journeys to and from the capital, and there-

37

fore in the eyes of the Japanese authorities at that time, not a desirable or a suitable site for the residence of foreigners.

Those familiar with Hiroshige's series of pictures of the *Fifty-three Stages of the Tokaido* will recall that Number Four in the series depicts Kanagawa as a coast town on top of a cliff overlooking Tokyo Bay, with female touts endeavouring to drag male travellers into the tea-houses.

The treaties having laid down that Kanagawa would be the port to be opened, and with the approach of the agreed date, the British, U.S., French, and Dutch Ministers landed there and established their offices and places of residence in various temples, there being no other suitable accommodation available.

A number of Christian missionaries were among the first arrivals and they also took up residence in Buddhist temples around Kanagawa. One of them, Dr. J. C. Hepburn, later compiled one of the first comprehensive English-Japanese dictionaries and introduced order into the Romanised spelling of Japanese words. His system known as the Hepburn System, although not receiving the mark of official approval in Japan, has been in general use both here and abroad, despite spasmodic efforts to establish the official system, and is likely to remain in common use so long as the average person prefers to be guided in scholastic matters by common sense rather than by the edicts of bureaucrats.

The Romanised spelling of Japanese words, by the Hepburn system, has become familiar to the world abroad, where people readily recognise Japan's famous mountain when written as *Fuji,* whereas few would recognise it, or be able correctly to pronounce it, when rendered under the official system as *Huzi.* Even the Emperor's brother, Prince Chichibu, swam against the stream of pre-war nationalism by objecting to his name being written as *Titibu.* In prewar days the N.Y.K. shipping company, in compliance with the demands of the nationalists that Japan dissociate herself from Western ways of thought, changed the spelling of the name of their Pacific passenger liner "Chichibu Maru" to "Titibu Maru," but in that form it became the butt of so many jokes that it proved to be bad publicity, and after one trip to Los Angeles the spelling was quickly changed to "Kamakura Maru." The N.Y.K. was forgiven, however, because dollars were involved!

But let us return to the earliest days of Yokohama. Whilst the foreign ministers were drawing up plans for the future foreign settlement in Kanagawa, the Japanese authorities had decided that it would be better that the foreigners should be relegated to the little fishing village of Yokohama, then located across the bay from Kanagawa. That bay has largely been reclaimed since those days and Kanagawa now merges into Yokohama. The village of Yokohama was then far removed from the Tokaido—the great artery of Japan—and was of no importance and without resources.

Whilst the foreign ministers were busy establishing their legations at Kanagawa, the Japanese authorities were even more busy on the outskirts of the fishing village at Yokohama in erecting buildings

The Early Years of Yokohama

suitable as residences, shops, and warehouses (or godowns as they are known in the East). Generally they were creating every inducement for the new-comers to foresake Kanagawa and settle down in Yokohama. The foreign ministers protested at those measures, but the official replies to their protests were sidetracked and long delayed. In the meantime merchants, shopkeepers, tradesmen, and plain adventurers were steadily arriving with merchandise or with their tools of trade, and were glad to take advantage of the facilities available at Yokohama, notwithstanding the exhortations of their consuls that they should settle at Kanagawa. In the early stages the consuls were thus located at Kanagawa, whilst most others, with the exception of the missionaries, were across the bay at Yokohama.

In course of time it came to be realised by all that Yokohama with its deeper water was better suited to meet the needs of a foreign port, and eventually the consuls moved out of the temples in Kanagawa and established themselves in Yokohama. However, they continued for many years to date their official correspondence as being from Kanagawa, rather than admit that they had acquiesced to any departure from the terms of the treaty that had specified Kanagawa as the foreign port.

To facilitate the establishment of the foreigners in their new homes, the Japanese Customs House performed many functions in addition to the receipt of customs. It served as a place of exchange for currency and bullion, an employment office, and a liaison office generally for all matters where the

40

activity of foreigners impinged upon native life. Also the officials there undertook such extra-curricular duties as the procuring of mistresses for those seeking them.

As an additional inducement for the foreigners to settle in Yokohama, the Japanese authorities then erected in an isolated area, known as "The Swamp," a dubious type of establishment called the Gankiro Teahouse, which thus became the first of Yokohama's many "Dirty Villages." After it was destroyed in the great fire of 1866 its place was taken by other establishments, each more elaborate than its predecessor, until finally Number Nine came into being, and gained fame of a kind from Rudyard Kipling having mentioned it in "MacAndrew's Hymn":

Judge not, O Lord, my steps aside at Gay Street in Hongkong....Jane Harrigan's an' Number Nine. The Reddicks an' Grant Road.

It is not surprising that the Bishop of Hongkong after visiting Yokohama in 1860, less than a year after its opening, wrote:

The Japanese officials...have also endeavoured to render Yokuhama (sic) an attractive locality to young unmarried foreigners by establishing at the edge of the settlement and on a site approached by a narrow drawbridge over the canal, one of those infamous public institutions which have been already adverted to, containing its two hundred female inmates dispersed over a spacious series of apartments and all under government regulation and control. Not content with these flagitious methods of corrupting the foreign residents, the

*native officials contributed every facility for the
perpetration of domestic vice and impurity. Young
men were encouraged to negotiate through the
customs-house the terms of payment and selection
of a partner in their dissolute mode of living. It is
feared that the snare has not been set in vain . . .
it is a deplorable scene of demoralisation and pro-
fligate life.*

Even although the Japanese authorities had
succeeded in placing the foreign settlement in Yokohama far from the main highway of Japan, nevertheless opposition to the entry of foreigners was strong,
and for this reason the next decade proved to be one
of turbulent years in Japan. With the outbreak of
a series of assassinations of foreigners, and also of
Japanese who had supported the treaties, it became
evident to all that the Japanese authorities had been
correct in seeking to confine the foreigners to the
quieter side of the bay and as far removed as possible
from the traffic of the Tokaido. As it was, the attacks by two-sworded *ronin* on foreigners at night
or in the countryside were all too frequent and many
died at the hands of those assassins.

The original settlement at Yokohama comprised a
narrow strip of land bounded to the north by the
sea, to the south by a swamp, and on both the east
and west by canals. It resembled an island, and this
in fact was one of the objections of the foreign ministers, who saw in it far too close a similarity to
the confined space of the island of Deshima in Nagasaki harbour to which the Dutch had been restricted
for about 240 years. However in the dangerous times

that were to follow it was soon seen that the location had advantages in that it was easily defended against assassins. At first there were only three entrances to Yokohama, each across a bridge, where guards were posted. At times of tension all two-sworded men were required to park their swords at the guard houses before entering.

Within the first year, five foreigners were assassinated within the Settlement. Later there were many others both there and in the countryside roundabout. Legations at Yedo were also attacked and burnt. These happenings convinced the consular authorities of the necessity of having their own guards, and eventually gave rise to detachments of English and French troops being quartered in Yokohama. At one period of tension there were over one thousand English and three hundred French troops garrisoned in Yokohama. In those days there were five hotels and twenty-four grog shops, the latter mostly in what was known as "Blood Town."

It was a period of adjustment and re-adjustment on all sides. Japan's sudden excursion into international trade after having existed behind locked doors for two and a half centuries was not accomplished without grievous troubles on both sides.

Even the discontent and clamour among the noodle dealers in Yedo, at the Yokohama foreigners, for buying up wheat and flour and exporting it to Shanghai, cost a governor his life. When the price of noodles advanced there was a demand from the noodle-makers and the public of Yedo that the export of flour be prohibited, and the Governor of Kanagawa

Prefecture became so involved in the dispute, by having to point out to his superiors in Yedo that the action of the foreigners in exporting wheat and flour was not a violation of the treaty and therefore should not be interfered with, that he left Yedo fully aware that his attitude had caused displeasure at the Court. When the Shogun heard of what had transpired, and fearing that the Governor might commit hara-kiri, he sent a messenger posthaste to assure the Governor that he was pardoned. The Shogun's messenger overtook the Governor's palanquin just as the bearers put it down at the entrance to the Governor's home. When the door of the palanquin was opened the Governor's body rolled out with a short dirk stuck fast into his abdomen.

In the earliest years of the Yokohama Settlement, plenty of snipe and other birds were to be had in the swamp that bordered the Settlement just south of where Ota-machi and Benten-dori are to-day. Later, drainage canals were cut and in 1867 the swamp was filled in and reclaimed with the debris from a great fire that wiped out most of early Yokohama. The city was then able to expand southwards. In those early days the Bluff was heavily wooded with pines and other trees, and there was an abundance of pheasants, woodcock and wild pigeons. The early foreign sportsmen were, however, responsible for the disappearance of bird life, but the trees remained for a long while. Alas, the fires following the earthquake of 1923 destroyed the trees of Yokohama and the air-raid fires of 1945 added to the bleakness of the city. An idea of the abundance of bird life in those days may be gained from the fact that some foreign firms specialised in the export of birdskins and feathers, a trade which unhappily eventually robbed the countryside of much of its bird life.

In November, 1868, the Mikado—the term by which the sovereign of Japan was then known to the outer world—passed along the Tokaido through Hodogaya and Kanagawa to make his first entrance into Yedo, which thereafter was named Tokyo, the eastern capital. A number of foreigners, together with a military band and a guard of honour from the English and French troops in Yokohama, went to Hodogaya to view the Imperial procession. When the palanquin in which the Emperor was believed to be came in sight, the band struck up the lively tune of "The British Grenadiers," that being the best they could do, as there was at that time no Japanese national anthem.

It was not until sometime later that thought was given by the Japanese authorities to the matter of a national anthem. It was then that a verse beginning *Kimi-ga-yo-wa* was selected from an ancient anthology. The Japanese tune to which the words were sung was then harmonised by a German bandmaster, and the *Kimigayo* as known to-day was created.

A pleasing feature of this early period in the life of Yokohama was the excellent relations that developed between the foreign troops and the Japanese soldiers who were quartered near Yokohama. The Japanese troops occasionally joined the English troops in route marches and sham fights, and on several occasions participated in their reviews. There are a number of rare old Japanese woodblock colour prints still to be had depicting the English red-coated soldiers and these happy relationships with the Japanese troops.

In the early eighteen seventies when the foreign troops were finally withdrawn, the parades and the performances of their regimental bands came to an end. Much of the attractive colour then disappeared from the social life of the port, and the end of an era in the history of Yokohama was reached.

THE
YOKO'AMA
'UNT

*There's no sport like 'unting, and
no 'ounds like those of the Yoko'ama
'unt.*

The world has changed a great deal in most countries during the past century, but in few have the changes been as great as in Japan. The Japanese of these days must look with amazement at the state of almost complete undress in which a considerable percentage of their male population spent a large part of their time a hundred years ago. The foreigners of to-day, who know anything of the habits of their predecessors of those same times, must, on the other hand, be no less amazed at the excess quantity of clothes which the Western male wore, or at the super-abundance of garments of the Western female of those same days. But whether European ladies then wore as many petticoats as Japanese court ladies wore under-kimono, is a matter for decision by the experts.

If, in these chapters, I more often relate the queer doings of foreigners in Japan nearly a century ago rather than those of the natives, it is merely because I recognize that, if Japanese are able to laugh at themselves, their own writers could poke a finger of fun at their own nationals of those far-off days more effectively than I. From the time Westerners first came to Japan both sides in fact have viewed the customs and habits of the other with never-ending amazement.

The early foreigner was a person of habits. He smoked one brand of cheroots, and always insisted on one particular brand of whisky, although in emergencies he was prepared to extend the range. He associated only with friends in his own caste. He bought his clothes from one particular Chinese tailor. Each day he had his drinks at the same club, hotel or saloon, depending upon his social standing, and always patronised the same rickshaw stand. Some historians have said that only in his love affairs was he inconstant. However that may be, at the conclusion of each of those transactions he signed a chit.

The signing of chits was a carry-over from the early China days, and fitted in well enough with life in Japan where the great men of this land had considered it beneath their dignity to handle money, although often they were not inept at making it. Considering the size, weight and multiplicity of coinage in those days, there was some reason for the custom of signing chits, and more reason perhaps among the foreigners than the Japanese of the upper brackets. The Japanese dignitary did have the copious folds of his kimono or the deep depths of his sleeves in which to carry the price of a night's fun. But five or six dollars in silver coinage would put out of shape, or might even burst the buttons of the tight fitting stove-pipe trousers of a foreigner of those days, and if carried in small change the weight would have anchored him to the floor.

The railways (when they came into being) and the

beggars were the only people who perversely refused
to accept chits. In a pinch you could drop a chit in
the church plate. The rickshaw-man and the barber
accepted them, as did many other categories who
contributed to life and pleasure. And so it was that
in those days one could start off on a "night-out"
that might easily carry on to waking up the following
morning in some obscure place, and finance the whole
proceeding with the scratch of a pencil. (There were
of course in those days no fountain pens to run out
of ink). All the chits signed during that night and
early morning would filter back sooner or later, just
depending upon the credit standing or state of health
of the signers. Chits signed by those whose health
or credit showed signs of expiring, bounced back
more quickly.

Those who thought anything of their credit,
squared up all outstanding chits before midnight on
31st December each year, and thereby became
patterns of regularity.

Some few who were known to be carrying paid-
up insurance policies might be able to drift on for
ten years without a settlement, but three years was
generally the limit of endurance. After that, the
signer lost some face and all credit, and drifted into
the unfortunate hands of his consul who shipped him
home steerage at government expense. He thus
again became the responsibility of his family, who
more often than not had originally sent him out East
to be rid of him.

If he was fortunate enough to have friends at the
Club who thought steerage was not good enough for

him, they might circulate a list and collect sufficient funds to procure for him a second-class passage, plus an extra "fiver" which was given to the captain to hand over when he walked down the gang-plank in his home country. Pocket money en route was not usually considered necessary, because it was assumed that he already had sufficient experience to be able to sponge on his fellow passengers for a period of eight or nine weeks whilst homeward bound.

Those who felt they could not face a return to their home country and families in such circumstances sometimes sought a permanent solution to their problem, which was generally a bloody operation carried out with a razor. On dying here they could be sure that the foreign residents would subscribe to bury them decently. At such funerals others of the same class, whilst mourning the loss of the deceased, would be hoping that some day other subscribers would be doing the same for them. That category of foreign resident became less in evidence each year and most of them passed away a long time ago, about the same time as the Gold Standard. Shortly afterwards exchange control regulations throughout most of the world brought to an end that other, but somewhat more picturesque, class in the East known as remittance men.

The earliest merchants were often a genial lot, probably because mails were infrequent. The nearest cable office was at Colombo, and their home directors in point of time were nearly three months distant from them. Important visitors, buyers, and other such trials were infrequent. The early residents, except those who were gouty and liverish, were fond of outdoor life, perhaps because in those very early days, radio, television, and other so-called attractions of modern indoor life did not exist. In any case the first homes provided for foreigners in Yokohama were built by the Japanese authorities and were clapboard affairs approximating a cross between a European-styled house and a Japanese building. Until a great fire destroyed them all, the first foreign residential section in Yokohama offered about as much comfort as a mushroom gold mining town of a century ago in America.

The merchants generally arrived at their offices, if at all, around 10 A.M. and quit at four, but out of those six hours, at least two would have been spent at the club or in one of the hotels. Before attending office they would perhaps do an hour's horse riding. The more athletic of them rode their own horses at the races which were held twice a year. As most of the community attended the race-meetings, all business and banking was necessarily at a standstill on those days.

After the first English regiment arrived in Yokohama, which was in 1864, and had made itself as comfortable as those uncomfortable times permitted, the officers gave thought to hunting. A pack of hounds, or rather a mixed lot of harriers, long-eared beagles, and several dwarf fox-hounds, all of doubtful lineage, were imported from Shanghai. Thereafter, they suffered, as did their masters, from the ills of the East, which in those early days took a greater toll of life than now. For the dogs, castor oil, sulphur ointment, and plenty of exercise were the only known cures. The remedies available to their masters were not much more varied.

So enthusiastic was the Yokohama Hunt Club that even drag-hunts by moonlight became a feature of the community life. Falls were frequent and occasionally broken collarbones had to be set, but the meetings were generally pronounced a great success, or as the batman of one of the English regimental officers put it—

There's no sport like 'unting, and no 'ounds like those of the Yoko'ama 'unt.

The hunt was followed by a dinner party of such gaiety and colour as has not been known in foreign circles in Japan since those days. The regimental band was of course in attendance and played its gayest airs, some of the same lively pieces as were played when the band came marching down Camp Hill Road, on returning from a funeral in the Bluff Cemetery. Fevers and contagious diseases took their toll among those English regiments in Japan, as can still be seen from the many tombstones of British soldiers buried in the Yokohama Cemetery.

Nevertheless those days must have been pleasant times, for all except the farmer, whose crops and agricultural interests must have suffered when the Yokohama 'unt staged a meet.

Foreigners were restricted in residence and travel to an area which was roughly within a radius of about twenty-four miles of the treaty port. Passports were required for travel or residence beyond that area, and residence was only permitted for health reasons or for those employed by Japanese nationals. The latter condition inevitably gave rise to one of the first rackets, whereby a foreigner was able to live in the interior on production of a certificate to the effect that he was employed as a teacher, or in some other capacity—such certificates being issued by their Japanese friends, for a consideration.

By way of assisting tourists who wished to visit the interior, but who were without any accommodating Japanese friends who would furnish them with a certificate, the English language guidebooks of those days helpfully advised the tourist to add to every application for travel in the interior, which they might lodge with the Japanese authorities, a statement that the reason for travel was "for benefit of health" or "for scientific investigation."

Shooting in the early days was restricted to the treaty limits, which areas were so shot over for several decades that by 1890 we find Murray's *Guide to Japan* remarking that "the majority of resident sportsmen have abandoned the field," and warning tourists and visitors that "meanwhile, a gun case is a useless piece of baggage to the foreign visitor."

When Yokohama was first opened the countryside gave excellent bags of pheasants. A hard worker and a good shot was always sure of fifteen to twenty brace in a day.

There were also deer and wild boar to be shot even in the nearby countryside stretching behind Yokohama to Kamakura or *Daiboots*, which in those days was the commonly accepted foreign spelling of the Great Buddha. Also there were innumerable wild

geese and ducks feeding in the swamps near Kanagawa. Such were the ravages committed by those
early hunters that the priests, in the temples scattered
throughout the countryside around Yokohama,
erected notices forbidding hunting and warning that
birds and other animals were not to be slaughtered
within the sanctuary of the temple grounds. Some
of those old signboards could still be seen in pre-war
days in some of the old temples.

Occasionally some of the diplomatic corps were
invited by provincial governors to shooting parties
on private lands. On one occasion in 1866, some of
the officers of the English regiment then stationed in
Yokohama were invited to visit the domains of the
Prince of Satsuma, when he threw open his preserves
for a day's sport. The shooting was not considered
a great success because the total bag consisted of
only seven deer and five wild boar—a poor day's sport
in those days of abundance. On another occasion
when invited by another Daimyo to beat a small island, the same party knocked over more than fifty
head of deer—a circumstance reported at the time
without shame.

Shooting as a sport in those early days was hardly
known at all to the Japanese. They skillfully netted
birds, or using live decoys caught them in ingenious
bamboo traps or nets. Some entangled them in
birdlime, which incidentally the early foreigners discovered was also effective for catching fleas, flies
and rats. There were plenty of monkeys in Japan
in those days, the flesh of which had an appeal to
some people. When the Japanese went hunting

monkeys they had a method of their own. They would place several bowls full of *sake* among the trees in a forest where there was known to be a troop of monkeys, and then retire to some place where they themselves would rest, sleep, or imbibe. When they returned to the forest some hours later they would pick up the empty bowls and also several sleeping monkeys. Such methods whilst undeniably effective were but crude affairs in comparison with the colorful outings with the " 'ounds of the Yoko'ama 'unt."

6 ¼
CENTS
DAMAGES

> *To-day being Sunday, all the Eng-*
> *lishmen put on different clothes.*
> Japanese account of Europeans,
> 1862

Yokohama Settlement during the first few years of its existence was an extraordinary place—extraordinary by any standards anywhere, and rendered the more so by the unusual conglomeration of foreigners, mostly males, who by force of circumstances were compelled to live in close proximity to one another.

It would seem that in those first years of Yokohama, the more respectable elements that formed the backbone of foreign settlements in the Far East were in the minority in Yokohama.

Many, even by the most generous standards, were poor types. The rest were a diverse body of men, most of whom suffered from boredom or the irritating necessity of having to rub shoulders too closely with others with whom they had little in common, some of whom annoyed them by assuming airs as pompous as their own. Sir Rutherford Alcock, the first British Minister to Japan, referring to the first arrivals in Japan, wrote:

Nowhere is there a greater influx, unless it be at some gold diggings, of the lawless and dissolute from all countries—and nowhere is the danger and

*the mischief they are calculated to inflict on whole
communities and national interests greater than in
these regions.*

The consuls were responsible for the maintenance
of order and the dispensation of justice among their
own nationals, who generally were far from co-
operative. Our sympathies must be with the consuls,
for how could they be popular when, in addition to
their consular duties, they often had to play the parts
of judge, assessor, magistrate, arbitrator, coroner,
jailer and turnkey. The merchants and the tradesmen, no less than the remittance men, and the sots
who parked themselves in the saloons of Bloodtown,
were slightly resentful of the privileges enjoyed by
the consuls, whilst the consuls in turn were ever
watchful that some other country's representative did
not gain some greater concession from the Japanese
than they. To all who stood on the sidelines and
watched the drama of settlement life, the antics of
some of the lesser honorary consuls, a few of whom
were frank adventurers, were matters to marvel at.

There were a number of men, however, mostly
among the missionaries and the diplomatic corps, who
withdrew to their studies and immersed themselves
in researches into Japanese history, culture, and
language, and so it was that apart from the vast
majority of foreigners who came to Japan in those
early days and left again (or died here) without
knowing anything more about Japan than when they
first arrived, there did emerge a number of most
noteworthy scholars whose researches are standard
works of reference to-day.

The Yokohama Settlement was a low-lying area ditched all over with drainage channels that led into broad canals which soon became concentrated with the essences from the drainage and refuse of an Oriental city having the sanitation of the feudal ages. The daily tides occasionally succeeded in carrying some of the contents out to sea, but generally only kept it gently stirring. A broad and deep canal had been dug around the town, across which were bridges, each with a guard house. While this canal therefore served as some protection against assassins, it did little to sweeten the Yokohama summer air.

Despite the primitive standards of sanitation which people were accustomed to in those days, it would seem that conditions in Yokohama were unusually trying. The *Japan Times Overland Mail* of 10 March, 1869, offered advice which it was thought would relieve some of the sufferings of its readers:

In moving abroad carry a vinaigrette with aromatic spirits of vinegar to smell at when exposed to noxious and unpleasant odours. This simple but effective remedy deservedly holds a high place among the preventatives of fever."

This discovery on the part of the *Japan Times* was not original, because it has been recorded elsewhere that somewhat earlier in Europe, body-snatchers, whose trade required that they should supply subjects from graveyards to aspirants to the medical profession, had great faith in the efficacy of smelling salts. Some of the resurrection men, however, preferred to chew garlic!

The learned *Japan Times* also recommended that its

readers avoid walking about in the early morning or evening with an empty stomach, because at such times *"the body is in an unprepared state to throw off miasmatic influences and that at those times of the day miasmal effluvia are in a state of concentration in the air."*

In spite of all this it would appear that Yokohama with its odoriferous canals was a model of sanitation as compared with Yedo and other Japanese cities. A year before Yokohama was opened, an outbreak of cholera accounted for the loss of thirty thousand lives in Yedo. In the summer of the previous year over half a million people in Yedo contracted measles of which over seventy-three thousand died. Smallpox, dysentery and diphtheria were constantly raging.

Outside the Settlement there were swamps that abounded with bird life; there were also two-sworded assassins out there awaiting the opportunity to test their swords on the neck of a foreigner. Nevertheless hunting was popular and the early foreigners were primarily responsible for the killing off of so many of the fine-plumaged birds that once enlivened the Japanese countryside.

Within the Settlement there were the bungalows of the foreign merchants, the *hongs* and the godowns, the banks and the Chinese exchange shops, the shops of the foreign tradesmen with sleeping quarters in the rear or upstairs, the hotels and the grog shops, and the riffraff lodging houses. Within a couple of years Yokohama rather resembled a Wild West town of clapboard buildings. The behaviour of some of the residents also seems to have been along Wild

West patterns, because on 5th Dec., 1861, the British Consul found it necessary to issue the following announcement:—

The undersigned is further called upon to remark upon the common practice of carrying fire-arms during the day and in the most ostentatious manner. ...There is something especially provocative and irritating in such ostentatious display of fire-arms, for men supposed to be following the avocations of merchants, which are or ought to be entirely peaceable....British subjects are hereby prohibited from so offending under penalty of fines and imprisonment....Furious horse riding in the streets of Yokohama is a common practice among foreigners, and not only among them but among their Chinese servants....The undersigned can see no adequate justification for this....

The British consul was not the only one having trouble with his nationals. In the previous year, with the approach of the glorious Fourth of July, the U.S. Consul had ruled that only U.S. officials would be permitted to fly the *Stars and Stripes* in the Settlement, and that if anyone else should hoist the American flag in Yokohama he personally would pull it down. This so enraged the American residents that during the night they had all the Chinese tailors busy making U.S. flags, and in the morning the *Stars and Stripes* were gaily flying over every American residence in the Settlement.

In 1866 a great fire destroyed this clapboard town and burnt out most of the foreign adventurers. Thereafter Yokohama Settlement threw off any likeness it

had to a Wild West town. It was rebuilt with firms
and persons of greater respectability taking their
proper place in a town of mortar, brick and stone,
with stately hongs and solid godowns.

Generally speaking the community quickly formed
itself into groups representing various social strata
and by each withdrawing to its favourite club, meet-
inghouse, or saloon, they hoped to avoid too much
contact with those whom they believed to be beneath
them. And so the caste system in the Foreign
Settlements developed.

When the English and the French began in 1862
to station troops in Yokohama and it became safe
enough to live outside the confines of the swampy
Settlement, stately homes began to develop on
the Bluff. Thereafter many residents built their
homes on the Bluff, where they were as far removed
as possible from the riffraff who came ashore as
transients and then remained to infest the Settlement. Nevertheless the area available to foreigners
was restricted, and many of the streets were as
narrow as the minds of some of the residents, but
the columns of the local newspapers were wide open
to correspondents anxious to air their grievances.
The editors so lacked copy that they devoted much
of their time and space to taking sides and fanning
the flames in the innumerable petty feuds that
developed. One feud ended in a duel and a life was
lost, but most just ended up in the Consular Courts
in actions for damages or in complaints of assault
and battery, of which the following was an example.

An English merchant, who happened to be one of

the minor pillars in the local community, suspected
his assistant of petty theft, and was able to make
such a convincing case of his complaint to the British
Consul, that the latter had the assistant arrested and
lodged in the British jail. Inasmuch as the assistant
was subsequently able to prove American nationality,
his arrest was quite illegal, and so he was quick to
bring an action against his employer for illegal imprisonment, though he had to seek justice in the
English court. To assist his case he employed as
counsel the only American lawyer in Yokohama, who
happened to be the American Consul. During the
course of this legal mix-up, the editor of the local
English newspaper was glad of the opportunity to
even up some old scores by publishing some scath-
ing remarks concerning the American assistant's character, whereupon the latter lay in wait for the editor
and gave him a horsewhipping on the steps of the
Yokohama Club.

The editor thereupon brought an action for assault
and battery against the assistant, but as the latter
was an American citizen, the editor had to seek
justice in the American Court where the American
Consul, who had previously played the part of counsel
for the defence in the English court, was now the
judge. Tempers flared, sparks flew, and the local
press thundered. Some English residents called as
witnesses refused to answer pertinent questions put
by the American judge, and walked out of the Court
free from any danger of contempt.

The learned judge, after treating all present to a
lengthy dissertation on what he declared to be perti-

nent English and American cases, ordered the assistant to pay to the English editor 6¼ cents damages. Then by way of settling some outstanding differences with the English editor and his English lawyer he slyly added "....*it is further ordered, adjudged and decreed by the Court that the Defendant further pay costs to the Plaintiff in a sum equal to his damages recovered,*" thereby going on record as estimating the legal services of the English lawyer to be worth something less than 6¼ cents.

As might have been expected that decision raised a storm of protests within the foreign community. Public meetings were held and much correspondence of an undisclosed nature took place between a certain two consuls, but in course of time that storm also blew itself out like all typhoons.

THE KOBE FOREIGN SETTLEMENT

We returned home through the main street of Hiogo, but without seeing anything in the shops of much interest or novelty.

Sir RUTHERFORD ALCOCK, 1861

Most people know that Commodore Perry forced the doors of Japan. That was more than a hundred years ago in 1853. In the following year he returned and signed a treaty on behalf of the United States with the Tokugawa Shogunate—the Emperor at that time being kept in comparative obscurity in Kyoto.

Shortly afterwards, England and Russia concluded similar trading pacts. Several years later Townsend Harris on behalf of the United States, Lord Elgin on behalf of England, and others acting for their respective governments concluded more exacting treaties which provided for the opening of certain ports to foreign trade.

Yokohama was opened in 1859, and Kobe, or rather Hyogo as it was then known, was due to be opened on New Year's Day, 1863. When the time for the opening of Hyogo approached, the Shogunate becoming fearful that their opponents would seize upon the extension of trading facilities with the Occidental nations as an excuse for the overthrow of the Shogun, procrastinated and sought a postponement. The

Treaty Powers agreed to such postponements. Kobe, therefore, was not eventually opened until 1868, or nine years after Yokohama.

The first years of trading in Yokohama had proved disappointing and a number of merchants in that port were waiting to try their luck in Kobe. Before the new year of 1868 was born, several foreign merchant vessels, carrying a considerable number of merchants from Yokohama and other ports in the Far East, had anchored off Kobe. There were also some British and American men-of-war.

The merchants on board the vessels were gazing at the sandy waste that was to be their home, and at the long sandy beach, lined for most of the way with old gnarled pine trees, that stretched towards Osaka. They were contemplating with some misgivings the immense amount of work that would have to be undertaken to raise the level of their settlement, to make it safe from invasion by the sea during typhoons, and to turn a barren sandy waste into a mercantile centre. As the merchants awaited the appointed hour of landing, their thoughts turned to the problem of accommodation.

To the east of their future settlement, towards Osaka, there were mostly fields. To the west the straggling village of Kobe, a few *sake* breweries and godowns, and some straw-thatched fishing huts. Motomachi was a narrow and odoriferous street inches deep in mud and lined with poor mean buildings. Above the village towards the hills a few temples were seen, each set in its own forest of trees—all of which forests, alas, have long since disappeared.

The Kobe Foreign Settlement

The merchants landed and Kobe was formally opened on 1st January, 1868. A few were able to rent some of the *sake* godowns as places of business and residence, although at extortionate rentals, which increased far quicker than did trade. Seemingly the problem of increased rentals for foreign residents was a trial and an annoyance born about eighty-seven years ago.

Others sought temporary accommodation in some of the temples. For a long while the problem of housing remained acute, but as urgent as was the matter of a place for the living, a place of burial for the dead had already proved to be of greater urgency. Several days before the landing, it had been necessary to negotiate with the Japanese authorities for a burial place for two officers, one a Britisher, the other an American, who had died on board the men-of-war. The cemetery site at Ono—the same cemetery that has figured so much in the life of the foreign community and which was recently transferred to Futatabi—was hastily selected and the two burials conducted. Before a month had passed there were about twenty graves in Ono cemetery. Such was the early end to the high hopes with which some foreigners came to establish businesses in Kobe.

The site at Ono had never been popular. Originally it was so close to the sea that water was found at about four feet. This necessitated the digging of shallow graves and at night the foxes came down from the hills and scraped the earth away and gnawed at newly buried coffins. Indeed so close were the coffins to the surface that on one occasion thieves

66

exhumed a body apparently searching for the treasure that was imagined to be buried with foreigners.

The first reports that reached Yokohama from the new settlement in Kobe were full of complaints and disappointment. The *Japan Times Overland Mail* of Yokohama, on 29th January, 1868, carried the following:—

The latest intelligence from the new port is depressing in the extreme. Death has been busy among high and low, danger from political strife hovers near and commerce cannot struggle into life among the numberless disadvantages which retard her birth....The meat of course comes from Yokohama....The trouble about houses and house rents, however, still continues. Extraordinary prices are still asked for sheds of the meanest description and the position of some representatives of the leading firms of Yokohama is positively ludicrous. One such writes to a personal friend here: "I have to work under great difficulty as my office is in the kitchen of a Japanese tea-house, and open to the street so that a crowd is constantly round the door watching me and making disparaging remarks." No accommodation is yet provided for goods and the merchandise which has already been landed lies in a roofless godown, hereafter to be a Bonded warehouse and protected from falling rain only by temporary expedients.

Another correspondent wrote:—

Hiogo is two miles distant from where foreigners will be allowed to reside. All Japanese merchants of any standing or wealth reside in Hiogo, so that any person who wishes to have any conversation with this class has to walk to Hiogo. This is not all—when he is about a mile on the road, if he chances to look back he finds a Japanese officer (spy) following him, wherever he may go, during which time if he happens to talk to a Japanese, this spy comes up and quietly listens to the conversation.

On the 12th February, six weeks after the port was opened, one of the performers at an amateur dramatic performance, attempted to lift the spirits of those present with the following prophetic *jeu d'esprit:*—

Sweet Kobe! Loveliest spot in fare Japan.
Who lives in thee indeed's happy man.
As through thy pleasant lanes, I take my way,
Or by the rills pellucid musing stray,
I think in search of bliss, why further roam.
Here let me dwell, here make my future home.

Now with prophetic vision I descry
A noble city tow'ring towards the sky,
Palatial godowns meet th'enraptured view,
Cramm'd with the wealth of India and Peru,
When Yokohama's crumbled to decay
And Nagasaki too has had its day.
This Settlement renowned as Kobeopolis
Shall be of Nippon then the proud metropolis.

Apparently it required more than that to raise the morale of the settlers, because two weeks later there was another despatch to the *Japan Times Overland Mail:*

The Kobe Foreign Settlement

...Every day shows us more clearly the disadvantages of the position chosen for the settlement and within the last few days we have had proof that even the enormous sum of money said to have been expended upon it has been literally thrown away. 36 hours rain has converted one third of it into a swamp and shows that the fall of land, instead of being towards the sea, leads inland towards the hills which will of course render drainage most difficult and expensive. No one who sees the place can deny that in placing the foreign settlement at Kobe the least eligible site has been chosen....Here according to treaty we are compelled to settle....Many are of the opinion that the land is not worth the rent they have to pay for it.

Three months later a correspondent wrote:—

Questions are being asked as to why Kobe should have been selected as the port of Osaka instead of the more convenient Sakai....Kobe has been weighed and found wanting. The Concession is a swamp and a quicksand knee deep with water in the rainy season, and a scorched dusty plain under the summer sun.

Another wrote:—

The foreign concession, or the "Sand Path". "Swamp" or "Desert", as the residents appropriately term it, remains an incubus upon the hands of the officials and those who planned it.

One year later in January, 1869, the first foreign baby was born in Kobe. In the years to come many more were born, but it is sad to relate that the number of deaths during infancy and childhood was, according to our modern standards, appalling. Sanitation was primitive and for water the residents were dependent upon wells, most of which were contaminated. Dysentery and diphtheria took a dreadful toll of young lives as is pathetically recorded on the tombstones of the old cemetery.

After their initial difficulties had been overcome, the early foreigners, most of whom had arrived from Yokohama or less attractive foreign settlements in the Far East, were agreeably surprised to note some of the unexpected attractions of Kobe. There being no reservoir at Nunobiki in those days, the waterfall was a grand sight especially during rainy seasons, and no visitor to Kobe would have thought of leaving without seeing it. Little wonder that the Nunobiki waterfall was given such prominence in the early guidebooks, although the claim that it was world famous was a gross exaggeration. In those days there were troops of monkeys in the great trees around Nunobiki. There were deer on Mayasan, and in nearby places mallard duck, snipe, and teal in abundance. Many fine pheasants were to be flushed in the middle reaches of Minatogawa (the port river) within a mile of what is to-day the neon-lighted amusement centre of Kobe.

Within nine months of arrival, sufficient progress had been made in laying out the Foreign Settlement to enable the first land sales to be conducted. Some attention had been given to the drainage, the level had been raised and a sea-wall constructed. The boundaries of the old Settlement can be plainly seen to-day and are in fact exactly where the roads cease to run at right angles one to the other and cease to form regular city blocks. The Settlement was divided into 126 lots to each of which was given a number, which number, for more than fifty years to come was quite sufficient as an address.

When Kobe was first opened, accommodation was a critical problem, even for the foreign consuls. The first British Consulate was located in an old Japanese *yashiki*—a Japanese mansion—near the Customs, whilst the French Consulate was at first established in the grounds of the Ikuta Shrine. The United States did not at that time have a Consul, but had a Consular Agency in a building on the site now occupied by the Nippon Yusen Kaisha, thereby giving the name of *Merikan Hatoba* to the landing stage opposite. Germany was then a mere geographical expression; however Prussia and North Germany were represented by a Consular Agent.

The community, having solved the immediate problem of accommodation, then commenced to organize the amenities, the recreational facilities, and the community organizations that have played such an important part in the life of the foreign community in Kobe ever since.

The first pony race was staged on Christmas Day, 1868, on a sand patch near the northeast corner of the Concession. Shortly afterwards a race club was formed and a permanent racecourse constructed east of Ikuta Shrine and north of the present-day Hankyu Terminus. The first cricket match was arranged in October, 1869.

71

The Kobe Foreign Settlement

In January, 1869, the Hyogo and Osaka Amateur Corps Dramatique announced the presentation of "Cool as a Cucumber" and "Ticket of Leave," the first of many hundreds of plays that have since been performed in Kobe by foreign amateur dramatic societies. The first professional foreign theatrical troupe to visit Kobe from abroad was in November 1868. By 1869 there were three billiard tables and one bowling alley in the Concession. The ratio of bars and saloons in Kobe to other establishments was unusually large even for those times, but is not accurately recorded.

Within four months of the opening of the port there were already two foreign newspapers, *The Hiogo and Osaka Herald* and the *Hiogo News,* both weeklies. The first foreign religious service conducted in Kobe was on Christmas Day, 1867, seven days before the formal opening of the port, when occurred the first burials in the old Ono Cemetery. In the months that followed there were a number of other burial services, and while no doubt there must have been some privately arranged Sunday services, the first actual announcement in the foreign press of a religious service was on 3rd July, 1868, when the community was informed that a Roman Catholic mass would be celebrated on the French warship H.I.M. "Dupleix"—Napoleon II was then Emperor of France.

Although there were as yet few organised religious services, nevertheless convention demanded that Sunday be observed as a closed day so far as sports, but not business, were concerned. One of the first of many storms-in-a-tea-cup which stirred the foreign community in Kobe was in August, 1869, when a few daring young men defied convention and held some boat races on a Sunday. In condemnation of their action, the *Hiogo News* when reporting the happening, caused them to suffer the penalty of anonymity by omitting mention of their names, but censuring them with the astonishing blast:

In some minds of a conscientious cast there will also be a feeling of shame that, whilst the ignorant heathen amongst whom we live are strict in the observance of their various religious festivals, we, the pioneers of civilization and propagandists of the true faith, should, so far as outward appearance goes, be greater heathen than they.

The first regular Protestant services were conducted in May, 1870, in a room loaned by the Masons. The attendance at the first Sabbath service was twenty-five, but thereafter it fluctuated widely. The only regular steamship company then plying to Kobe was the Pacific Mail S. S. Co., with a bi-monthly service, and as mail day was an all important event in the life of the community it was noted that the attendance at church service was negligible when services fell on a mail day.

On 22nd April, 1871, at a meeting of some twenty residents in the Masonic Lodge room, plans were made for the building of a Union Church. By early 1872, a red brick church, an imposing structure in those days, had been built at a cost of $4,121 Mex. on the corner opposite the present-day Daimaru Department Store, now the site of the Mitsubishi Bank.

The Roman Catholic Church had already been built on Lot No. 37 at the rear of the present Daimaru Store. In the early nineteen-twenties when both of those quaint old-fashioned churches were pulled down to make way for big business, the transition of an early settlement to a modern mercantile centre was finally marked.

The Anglicans co-operated in the use of the Union Church until 1897 when they were able to erect All Saints Church on a lot outside the Settlement, half-way up what is now known as Tor Road. That consecrated ground—shameful though it is to relate—was made available in the immediate post-war days to the hucksters and worse as a place on which to carry on businesses that would have been better hidden in the back streets. At the time of writing it has still not been restored to the foreign community, the Peace Treaty conditions notwithstanding.

In 1871 a foreign International Hospital was established in a house at the beginning of the thorough-fare leading to Ikuta Shrine—then an avenue running through fields and bordered with many old stone lanterns and with cherry trees.

Do not let it be imagined that wealth fell into the laps of all those early merchants and adventurers who came to Kobe seventy or eighty years ago. Most of what was achieved was the result of perseverance, enterprise, and a strong co-operative spirit which marked the life of the foreign community from the beginning. That same civic and co-operative spirit of many thousands of honorary workers over a long period of time also built up a Municipal Council, a fire brigade, and in addition many institutions that have progressed and live even to this day—schools, churches, a hospital, social and athletic clubs, a Chamber of Commerce and various philanthropic institutions.

The Settlement also had its own Volunteer Fire Brigade which was so efficiently operated that fire insurance rates declined from the high level of around 5% that had been quoted for a while. A monument erected to the memory of Mr. A. C. Sim, the local pharmacist and for many years Captain of the Fire Brigade, still stands in the Recreation Ground, and until the new buildings of the K.R. & A.C. were erected, his fireman's helmet adorned one of the rooms of that club.

Of necessity the Settlement had its own municipal police force and of course its own jail, all being controlled by the foreign Municipal Council that was elected by the foreign residents.

The foreigners were confined to Kobe and in some directions up to twenty-five miles beyond, and they were not permitted to approach the sacred and Imperial City of Kyoto unless with a special passport. A notice board stood in Takarazuka announcing that town as the farthest point foreigners could go without a permit. Not at all times, however, were the regulations obeyed or strictly enforced. It was not until 1899, when extra-territoriality lapsed, that foreigners were permitted to travel and reside anywhere in Japan. At the same time the control of the Foreign Settlement was handed over to the Japanese authorities.

That the foreign community in Kobe enjoys exceptional sporting and social clubs, despite the ravages of war, is undeniably a fact, but it should not be imagined that these are the creations of wealthy people. Rather they are the result of about ninety years of community effort and the unselfish labour of a great number of honorary workers. As each generation shared in the work, so it handed on the traditions of the institution to the next generation to carry on. To that extent the life of the foreign community in Kobe is well worthy of study.

The K.R. & A.C. for example is the result of over eighty years of effort on the part of some thousands of honorary workers. Most of what was achieved was lost during the World War II years and the period of Occupation, but the same spirit that created it, has again been at work rebuilding it.

The early years proved disappointing in business. Death and bankruptcy took its toll and thirty years after the port was opened only one Settlement lot was still owned by the original purchaser. During the big depressions that assailed the world during the second half of the last century, when many banking institutions in various parts of the world failed, some Settlement lots could be bought for as little as fifty *sen* a *tsubo,* provided the buyer paid the tax arrears. It was thus possible to acquire then, for an outlay of a few *yen* a *tsubo,* land which eventually became worth eight hundred *yen* a *tsubo* in the pre-war years and around fifty thousand *yen* or more per *tsubo* today.

There were Consular Courts, and as the community,

according to our standards, was definitely litigious there were generally four or five lawyers and solicitors, several of whom conducted newspapers in addition to pleading in the Consular Courts of Kobe.

So slowly did business develop in Kobe that by 1878, which was ten years after the port was first opened, the total foreign resident population including women and children, exclusive of Chinese, was less than 250. That number comprised mainly British, American and Germans, about equally divided. In the earliest years, the trade done by the German firms was probably the greatest. There were always a number of transients in the port, some desirable but many not.

Bricks for the building of godowns were first imported from Shanghai, and in fact some of those bricks are still to be seen in the ruins of the Settlement. But many thousands of Glasgow bricks also could once be seen—Scottish bricks, brought all the way to the East by tea-ships in lieu of ballast. Now that the World War II air raid damage has been cleaned up, those reminders of the past have mostly disappeared.

The telegraph service with Osaka was not opened until 1870. Up to then letters were carried from Kobe to Osaka by couriers in about twelve hours. The railway linking Kobe with Kyoto was completed in 1876. The Tokyo-Yokohama line having been in operation for several years, the Kansai trains did not attract the same crowds as did the first trains in the Tokyo-Yokohama area.

The early foreign residents brought in many of

The Kobe Foreign Settlement

their native trees, and up to a few years ago a great
number of Australian gum trees and acacias were to
be seen in the gardens of foreign residents in Kobe
and Ichi-no-tani. Most of them have since disappeared, but there are several Australian gum trees
still to be seen in Shioya and other places.

The Kobe Concession, having come into being so
much later than the Yokohama Concession, pro-
fited by the mistakes that were made there, where
the administration was left in the hands of the Japanese. In Kobe the foreigners had administered their
Concession through their own Municipal Council,
which functioned so well that in 1899 the French
Consul speaking on behalf of the Consular Corps,
when handing back the Settlement, was able to say,
with pride:—

*Thirty years ago when the Japanese Authorities
handed over the Concession of Kobe to the foreigners, the site was practically a stretch of sand, just
cleared of the pine-trees that spread down to the
beach, so waste and desolate and out of the way
that the land was all but valueless. To-day we
hand back to the Japanese Authorities the very
same site transformed into a regular town, every
square foot of which is worth tens of dollars, built
over with handsome houses and godowns filled with
merchandise.... The work of the Council speaks
for itself to-day; the broad and well laid streets,
with rows of handsome trees, their neat brick foot-
paths...brightly lighted with gas at night, the
carefully kept Recreation Ground,...the general
appearance of order and cleanliness to be noted*

*everywhere, have won for the Concession the name
of the Model Settlement of the Far East....*

Right on the borders of this model settlement was
the Japanese town where sanitation conditions were
then not much better than in the feudal ages, which
conditions were described in the local Foreign Press
of those days as follows:—

*Let anyone afflicted with a squeamish stomach
venture to walk through the lower portion of the
narrow lane which runs from the Native Bund to
the Main Street of the native town and we venture
to say he will agree with us that the worst slums
of Liverpool or London are as lavender fields to it,
and the evil-odoured fields of a Chinese city are
scarcely as noisome.*

In 1899 the streets of the model settlement of Kobe
were lined with great trees, but the mountains behind
Kobe were bare. After the Settlement was handed
back to the Japanese it passed through a period of
neglect, the trees all eventually disappeared, but
curiously enough, while the Japanese authorities
neglected the trees within the city, they reforested
the mountains. To-day those mountains are well
wooded and in pleasant contrast to the bleak barren
sides of half a century ago.

When the Foreign Concession was handed back to
the Japanese in 1899 the foundations for the future
had been well laid. Little wonder is it that with the
opening of the twentieth century Kobe moved into an
era of growth and prosperity and that the old Foreign
Concession has become the finest section of the city.

EVEN FLOWERS WEEP IN KOBE

> *This great centre with its port of Hyogo (Kobe) must be worth more to foreign commerce than all the other ports put together.*
> Sir RUTHERFORD ALCOCK, 1861

When the foreign merchants first landed in Kobe on 1st January, 1868, it was a village of small houses, many with roofs of thatched straw, straggling along a mean narrow road that was later twice widened into the Moto-machi of to-day. Between the road and the beach were a few *sake* breweries and warehouses. The population of Kobe village was then less than one thousand.

To the west was the ancient port of Hyogo. To the east, the sandy waste that was to serve as the Settlement for the foreign merchants, and touching that Settlement on its northern edge were the extensive grounds of Ikuta Shrine. Leading to the Shrine was an avenue lined with cherry trees and stone lanterns. Three stone *torii* marked the approach where to-day are the shops, bars and cabarets of Ikuta-mae. Surrounding the Shrine was a forest of cryptomeria and camphor trees, a portion of which survived, even until pre-war days, the dangers of a developing city that pressed in upon it on all sides.

Even Flowers Weep in Kobe

Eventually most of the old trees died a sudden and violent death in the air raids of 1945. To-day all that remains of the majestic forest of camphor trees are eight battered trunks, from which the young leaves are tenaciously sprouting forth again.

The splendid avenue which led to the Shrine is said to have marked the path that the Empress Jingo took when she returned from the subjugation of Korea in the third century. Although the event goes back to mythological times, it must be of considerable interest still to medical men and especially to gynæcologists because it is one of the first recorded cases of birth control! The blessed event, it is written, was postponed for a period of three years after conception owing to the exigencies of the military invasion which she led into Korea!

There were no pine-trees in Ikuta, and there are none there to-day, because the god of Ikuta dislikes pines.

In the 12th century a battle was fought at Ikuta and it is still told in song and drama how the fifteen year old son of Kajiwara Kagetoki plucking a small branch of blossoming plum and thrusting it into his quiver, charged into the fray. Wherever the battle was fiercest, there was the young samurai mounted on his horse and with the plum blossom fluttering high in his quiver. The lyrics tell us that the heart of the youth being as pure and guileless as the plum blossom, the gods protected him.

Even as late as 1868 when Kobe was opened to foreign trade, the highway to Osaka was narrow and unsuitable for wheeled traffic. With the exception of a few of the rivers over which there were rickety bridges, most had to be forded or crossed in ferries. The Tokugawa Shoguns were not bridge builders and did not encourage too many highways. They knew that poor communications hampered the movements of subversive troops and rendered the control of those moving on the capital easier to maintain. Even so, as on all roads in Japan in feudal times, there was a constant stream of porters, pilgrims, couriers and travellers on foot, on horse or in palanquins.

Daimyo processions and travellers moving overland from Hyogo to Osaka would turn into the avenue leading to Ikuta Shrine, where the porters and others would rest under the stately trees. The theatres and amusement quarters had been left behind and there was nothing ahead of much importance in the way of amusement until they reached Osaka.

In those days the more renowned of the gay ladies of the amusement quarters in the great cities gilded their lips, blackened their teeth, painted their faces with false eyebrows, pushed half a dozen or more large tortoise-shell hairpins into their elaborate coiffures, dressed in heavy silk brocaded kimono, and tied their *obi* in front in a large bow which gave them the appearance of being enceinte even when they were not. As a seductive device they whitened with a heavy layer of powder their bosoms, and more especially the backs of their necks—that being then a much admired part of the female form.

These adornments were among the badges of high rank in their profession. Their more unfortunate sisters in the common stews wore less elaborate dresses, had ungilded lips and were satisfied with the less fashionable white teeth.

Then of course among the hierarchy of the amusement quarters were the geisha, the actors, and other professional entertainers who also had their own distinctive coiffures and elaborate dress styles. But there were no amusement quarters near Ikuta and the music of the populace was seldom heard there except when wandering minstrels chanced along, or at festival times.

The quietness of the Ikuta Shrine grounds has however long since vanished and to-day there are gaudy cabarets where once there were stately camphor trees. Fashions also have changed, and the entertainers in the cabarets now bordering Ikuta, where the cherry trees and stone lanterns once stood, have retained the powder, added false eyelashes and a pair of shoes, but discarded most else! Jazz music now blares through the temple grounds late into the night. Neon lighting gives the approach the glitter of cheap tinsel. The doves have departed and flowers no longer bloom in Ikuta.

There are over fifty varieties of cherry trees, but it is said that the particular variety which once lined the avenue to Ikuta no longer blossoms well in Kobe. The petals fall to the ground before the buds have fully opened. Even the flowers weep in Kobe at the high price that must be paid for progress.

THE
PARK
LANDS
OF
THE
KOBE
SETTLEMENT

Thirty years ago when the Japanese authorities handed over the Concession to the foreigners... the land was all but valueless.... To-day we hand back to the Japanese authorities the very same site transformed into a regular town.
French Consul, Doyen of Consular Corps, 17th July, 1899

When the foreigners first came to Kobe, feudal Japan was to be seen right at their doorsteps. Large notice-boards were still to be found warning the native population against turning Christian; other notices offered rewards for information leading to the apprehension of Christians. Public execution grounds were still to be seen in front of the Kencho

---

This chapter first appeared in *The Mainichi* newspaper on Feb. 9, 1955.

Since it was written in 1955, a large portion of the park lands of the former Kobe Settlement, which by international treaty were set apart as a perpetual trust to be maintained as park lands for the public use, has been alienated.

and also on the beach at Wada Point where criminals were decapitated. At the latter place a show of heads, half putrefied and half devoured by the ravens and crows, could at times be seen affixed to long pikes. Floggings were common and criminals were transported in bamboo cages, much like so many fowls.

Although the people of Japan had long been forbidden to leave the country, a number had managed to slip out through Nagasaki and Yokohama. The most notorious case occurred in 1862 when five young nobles succeeded in getting themselves smuggled out of Nagasaki on a British ship with the connivance of an English merchant, Mr. T.B. Glover. Then, with the assistance of Jardine Matheson & Co., they finally reached London serving as common sailors during the voyage. In England they studied British methods of rule and government. In having left Japan these five young men had committed what was at that time a capital offence. The Tokugawa Government made vigorous protests at this connivance by foreigners at such a breach of the law, but all ended well, because a few years later when the Tokugawa Shogunate was approaching its fall they were able to return, and took their places in the task of assisting Japan to emerge from a feudal to a modern age.

In February, 1868, one of these young men, Ito Shunsuke, became the first governor of Hyogo Prefecture, and it was his breadth of vision gained from his trip abroad, and his ability to visualize Kobe as a great international trading centre of the future, that contributed to a solution of some of the prob-

lems that faced the Foreign Municipal Council of
the Kobe Foreign Settlement. Later, as Prince Ito
Hirobumi, he became one of Japan's foremost statesmen. Of the others, two became famous under the
names of Marquis Inouye Bunda and Viscount Inouye Yakichi.

A statue of Prince Ito stands close to the Diet
Building in Tokyo and foreign visitors to that great
city look with some wonder at the only red-headed
Japanese in the nation! The statue having been cast
from a bronze in which there is a fairly large iron
content, the head of that worthy prince, which is
the part most exposed to rain and dew, has rusted a
brick red thus producing the startling and somewhat
ludicrous effect of a red-headed Japanese!

When the foreigners landed at Kobe on New Year's
Day 1868, they were disappointed to find that the
site given to them for a settlement was largely a
barren and undesirable sandy waste. They controlled
their Settlement through their own Foreign Municipal Council, and during the course of the next thirty
years transformed it into what came to be referred
to as the Model Settlement in the Far East. Parks,
recreational, sporting and social amenities were
gradually created. One of the earliest community
efforts took place on 23rd September, 1870, when
the Kobe Regatta & Athletic Club was formed,
undoubtedly one of the most important happenings
in the foreign community of Kobe, important too for
the Japanese. Just as the Foreign Concessions in
Japan served as the fountains from which Western
learning and ideas flooded into feudal Japan, so also

was the K.R. & A.C. and similar foreign sporting clubs elsewhere in Japan the fountains through which a knowledge of rowing, swimming, rugby, soccer, hockey, field and track events, and in fact most western sports first came to the Japanese. The Japanese learned so well that in many events they soon surpassed those who had been their teachers. In this connection it is of interest to recall that in 1916 E.W. Slade introduced into Japan through the K.R. & A.C. the crawl stroke in swimming. The Japanese quickly learned modern swimming techniques and within a decade had broken into international swimming contests.

But let us return to the events of 1870. A boathouse and a gymnasium were built at what was then known as Eastern Camber, located just south of the present club, very close to what is to-day the main entrance to the Customs.

In 1872 an arrangement was entered into between the Foreign Consuls and the Japanese authorities for the use of a piece of ground but which later came to be known as the Recreation Ground. It was over nine thousand *tsubo* in area and extended along the eastern side of the Concession. It thus became one of the public grounds of the Foreign Settlement. On 19th August, 1875, a formal treaty was entered into by the foreign powers with the Japanese Government whereby this land was designated as public ground or garden to be maintained and managed by the Foreign Municipal Council *"as a perpetual trust for the common recreation of Foreigners and Japanese."* The treaty was signed at Yedo by Terashima Munenori for the Japanese, by Sir Harry S. Parkes for the British, by John A. Bingham for the United States of America and by the diplomatic representatives of Belgium, France, Italy, Russia, Spain and others.

In 1878 an arrangement was legally approved whereby the K.R. & A.C. Gymnasium should be moved to a corner of the Recreation Ground, where the club has been located ever since. Thereafter the K.R. & A.C. assumed much of the responsibility for maintenance of the Recreation Ground.

In 1899 when the era of extra-territoriality came to an end and foreigners were brought under Japanese jurisdiction, the Foreign Municipal Council transferred the administration of the Foreign Concession to the Japanese municipal authorities, who then became responsible for the maintenance of the Recreation Ground and other park lands in the Concession, as provided for in the Treaty of 1875. On that occasion under date of 17th July, 1899, the Governor of Hyogo Prefecture despatched to the Mayor of Kobe Instruction No. 467 stating, *inter alia,* that the City is responsible for the preservation of the parks and:

> *In regard to the upkeep and administration of Parks you are requested to exercise great care. . . . so as not to give occasion to cause any feelings that by coming under my Prefectural Government's administration the arrangements for such institutions were not being carried out.*

At that time about the only public park lands in Kobe city were those which the foreigners had created. Vacant land for the public use hardly ex-

The Park Lands of the Kobe Settlement

isted. Certainly the main temples in Kobe, such as
Ikuta Temple, Ninomiya and others, were surrounded
by forests belonging to the temples, but as the city
grew the trees were cut down and the land sold or
rented out for building. The treaty arrangements
respecting the park lands of the Kobe Foreign Settlement were possibly the first opportunity the people
of Japan had of observing a principle that has been
jealously guarded, and fought over too, in England
from early Saxon times, and possibly in other countries also, and that is that the common lands—the
public lands—belong to the common people and
must not be filched by those in power. Although
the park lands which the foreigners handed back to
the Japanese were pitifully small for a great city,
they have nevertheless been the object of landgrab-
bing from time to time by the city fathers.

There does stand out in sharp relief, however, one
interesting example—unfortunately a rare example—
of meticulous care taken by the Japanese authorities
to observe the principles of the treaty, whereby those
park lands are to be held in perpetuity for *"the common recreation of Foreigners and Japanese."*

Along the centre of the so-called Bund in Kobe, in
front of the Oriental Hotel, are a number of grassed
plots, not particularly well cared for, that form islands in the centre of the roadway. In the balmy
days of spring the *rumpen* gather there, drowse,
scratch themselves and crack the lice hiding in the
seams of their clothing. (*Rumpen,* a corruption of
the German word *lumpen,* is now used by Japanese
to describe beggars and tramps in tattered clothing.)

That same place was once the favourite promenade of European ladies dressed in crinolines, but later more fashionably gowned with flounces, bustles and long trains.

To understand this transformation and the reason for those grassed plots, one must go back over ninety years to 1868 when Hyogo was first opened to foreign trade. Kobe then consisted of little more than a straggling fishing village. A wide sandy beach extended from the present day Kawasaki Dockyard to the mouth of the Ikuta River which was then close to the present day K.R. & A.C. The fishermen hauled their nets up onto this beach and landed large catches of sardines (*iwashi*) which nowadays, owing to the pollution of the sea arising from the drains of the city of Kobe, do not normally come much further up the bay than Shioya and Suma.

In those days at the typhoon season the sea waves swept over the beach and flooded portions of the low sandy waste that was to be the future Kobe. Water also flowed in from the hills, and in the absence of drainage channels the whole area was often waterlogged, and is described in the early records as having contained many quicksands. Eventually the area was drained, the level raised and a sea wall constructed. When the first land sales were held, the first lots of land sold were those stretching along the sea front. The most attractive houses and business premises in the Settlement were built on those sites, all of which commanded a fine view of the sea across the Bund.

The narrow strip of land between the Bund road and the sea wall was then turfed, and benches were erected. It thus became one of the parks maintained by the Kobe Foreign Municipal Council where little girls in lace-edged pantaloons romped in the daytime, and where the foreign ladies and gentlemen strolled in the evening and listened to the local band or to one of the bands from visiting warships.

This narrow strip of lawn was thus one of the park lands eventually handed back to the Japanese, to be maintained in perpetuity for *"the common recreation of Foreigners and Japanese."*

In the nineteen-twenties extensive reclamation schemes along the water front were undertaken, and a railway line was laid down on the reclaimed ground. The former Bund thus became a road far removed from the sea. The sea wall had of course been pulled down and the road widened, but the Japanese authorities meticulously observed the principles of the treaty and the narrow strip of turf, which had once served as the fashionable promenade on which the bands had played over fifty years before, was converted into islands, such as you see to-day, and so in accordance with the treaty the land is being preserved as park land for the joint use of foreigners and Japanese alike.

THE
OPENING
OF
OSAKA

> *This great centre, Osaka, with its port of Hyogo must be worth more to foreign commerce than all the other ports put together.*
>
> Sir RUTHERFORD ALCOCK 1861

Osaka was opened to foreign trade on the same day as Kobe, which was January 1st, 1868, but for centuries before that time it had been a flourishing trading centre.

Will Adams described it in 1600 as being *"a very great towne as great as London."* The English East India Company opened an agency there a few years later, but the Portuguese, Dutch, and Chinese had agents in Osaka before the English. The English were thus the last in the field and the least experienced in the market. They did not find trading easy and Richard Cocks, manager of the company, described his difficulties as follows:

> *That which chiefly spoiled the Japon trade is a company of rich usurers whoe have gotten all the trade of Japon into their own hands...which maketh me altogether aweary of Japon.*

After ten years of unprofitable trading the English East India Company closed down and left Japan. Shortly afterwards Japan made her momentous decision to shut herself off from the Western World, and started by ordering the Portuguese out of the country. Apart from the Chinese Trading Guild, only the Dutch were allowed to remain, but they had to give up their agencies in Osaka and other places, and were confined to the tiny island of Deshima, in Nagasaki harbour, which had just been vacated by the Portuguese. During the two centuries or so that the Dutch remained there, they frequently passed through Osaka on the occasion of their periodical visits to Yedo to pay tribute to the Shogun. Dr. Engelbert Kaempfer, the physician, who saw Osaka on one such occasion, has left the following description of that city:

Osaca is extremely populous, and if we can believe what the boasting Japanese tell us, can raise an army of eighty thousand men among its inhabitants. It is the best trading town in Japan, being extraordinarily well situated for carrying on commerce both by land and water. This is the reason why it is so well inhabited by rich merchants, artificers and manufacturers. . . .Whatever tends to promote luxury or to gratify sensual pleasure, may be had at as easy a rate here as elsewhere, and for this reason the Japanese call Osaca the universal theatre of pleasurers and diversions. Plays are to be seen daily. . . .

The re-opening of Osaka to foreigners in 1868 took place, as already mentioned, on the same day as Kobe, but little ceremony was attached to the occasion because the sandbanks across the entrance to Osaka made the sea approach too dangerous for large vessels.

The Opening of Osaka

The foreign merchants and others intending to go to Osaka therefore had to disembark at Kobe and proceed either overland or by junks.

As in Yokohama and Kobe, and later in Tokio, the site allotted in Osaka for the future foreign settlement was at the time a worthless stretch of waste land. Nevertheless it was pleasantly situated. It was known as Kawaguchi and lay outside of what was then the city of Osaka. It was bounded on three sides by rivers, along which passed great fleets of junks and other vessels.

Land communications in those days were so poor that there was even greater emphasis then than now in Japan on sea and river communications. The early foreign residents in the Osaka Settlement used to sit on their front verandahs and watch that never-ending traffic on the rivers.

The *Japan Times Overland Mail* of 27th January, 1868, presented to its readers in Yokohama and Tokio a description of Osaka received from one of the first arrivals there:

Osaka is a fine place of, according to Japanese accounts, some 300,000 inhabitants.... The streets are almost perfectly straight, crossing each other at right angles, and of a uniform breadth of 15 to 20 feet. There is nothing grand or stately in its appearance except the castle and temples of which there are upwards of 1,000, but it is undoubtedly a place of trade, almost every house being a shop or godown.

The river is lined with junks, some of a size which makes it a matter of wonder, as in the case

94

of King George's apples in the dumplings, how on earth they got in there.

The foreign settlement is in a well chosen position, and the Ministers really deserve great credit for selecting the best site in the whole city for the purpose.

The new arrivals did not imagine that a few weeks later they would be within a short distance of a civil war battlefield. The clans were struggling for possession of the Person of the Emperor, who up to that time had been cooped up in Kyoto by the Tokugawa clan. A new constitution had been proclaimed and a return to the ancient system of rule by the Mikado. The Shogun's power had waned. He almost had been driven from power and had retired to his powerful castle in Osaka. Then it was that the strongest clans from southern Japan began to concentrate their forces against him. Battle raged for three days in the Kyoto area, until one of the *daimyo* defected to the other side. The issue was then certain. The days of the Tokugawas were over. Their control of Japan was at an end. They abandoned Osaka and the victorious Imperial forces entered the city and burnt and pillaged the great castle.

And so within less than thirty days of their arrival in the new Settlement at Osaka, the foreign merchants who had come to open up foreign trade, fled back to Kobe. Most of them decided to stay there.

A new-comer to Japan four years later was much impressed with the growth of Kobe, which he described as a modern town, but he was less impressed with Osaka:—

The Opening of Osaka

Osaka was formerly the chief commercial town of Japan and is still a city of not less than 400,000 inhabitants, boasting of a very old moated castle of much historical interest, a modern mint, an arsenal, and a considerable garrison. Few foreigners live there, and those are chiefly either missionaries or government employees.

Those interested in shooting had almost a virgin field within a short distance of the Settlement. Plenty of wild duck were to be found in the marshes around what is to-day the Osaka Railway Station. One of the favourite Sunday excursions for those not interested in hunting was a walk to the famous nursery gardens at the top of Dotonbori, which is now the amusement and night centre of Osaka. Those gardens were then the best in Osaka. On the way they would stop at Mitsui's drapery store and make a few purchases.

In the early days of the foreign settlements, foreigners were restricted in travel to distances of about twenty-five miles, but were not permitted to approach the Imperial City of Kyoto, not because the Emperor was then deemed too sacred to be seen, but because the Tokugawa Shogunate would not permit any approach to Kyoto except through their own officials. Furthermore, for the purpose of assuring their own survival, they had posted "No Thoroughfare" notices at all the seven principal entrances to Kyoto. Later after the Emperor established his capital in Tokyo, the prohibition on foreigners entering Kyoto was gradually abated.

The journey by jinrikisha was tiring and so it be-

came customary, especially in summertime, to travel
from Osaka to Kyoto up the Yodogawa by river boat
during the night rather than to be jolted about in a
jinrikisha. The boats were flat-bottom houseboats
such as may be seen to-day on some rivers. The
larger ones were pushed upstream by eight men with
poles twelve to sixteen feet in length.

*They would start together at the bow of the boat,
each with a pole braced against his shoulders and
then with a yell they would plunge their poles into
the shallow river-bed and rush together towards
the stern making the boat fairly jump on its course.*

*It was ludicrous to us who sat within to see this
continuous procession of naked legs passing to and
fro, for our windows being low, we could see the
biped extremities of the human propellers with the
least possible clothing.*

In places, where towing was possible, the crew went
ashore and began hauling the boat with long ropes.

In summer such trips usually started at sundown,
so that the crew could escape the heat of day. Of a
summer night that part of the river near Osaka was
lively with many pleasure parties on boats lighted
with lanterns and enlivened with fireworks. The
boats bound for Kyoto travelled on during the night
and arrived at Fushimi, a suburb of Kyoto, at about
6 a.m. the following morning. Such trips to Kyoto
were for the foreigners very much in the way of an
adventure, for it was not until Kyoto was linked to
Osaka by railway that many foreigners visited that
place.

There were not many foreign merchants who went

to Osaka on its opening, and as the years passed by more left than remained, until eventually Kawaguchi became more of a missionary than a trading centre. Still later its character changed again and Kawaguchi and the adjoining district became a sort of Chinatown. The foreign merchants had soon found that they could equally as well transact their business from the more favourably located and congenial settlement in Kobe, where they also enjoyed a greater measure of security than in Osaka. Foreign men-of-war were generally anchored off Kobe in those troubled times for the protection of the Settlement. Most of the foreign merchants continued to maintain their offices in Kobe until after the First World War. From then on, with changing circumstances, trade gradually began to move towards Osaka, with Kobe maintaining its position of importance as a shipping port.

THE
TOKYO
FOREIGN
SETTLEMENT

Edoo, a Citie of Japan as bigge as London.

RICHARD COCKS' letter, 1614

The astute Tokugawa Shoguns maintained their control over Japan for about 265 years by the introduction of a number of novel security measures. One which they developed was the requirement that each *daimyo* (the feudal lords who governed the provinces) should maintain an establishment in Yedo and spend part of each year there. When they departed they were required to leave some of their womenfolk and children behind as hostages.

One of the districts in Yedo where some of the *daimyo* residences had been located was at Tsukiji, meaning reclaimed ground, so named because many years before the flats between the branches of the Sumida river had been reclaimed and built on.

The trade of the city of Yedo had been maintained mostly by means of its shipping which was very large, and in fact the vessels lying in the port were said to be *"as thick as the scales upon the back of a fish, while the masts presented the appearance of a dense forest."*

After Tsukiji was reclaimed many fishermen built their huts there. Their catches of fish were landed and auctioned on the beach nearby, out of which humble beginnings developed the odoriferous fish-market of Tokyo, which is located close by to-day. A hundred years ago the district was sparsely populated, because it was one of the least desirable parts of Yedo. The wells were brackish and noisome. The cleansing of the place was largely done by armies of raven-beaked crows and kites. A little beyond Tsukiji, at each ebb tide, miles of mud flats were laid bare, from which arose a festering stench. In the middle of this section of the city there was a large area of vacant ground used as a dump for all manner of evil refuse—the so-called Tsukiji-no-hara. When negotiations were opened between Japan and the foreign powers, and the foreigners wanted to reside in Tokyo to carry on business, the Japanese Government offered them Tsukiji-no-hara as the only vacant ground at their disposal. The rubbish was cleared away. Well laid out streets and fine houses were subsequently built where previously was squalor and rubbish tips. After the foreigners had settled there, a Japanese writer described the transformation:

The new Settlement increased in size day by day, month by month, until the new buildings resembled the teeth of a comb in closeness and orderliness. There was no longer any stinking refuse or hollow places filled with stagnant water at Tsukiji.

Yokohama had been opened in 1859 to foreign trade and as a place of residence for foreigners; Kobe was opened on 1st January, 1868, but it was not until exactly one year later that Tokyo was opened. By that time much of the opposition within Japan to the entry of foreigners had been overcome, but during the ten years that the merchants in Yokohama had been waiting for Yedo to be opened, their enthusiasm had cooled and they had begun to reconsider whether it offered the great trading possibilities that they had at first imagined. Many decided that their trading operations could equally as well be conducted from the more pleasantly located settlement in Yokohama. Tsukiji therefore did not attract as many merchants as was at first anticipated.

Those firms with steamship agencies had been impatient at first to establish branches in Tokyo, but by 1869 they were no longer much interested in going there. The times were changing rapidly and the lucrative charterage business that they had hoped to do in Tokyo with the *daimyo's* representatives was by then a thing of the past.

Prior to the arrival of the foreigners in Yokohama it had been customary for the *daimyo* processions on their trips to and from Yedo to take the dangerous and uncomfortable sea voyage in junks or the tedious and expensive land route over the Tokaido. After the arrival of the foreigners it became fashionable for the more wealthy *daimyo* to arrange for a foreign vessel to be chartered through one of the local foreign firms, and for their retinue, often amounting to several hundred persons, to travel by steamer in greater comfort and with more speed. This innovation in travel did, however, present an added responsibility and hazard for the unfortunate steward or transport officer on the *daimyo's* staff, because, while an order from the *daimyo* was an order that could not be lightly disregarded, the unfortunate steward had no control over the arrival and sailing dates of oversea vessels. After the overthrow of the Shogunate and transfer of the residence of the Emperor to Tokyo, the *daimyo* were no longer required to maintain establishments in Tokyo. The *daimyo* processions to and from Tokyo, which had been a feature of the feudal days, then ceased.

Following the decline in power of the Tokugawa Shoguns, the *daimyo* who had been compelled to stay in Yedo closed down their establishments and moved their families and their retainers back to their own provinces. There was then such an exodus that Yedo was left almost in the hands of robbers and *ronin.* The latter thereupon began to occupy the mansions which had been deserted by their owners, and from those strongholds they set out to plunder and kill. The civilians thereupon commenced to leave and the tradespeople began to shut up their shops. Trade slumped. The ancient splendour of Yedo was paling, as fast as were the fortunes of the House of the Tokugawa Shoguns. Yedo had reached its lowest ebb.

Then on 29th October, 1868, the Emperor left Kyoto to take up residence in Yedo, thereafter to be known as Tokyo, or eastern capital. He travelled in a palanquin, guarded by one thousand soldiers. Except for eight bands of Japanese drums and fifes, which played the same single strain over and over again, the procession passed on unobtrusively through the country for twenty-eight days. The Emperor entered Tokyo on 26th November, 1868. Shortly afterwards preparations were made for him to receive the representatives of the foreign powers. In the words of the *Japan Times Overland Mail* of 13th January, 1869:

> *In January an Imperial demi-god, unapproachable, sacred from the eyes even of his own nobles: in December asking admission within the circle of civilized sovereigns, attempting the part of a constitutional monarch and preparing to receive the representatives of a score of foreign nations and foreign services, every individual of which the law, but a few short years ago, enjoined each true Japanese to slay, should he dare to pollute the soil of Nippon with unholy tread.*

So hesitant were the foreign merchants to establish themselves in business in the capital that on 2nd June, 1870, when the first land sale was conducted it took the auctioneer an hour to sell the first lot. During the remainder of the day twenty-four lots in all were sold, but few to merchants. As a foreign commercial centre, early Tokyo was a failure. From the beginning the shallowness of Tokyo Harbour doomed to failure the Tsukiji Foreign Settlement as a center of trade.

The Settlement faced the river and was moated on all sides by canals. It reminded the foreigners far too much of the island of Deshima in Nagasaki, on which the Dutch had been confined for over two hundred years, and created in the minds of some the impression that another Deshima was being attempted in Tokyo.

The land entrance to the Settlement was guarded

by a watch house with Japanese soldiers, but as they were generally more afraid of the two-sworded *ronin,* than the *ronin* were of them, they were not always effective.

Although the name of the city had been changed to Tokyo (or Tokio as was the commonly accepted Romanised spelling of those days) some of the legations, including the British Legation, for reasons tied up with the early treaties, persisted for about another ten years in using the word Yedo, notwithstanding the fact that the Japanese insisted that such address no longer had any legal application.

By 1880 the city named Tokio had found its way into most school geography books in the Western World, where it was generally described as "the largest city in the world." Tourists certainly found it to be large and sprawling, but as quiet and backward as a country town abroad. They were struck with the extreme quietude of the place, which they explained by the absence of horse-drawn vehicles or any noise of horses' hoofs on cobblestones. The carts were mostly man-drawn over mud roads.

In 1872, fire, the hazard of Tokyo over the centuries, wiped out a great part of the city including a considerable portion of the Foreign Settlement and so marked the end of that Settlement as a trading community. Most of the foreigners who were burnt out never thought it worth their while to re-establish themselves in Tokyo.

Among the many fine edifices of feudal days that were destroyed in that same fire was the old Nishi Honganji Temple that was located near the edge of the Foreign Settlement. Several times previously it had been destroyed by fire, but it was always built again on a grander scale.

The earthquake and the fires of 1st September 1923, wiped out the few links that remained around Tsukiji of the old Settlement days, and once again the Nishi Honganji Temple was destroyed—the fifth occasion within its history of some six or seven hundred years. Wide roads were built where previously had been a crisscross of narrow streets and once again the priests rebuilt their temple, but this time as a fire-proof building in reinforced concrete and outwardly in an ancient Indian style of architecture. It withstood the air raids of 1945. And so when the Occupation troops and later their dependents came to Japan, this temple with its interior blend of Oriental and Western architecture and its foreign-styled seating accommodation for the congregation, became one of the wonders and most visited places in Tokyo.

Until the railway line connecting Yokohama and Shinagawa was opened in 1872, communications between the two foreign settlements were maintained by four-horse coaches, called the *Yedo Mail*. The journey took four hours and the terminal point in Tokyo was Hall's Store, which was located not far from the present site of St. Luke's Hospital. Cobb & Co. from Australia who had established themselves in Yokohama, ran a competitive service.

There was an alternative route by sea in a small steamer named the "City of Yedo" which left the English Hatoba in Yokohama in the morning for

Tsukiji and returned to Yokohama at night. One day her boiler burst, resulting in the death of seventy-one persons and she sank at the pier at Tsukiji.

The first trains were piloted by English engine drivers, and for quite some time the chief engine driver, an Englishman, was always called upon to pilot the train when the Emperor Meiji travelled by rail.

From the earliest times the Foreign Settlement in Tsukiji tended to become the centre of religious and educational bodies that had entered Japan concurrently with the merchants and were carrying on their work with great zeal. The present great St. Luke's Hospital grew out of modest beginnings there many decades ago.

Tsukiji continued to be the centre of foreign religionists. The diplomatic community gathered around Kojimachi-ku, but in the nineteen thirties when red-tape control began to take a firm grip on business, foreign firms drifted into Tokyo around Marunouchi. But it required the upheavals following a world war, the peculiar circumstances of an occupation, and the strangle hold of bureaucratic economic controls to really bring the foreign merchants to Tokyo in a big way. They came in a swarm following the Occupation, some with boxes of tricks hidden up their sleeves. A number have since departed with their carpetbags packed to overflowing. Fortunately they did not come to Tsukiji—the site of the old Foreign Settlement. There was neither room nor opportunities for them there, and so some of the greatest work in Japan continues to be carried

106

on from that old site—the relief of the sick and the suffering, admittedly work far greater and more noble than the few struggling merchants and shop-keepers had ever been able to do in Tsukiji.

If there be any shades of those early merchants wandering the highways and byways of Tokyo these days, they must be very lonely and troubled spirits, lost in a maze of streets and boulevards unknown to them when alive, with hardly a landmark standing that would be readily recognisable by them, their ethereal existence at all times endangered by the motor traffic of modern Tokyo, and their spiritual serenity driven to distraction by the noise and hulla-baloo of the most expensive city in the world.

LIFE
WAS
SIMPLE
THEN

Wee spent fortie days in learning
the Elements of the Japonian tongue
with great labour.
FRANCIS XAVIER, 1549

Life in Japan ninety years ago was so simple for
foreigners that if one possessed a Bible, a dictionary
and a copy of the *Hongkong Daily Press Directory*
it should have been possible to cope with any emer-
gency that might arise.

A copy of the Hongkong Directory for 1865 lies
before me. It is a sizeable volume of over five hundred pages bound in quarter leather and contains,
among many other features, an alphabetical list of all
"Foreign Residents in China, Japan and the Philippines" with occupations and addresses. Three thousand seven hundred and ninety-two adult males are
listed but the directory does not make mention of
any females as it was strictly a commercial directory.
The Smiths easily top the list—forty-one in all—
followed by Silva, Pereira, and Remedios with twenty-
eight, twenty, and eighteen respectively.

There are separate and detailed sections covering
each port. In Japan there are Yeddo (sic), Yokohama, Nagasaki, Deshima, and Hakodadi (sic). It
is interesting to note that in those days there were

six European policemen in Nagasaki. In Hakodate there were three European butcher shops, their clientele of course being the whalers and other ships. There is no reference to Kobe (Hyogo) which port had not at that time been opened to foreign trade. An examination of all sections covering Japan shows that with the exceptions of *Jardine Matheson & Co.* and the *Netherlands Trading Society* there was not a foreign bank or firm then operating in Japan that has survived the hazards of trading and is still in business to-day under the same name.

The Hongkong section covers fifty pages as against thirty-four pages for Shanghae (sic). Of all the ports in the Far East, Hongkong seems to have been the only one sufficiently organised to have an "Inspector of Brothels."

There are seperate sections for the China ports of Amoy, Canton, Chefoo, Chinkiang, Foochow, Hankow, Kiukiang, Newchwang, Ningpo, Pekin, Swatow, Tientsin, Whampoa, and Tamsui and Takao in Formosa.

The Macao section occupies four pages, which is more than that for the whole Philippines and almost as much as for Yokohama, but it is dull reading and conveys no hint as to whether there then existed the gambling and other joints upon which its fame rests today.

The Manila directory comprises only four and a half pages and it is to be noted that the United States then had so little interest in the place that they ran a joint consulate with Norway and Sweden. The mysterious matter of the U.S.S. "Maine" in Havana harbour twenty-three years later changed all that for the Spanish possession of the Philippines. Incidentally among the crew members of the ill-fated "Maine" when she blew up, there were nine with Japanese names, of whom seven lost their lives.

The directory also contains much information on international treaties including the Treaties of Friendship and Commerce between each of the great powers (Great Britain, United States, France) and Japan, all of which were reproduced for the benefit of the early traders, many of whom carried on their businesses with the aggressive opportunism of sea-lawyers. The regulations under which trade was conducted are set out in full and could be understood by any high school student in an hour—an astonishing contrast to the complications of life to-day. Nowadays the tax law of Japan alone represents a volume much greater and many times as expensive, and as most people know is couched in such language that it requires another volume of greater size for the guidance of taxation officials in interpreting the law.

In addition the directory contains a day by day calendar according to both the European and the Chinese systems, complete customs tariffs, postal rules and regulations, comparative tables of weights and measures, consular regulations, and exchange rates; five pages devoted to passenger and freight rates, terms of carriage and the complete sailing schedule of the P. & O. S. N. Company for all routes for that year; Japanese, Chinese, Mohammedan and Parsee festivals, fasts and observances; and a mass of other information down even to a schedule of the opium sales to be held in Calcutta for the year.

The whole cost for all this information was only four Hongkong Dollars.

The Yokohama section lists the names of two hundred and sixty-eight male residents, but in addition there were actually the British and French military garrisons, the drifting population of sailors and mariners, and the less respectable folk—male and female—including the ever-present beachcombers who never got their names in any directory other than those maintained by the local jails.

Listed among the foreign residents was Joseph Heco, originally a Japanese seaman named Hamada Hikozo, who was shipwrecked in 1850, rescued and carried to America where he lived for some years and probably was the first Japanese to become a naturalised citizen of the United States. He returned to Japan as an interpreter when the country was opened and became one of the earliest newspaper men in Japan, if the crude sheet he published could be termed a newspaper.

In those days riding hacks and ponies were as familiar a sight in Yokohama as in Rotten Row, but a new means of transportation was shortly to be born. An American Baptist named Jonathan Goble, half cobbler and half missionary, and originally a marine on the U.S.S. "Mississippi" when Commodore Perry made his expedition to Japan, finding it tiresomely uncomfortable to be carried around in a *kago*—a Japanese type of sedan chair—designed for himself an oversized perambulator drawn by one man. To

111

this contraption the Japanese gave the name *jin-riki-sha* (man power carriage) but this being too big a mouthful was contracted to *rikisha* which was later Anglicized to ricksha or rickshaw.

At first there was similar opposition to this new fangled method of transportation as to the introduction of railways in England, but the idea soon caught on and within three years there were over 25,000 licensed *jinrikisha* giving employment to far more men than those who formerly carried *kago*. From then on the number increased immensely, which fortunately relieved much of the distress among the porters on the Tokaido and other highways who were being thrown out of work by the introduction of railways. Ironically enough in the port cities, then, and even now, these vehicles and the men who drew them were often engaged in a pursuit that would never have been approved of by Jonathan Goble! From Japan the *jinrikisha* idea spread to China, but there also it at first met with opposition, particularly from the cart guilds.

It was not until as late as 1871 that the common people of Japan were permitted to ride on horseback; prior to that time only the samurai or military class were allowed that privilege. In the same year the people were also given permission to wear *hakama* (divided skirt-like loose trousers) and *haori* (type of tunic coat) which theretofore had been the distinctive garments of samurai.

Yokohama in 1865, the year of the directory described above, still looked very much like a small mining town that had blossomed into sudden pros-

perity. In 1866 much of the Settlement and most of
the Japanese town were destroyed by a fire, and
thereafter the Settlement was rebuilt in something
better than weatherboard style.

With the filling in of the swamp at the rear of the
Settlement and with the digging of many drainage
canals, the health of the community improved,
although if we are to believe much of what was
written about Yokohama in those early days, the
moral tone remained as low as ever.

More and more foreign women folk were coming
to Japan, and palatial homes and tasteful bungalows
were beginning to be built on the Bluff, whilst the
riffraff lodging houses in the Settlement were extending back to what was formerly the swamp.

The residents and transients in the Foreign Concession represented a varied bloc of humanity. Well
dressed merchants and bankers in suits from Saville
Row or tailored by Chinese from Shanghai and Hongkong, British soldiers in red, and French in blue,
French Catholic priests, Russian and Greek priests,
Japanese itinerant priests, Jews orthodox and otherwise from every nation, nuns, Yankees with carpetbags, drunken sailors of many countries, whaling
captains, blustering Russians and epaulet wearers of
all sorts, well dressed compradores, English butchers,
French bakers, German sausage-makers and Chinese
shroffs, a few sun-tanned Australians from the goldfields, missionaries, ladies of fashion, little girls in
pantaloons, Chinese amahs, Japanese porters, money-
changers, beachcombers and bums. Any samurai
entering the Settlement had to park his swords at

the guard houses at the entrance to the settlement. Customs duty was mostly at the rate of five percent but somewhat higher for intoxicants. Liquor was cheap, however, and never in short supply except on those rare occasions when shipwrecks caused temporary shortages. Taxation forms were unknown, and it was permissible to do business and to live without the necessity of filling in application forms and securing permits!

Food was plentiful and dieting unheard of. Certainly the water was bad, but as already stated liquor was cheap, both of which circumstances cut short many lives.

The tradesmen and shopkeepers were all foreigners and the womenfolk, for what few housekeeping duties they performed, were able to do their shopping and instruct the tradesmen in English. Most of the servants were Chinese. The supply of Japanese servants far exceeded the demand. Very few of the latter understood any English or had learnt to make the appropriate guesses, nor did they show any aptitude for learning pidgin—that mongrel talk as debasing to the dignity of the speaker as of the one spoken to. Residents in the foreign settlements later evolved a dialect of their own which came to be known as Yokohama Dialect, and thus some of them made their one and only contribution to cultural relations with Japan. The following delectable specimens are fair samples of that once dead, but recently partly resurrected, language:

"Moods cashey."   Is it too difficult for you to do?

114

Life Was Simple Then

"Oh terror arimasu."   I went to church, I am going to church, or I will go to church (and many others at speaker's option).

"Coconuts arimasu."   It is nine o'clock.

"Yakkamash sto."   A drunken sailor.

And incidentally *"Coots pom-pom otoko"* meant ....You could not guess it? A shoemaker.

Yokohama dialect was a tongue that largely ignored the existence of the kitchen. It was a curious circumstance but most foreign women then (and much later also) forgot how to fry a sausage or boil porridge—arts in which they were long experienced. From the time the P. & O. vessel pulled out of Tilbury Dock, and as she rounded the Cape of Good Hope (Suez Canal was not opened for traffic until 1869) and began to chug up the Indian Ocean, they had no fear of starving; they had already learnt that bountiful providence would take care of them in the form of Chinese cooks and house servants. Most of them never saw again the once familiar domestic sight of fat frizzling in the frying-pan, that appetizing spectacle being reserved thereafter for their Chinese cooks and for the myriads of cockcroaches that shared their kitchens.

115

THE CONSULAR COURTS

> *Japan being a country not only the most distant from us, but the most inaccessible to Europeans of any upon the face of the earth, it may be some time before we are rightly inform'd of the temper and genius of this people.*
>
> SALMON—*"Modern History or the Present State of All Nations"* (1725–1739)

"KNOW ALL MEN, THIS COURT STANDS ADJOURNED. GOD SAVE THE QUEEN."

These words read on 31st January, 1900, by the Clerk of Her Britannic Majesty's Court for Japan, marked the end of an era in that it was the last occasion on which a foreign court functioned in Japan until some forty-five years later when the Occupation commenced and various foreign military courts came into being for a while.

After Japan was opened to foreign trade in 1859, foreigners lived here under the system of extraterritoriality whereby they were exempt from the jurisdiction of Japanese law courts. Whilst that was a necessary provision when Japan was first opened and the Japanese legal system was that of the feudal ages with torture and all manner of other barbarous practices, the time eventually came when the Japanese began to believe that their legal system had developed to such a stage that a revision of the treaties could fairly be asked for. In 1877 the Japanese Government began its system of subsidizing an English language newspaper to present its case. The first was the *Tokio Times* which, according to its contemporaries, was a "puny periodical" which with "tedious verbosity and mawkish insipidity" began to attack extraterritoriality, week in and week out. The following is but a single specimen:—

> *Extra-territoriality—that fungoid and poisonous growth, of pride of race and conquest, a dying echo of medieval barbarism, an echo which will only cease to sound when the walls of prejudice reflecting it are thrown down.*

In the years that followed much headway was made in modernising Japan's legal system. Finally in 1899 the era of extraterritoriality came to an end, and from that date all foreigners in Japan became amenable to Japanese law. Actually Mexico showed the way by being the first to sign a new treaty with Japan, but as at that time there was only one Mexican national resident in Japan, some people were not slow to point out that Mexico did not have much at risk.

Dr. Engelbert Kaempfer, the German physician attached to the Dutch East India Trading Station on Deshima, in Nagasaki Harbour, complained in 1690:

> *It is an easy matter for anybody, whether native or foreigner to make his claims upon the Dutch, but we find it very difficult to obtain justice from others. . . . If we have a complaint to make we generally meet with so many difficulties and delays*

117

*as would deter anybody from pressing even the
most righteous cause.*

Two centuries later when Japan was opened and
foreigners lived here under the system of extra-
territoriality, many Japanese experienced the same
feelings of frustration owing to the difficulties of
procedure in securing justice where their complaints
were against foreigners. The foreigners likewise
encountered difficulties in attempting to sue Japanese
in the Japanese courts of that time.

Under the treaties the citizens of each foreign
Power were amenable to the laws of their respective
countries and justice was administered by Consular
Courts of the different nationalities. Under this system, for example, an American committing an offence
against a Japanese was tried in the U.S. Consular
Court, whereas a Japanese committing an offence
against an American was tried in a Japanese Court.

Towards the end of the last century when Consular
jurisdiction approached its end, some of the die-
hards in the foreign community professed apprehension at the idea "of abandoning the lives and property
of Europeans unreservedly to Oriental rule," but most
fair-minded men felt that the system of Consular
Courts had served a useful purpose during a period
of transition but was outdated and should go.

Among Japanese circles only the Buddhist priesthood were apprehensive of a revision of the treaties.
Under extraterritoriality foreigners were mainly
restricted to residence in the treaty port areas, and
passports were required for travel outside a radius
of ten *ri* (about twenty-five miles). Exceptions were

made in the case of those foreigners employed by Japanese, which included teachers and many telegraphists and other technicians in the employ of Japanese Government departments.

Special passports were given to those seeking to live in the interior for health reasons. The Buddhists at first feared that the end of extraterritoriality might result in an influx of foreigners into the interior in numbers so vast as to menace Buddhist influence.

Perhaps the vigour and the lack of good manners with which some of the early foreign missionaries had sought converts justified such fears. Some of the early missionaries have described how they used to attend Buddhist religious services at the temples, and distribute tracts among the worshippers, and enter into controversial arguments with the priests.

The foreign press of the Treaty ports, on the other hand, saw no advantages ahead and were lamenting the fate which they imagined awaited the foreign community once extraterritoriality was abolished. When the change actually came neither the fears of the Buddhist priests nor those of the foreign press materialised.

When the system first came into being all the Powers maintained purely consular courts presided over by the consul. However, the British Government at an early date saw the defects in such a system, and in 1865 established at Yokohama a branch of Her Majesty's Supreme Court of China presided over by a trained lawyer. In 1878 the Court was reorganized, provided with complete judicial machinery under the supervision of trained judges and thereafter was known as Her Majesty's Court of Japan. The high integrity of that court and the able manner in which the law of England was administered was an object lesson that was closely watched by the growing Japanese judiciary.

Most of the Powers however, left the administration of justice to their consuls and the courts that were convened were often of a makeshift nature, each with its own legal code and traditions, with which the Consul was all too frequently ill-informed, and not qualified to deal. Some of the honorary consuls in particular soon found themselves entangled in a mesh of legal procedure, especially complicated when the case involved parties of more than one nationality.

There were the extreme cases also where an honorary consul, whose personal interests conflicted with his official duties, heard and decided cases that were brought against himself. To carry a case to appeal involved considerable expense and many legal hurdles had first to be jumped. Little wonder that a Japanese editor once wrote with some bitterness:

Injustice is the general rule in some of these courts.
Justice is rare.

When two foreigners of different nationality were involved, the court had no power of enforcing its verdict against the party of the other nationality or of securing payment of costs, unless that party's national authority offered co-operation, which was not always forthcoming.

There were many defects in the system. For example, because of the absence of a statute of fraud under American law as administered by U.S. Consular Courts in Japan, the U.S. Consular Courts could not convict U.S. citizens who insisted on riding the Japanese railways without tickets.

Although appeals against verdicts in the British Court could be made to the British Supreme Court in Shanghai, in most other cases appeals had to be carried to the home countries. In the case of the U.S. Consular Courts appeals had to be made in San Francisco. While the heavy expenses involved in such appeals may have prevented some would-be appellants from securing justice, they undoubtedly must have discouraged much needless litigation. Seemingly some such deterrent was necessary because a perusal of the newspapers of those far-off days shows that the foreign community was astonishingly litigious. Four or five hundred foreigners in those early days could be depended upon to provide a good living for three or four foreign lawyers. The large amount of copy that reports on law cases provided for the local foreign newspapers may possibly explain why some of the lawyers combined law with the business of running a newspaper.

Judging from the number of libel suits that came before the consular courts, foreign residents must then have been rather touchy. One case that came before the British Court aroused much interest and stirred up some national feelings. It was brought by an Irish legal gentleman who complained that a certain Englishman had held him up to ridicule and contempt by the circulation of a caricature which represented him in his earlier days as hoeing potatoes!

There was little co-operation between the various Consular Courts and the results of bringing an identical complaint against persons of different nationality could not be foreseen. There was the unusual case where two Englishmen and one American indulged in a midnight frolic as a result of which a Chinaman lost his queue. The unfortunate man lodged a complaint at the British and American Consulates and in due course the cases were tried. The judge in the British Court was correctly dressed in wig and gown and after lengthy examination of the evidence handed out a very heavy fine to the two Englishmen with the alternative of imprisonment, whereas their American friend got off quickly with a nominal fine in an informal trial in the U.S. Court, a result which earned for British justice the admiration of the Chinatowns in Japan.

Lockups were maintained in the Foreign Settlements for dead beats and casuals, but when a prisoner was sentenced in the consular courts to a term of imprisonment, he was transported abroad to serve the sentence.

If a foreigner were of a nation with whom Japan had no treaty, any case against him had to be tried in the Japanese local court. It did at times arise that, where a sailor, a beachcomber or a resident, not registered at a consulate was charged with a serious offence, he might first endeavour to calculate whether he was likely to receive a lighter sentence in his own consular court or in the Japanese court. If he decided that the Japanese court would probably be the more lenient, he might refrain from establishing his nationality so that his case would have to be heard in the Japanese Court. There was an occasion where a German charged with murder decided to take his chance on Japanese justice rather than on German, and succeeded in having the case tried before a Japanese Court. The German Consul was, however, anxious to get his hands on the accused and by establishing that he had German nationality obtained his release from the Japanese Court. The German then confused the whole issue by appealing to the Japanese Supreme Court against his own release!

Sympathies must be with the Japanese courts in their efforts to deal with some of the complications that arose out of the system. There was the celebrated case where the Oriental Bank brought an action against a foreigner of a nation with which Japan had no treaty. The case therefore had to be heard in the Yokohama Local Court. During the course of the trial the Court summoned a former manager of the bank to give evidence. The gentleman in question appeared, but apparently was no longer friendly towards his former employers and refused to give testimony unless allowed $100 Mex. a day for expenses. This was impossible for the Court to allow because the Japanese scale of remuneration for witnesses was no more than fifty sen a day. Upon the former bank manager declining in the circumstances to give any evidence the Court adjourned to consider the problem, and later announced its decision, with the wisdom of Solomon:

A witness cannot be punished for declining to give

*evidence, but he can be punished for non-attend-
ance. He may therefore be required to attend day
after day until he chooses to open his mouth!*

On the very same day that the new treaties came
into force a beachcomber named Miller, a man of
doubtful antecedents but claiming American nationality, murdered three persons in a Yokohama saloon.
Miller had deserted his ship the "Tam O'Shanter" for
an easier life ashore and then conceived the idea of
marrying the Japanese proprietress of the saloon
"Rising Sun" in Bloodtown, Yokohama. He had
competition in that another American of about
equivalent character, but half his age, had the same
ambition and seemed to be making more headway in
his suit.

It was on the eve of the cessation of extraterritoriality that Milller, in a fit of rage, killed his rival
and then despatched the proprietress and another
Japanese girl on the premises with a razor and a
claw hammer. The saloon and the bedrooms upstairs
presented a ghastly appearance the next morning
when the crime was discovered. Miller was soon
arrested and in the course of time was tried in a
Japanese court.

While the manner in which justice was dispensed
in some Japanese courts in certain commercial suits
became, rightly or wrongly, a target of criticism in
the foreign press, there was nothing but commendation for the manner in which the Japanese court
handled their first foreign murder case. General
sympathy was also felt for the Japanese police force
in having a triple murder on their hands, on the

first day that they became responsible for the handling of foreigners.

There was a feeling of relief when Miller was given the death sentence, but it quickly turned to uneasiness when it was heard that Miller's Japanese counsel had lodged an appeal, which strangely enough was supported by counsel for the prosecution, on the unusual grounds:

(a) That as the murders had occurred on the day of the new treaties taking effect, the sentence should be commuted in order to make known the goodwill of the Japanese authorities towards foreigners.

(b) That of the three persons murdered, two were unlicensed prostitutes and the third an American swindler.

The dignity of the law was fortunately upheld by the Court of Appeal confirming the death sentence. On the day of his execution Miller ate a hearty breakfast comprising "a pound of bread with beef and other food instead of the forty *momme* of bread usually given."

Just before the execution Miller thanked his Japanese gaolers and the governor of the prison for their kindness, confirmed that he had no worldly possessions to will away, and then asked for a last drink, meaning an alcoholic drink. This was refused, but the Governor of the prison provided instead a glass of warm water, it being then winter time. Miller then requested permission to smoke a last cigar, which was granted, and curiously enough the missionary minister who was attending him was able to supply the cigar on the spot. When it was only half smoked, the Governor announced that time was up. The hood was pulled over Miller's head. His arms and feet were tied. He fell the calculated number of feet and precisely eight minutes later was declared dead. The hangman had done a neat job, and so deservedly died the first foreign criminal tried in Japanese courts after the days of extraterritoriality.

EXCITEMENT IN THE SETTLEMENTS

*Our entertaynment was good, only
the drinking was overmuch.*
RICHARD COCK's Dairy, 1615

The foreign community of Yokohama in the early days of nearly a century ago, and also that of Kobe when it was opened about nine years after Yokohama, comprised a more colourful and varied block of humanity than to-day. At the top—although this would have been strenuously denied at the time by the majority of the foreign community—were the diplomats and the consular corps. The order in which the remaining categories followed was a matter of personal opinion—and prejudices were strong in those days.

There were the numerous foreign experts attached to the various Japanese Government Departments such as the railways, telegraphs, lighthouses, public works, navy, etc. The mercantile community comprised members of old established and highly respected trading houses and banks, also more adventurous types and many rank carpetbaggers. There were the missionaries, included in whose number were many industrious students who later became authorities on the Japanese language, culture and history. There were the shopkeepers and tradesmen, the legation guards, the soldiers, the saloonkeepers of

Bloodtown, the demimonde down Creekside, and last of all the beachcombers.

Those were the days when the expression "The Reds" (or *Akatai* in Japanese) had an entirely different connotation than it has to-day. To the Japanese "The Reds" in those times were the red-coated soldiers of the English regiments who were then stationed in the little town of Yokohama, of whom at times there were over a thousand men. It was the military stationed in Yokohama who first organized sports and at an early date established a United Service Club, which ultimately merged into the Yokohama United Club.

In the early days of the foreign settlements, when very few Japanese knew English and when most were unfamiliar with Western customs, many Chinese from the Foreign Settlements in China came to Japan seeking employment. In those days when you entered a merchant's office or a foreign bank or knocked at the door of a foreign residence, the person who enquired your business was a Chinaman. The cooks invariably were Chinese and generally the house servants also. The butler, footman and cook at the British Legation were Chinese. When you exchanged your money at the bank or at the exchange shop or purchased a railway ticket, it was a Chinaman who attended to you. Their familiarity with the intricacies of coinage made them especially useful as cashiers in Japan at a time when Trade Dollars, Mexican Dollars, and a variety of Japanese coins and bullion were in circulation. Those were the days before currency restrictions had been thought of, and travellers carried coinage at will exchanging it wherever it suited them to do so, without being treated as criminals, as is so to-day.

The Chinese have always been the largest bloc in the foreign community. By 1878 there were over 2,500 in Japan of whom 1,100 were in Yokohama. Chinatown was beginning to take shape, and in fact in later years it became one of the tourist sights of Yokohama, much as Chinatown in San Francisco was on the other side of the Pacific. Then, as now, the Chinese were great gamblers, but for security they conducted their fan-tan schools in the servant-quarters at one of the local consulates, where they reckoned they enjoyed greater immunity from detection and arrest. It was a wise consul who knew as much about his servants as they knew about him.

Townsend Harris, the first U.S. Consul-General to Japan, was the first to make that discovery. He landed at Shimoda in 1856 accompanied by two Chinese servants, one a cook, the other a tailor. They were quick to learn all the angles of life in Japan and within a few months of their arrival had visited all the apothecary shops in Shimoda asking for opium. On being refused supplies they hunted through the shelves until they came upon containers bearing the Chinese characters for that drug, whereupon they demanded it in the name of the United States of America. When all this came to the notice of Townsend Harris he ordered that the opium be restored to the apothecaries, but by then his servants had converted it into a form suitable for smoking but no longer fit for medicinal purposes. He then directed that no opium, sake, or intoxicating beverages should be sold to his servants. That they were thereupon deprived of supplies is unlikely. Probably the good Townsend Harris, by curtailing the supply had merely succeeded in raising the market price of such commodities for his staff to such a level that one of the first blackmarkets came into being.

Apart from the risks of contagious and infectious diseases (and liquor, which the early arrivals did not admit was a danger to their mortal existence) the greatest hazard that they ran was that of assassination by two-sworded *ronin*. As soon as the dangers of assassination and violence decreased, more foreign women began to appear in Japan, but even before they had arrived in any great number, the Japanese had become aware of the difference in attitude towards womenfolk between the West and Japan. Many of the English soldiers quartered at Yokohama had badges on their caps depicting Britannia, and whilst individual Japanese opinions differed, some believing the figure was that of the Queen and some that of the colonel's wife, the general impression was one of amazement that so much respect should be shown by soldiers to a mere female.

In the early days of the Foreign Settlements people were expected to know their proper places in society and to remain there. The visiting theatrical shows usually advertised "select nights" when the upper crust attended and from which the *hoi polloi* gladly kept away; then there were the "ordinary nights" when the soldiers and the tradesmen and shopkeepers from down Creekside came along and when a junior of the *hongs* could get "lit-up" with a girl friend without fear of being seen by the *taipan's* wife.

Fortunately it was on a "select night," when the local doctor was in the audience, that a tenor on taking in a great breath, after having lingered long on a top note, sucked his false moustache down his throat. It blocked his windpipe and the startled man displayed every symptom of dramatically dying on the stage from suffocation. It was then that the doctor in the audience came to his rescue; there being no drop curtain to the stage the audience had the unusual experience of witnessing a laryngotomy being performed with a penknife.

The foreign volunteer fire brigades in Yokohama (and later in Kobe) were always busy and effective. And how they turned out in force to put out the fire and to rescue the girls whenever there was a report at night of a fire at one of the female establishments over at The Swamp! Sometimes it was learned later that the report was a false alarm. At any rate they had started out in good faith!

The beachcombers were always a problem to both the police of the Foreign Settlements and to the Japanese police outside. When they were drunk and found the foreign municipal police on their trail they would slip out of the Foreign Settlement and hope that the Japanese police would not chase them back again too quickly.

In 1904 a use was at last found for them. A play dealing with the Russo-Japanese War was being produced in Nagasaki by a Japanese theatrical party, and the beachcombers were approached as persons who might bear with fortitude the catcalls and the nasty things that might be shouted and thrown at them by angry Japanese audiences whilst they were acting the parts of Russians in the play. The beachcombers readily fell in with the idea of becoming actors, after first making clear that they did not much mind what they did so long as it was not hard work. They were thereupon engaged for the sum of "Yen 12 per month all found." A few whose voices had been so deeply corroded with cheap whisky, that they could only talk in husky whispers, had to be discarded, but the others made pretty convincing Russians.

Early in 1908 members of the foreign community in Japan were rocked with excitement, alarm, anxiety or amusement, depending on exactly which side of the fence one happened to be sitting, at the discovery that about thirty most respectable English couples were living in sin, or in a state of concubinage, as the newspapers more elegantly expressed it, and that no less a person than the Anglican Bishop of Tokyo was responsible for their predicament. The alarm of some of the couples who had imagined that they were married, whereas in fact they had been cohabiting for over seven years and had one or more children was very painful, because under English law at that time children born out of wedlock could not be divested of illegitimacy by the subsequent marriage of the parents. Quite apart from the stigma of illegitimacy there were also the grave disabilities placed on those children by English law.

All this came about when a divorce suit, *Marshall v. Marshall,* came before the court in England and the judge refused to grant a divorce on the grounds that there had been no valid marriage. The parties to the case had believed themselves to have been married by the Bishop of Tokyo, but as the learned judge pointed out they had merely participated in a religious ceremony of no legal significance.

During the years of extraterritoriality, that is to say up to July, 1899, religious marriages performed in the churches within the Foreign Concessions in Japan were regarded as valid in English law, but when the Concessions became incorporated within Japanese municipalities and foreigners came under Japanese law, the laws of the respective countries ceased to operate except within the embassies and consulates; consequently the laws of England in regard to marriages in the church also ceased to operate and all the marriages thereafter that had been performed in Anglican churches in Japan, without any civil ceremony at the Consulate, of which there were over thirty, were consequently invalid.

On 9th February, 1908, the Bishop of Tokyo delivered a long and brilliant sermon in Christ Church, Yokohama, in which he explained the full effect of the mistake made by himself and others in officiating at such marriages, and it was this news that spread throughout the foreign community engulfing it like a rising tidal wave. It burst, as it were, into the drawing rooms of the stately houses on the Bluff; it spouted into the Yokohama Club and splashed about in the saloons in Bloodtown; it even seeped into the houses in Dirty Village, where the news was so little understood that it at first gave rise to murmurs of disapproval on the quite erroneous but ludicrous misunderstanding on the part of the girls in those houses, that they had sisters in distress who had opened on the Bluff in competition.

When the news that they were not legally married hit the parties concerned, it is not known whether any of the "wives," who may have nagged, nagged less, or whether any of the "husbands" who may have been wayward, became more wayward; nor is it known with what feelings the various partners awaited the outcome of the efforts that were being made to legalize the marriages.

In due course of time, however, after a special act of Parliament was passed rendering those marriages retrospectively valid, the couples concerned found that the state of concubinage in which they had innocently been living had come to an end.

Since those days Britishers marrying in Japan who desire a religious ceremony are careful to have a civil ceremony carried out at the Consulate first, except maybe in a few rare and eccentric cases where they may go though a marriage ceremony in accordance with the *lex loci*.

In 1945 when the Occupation commenced the Allied soldiers thought that the military regulations forbidding fraternization with the Japanese were unduly strict, not that they were ever very rigidly enforced or obeyed. Many soldiers soon formed friendships with Japanese girls and began to make enquiries as to the manner in which wedding ceremonies were conducted in Japan. The information that they received was not always complete or accurate, often it was not genuine or disinterested advice. Many soldiers paid fees, generally demanded in canteen supplies through middlemen, for secret Shinto marriage services to be performed. There may have been occasions when the ceremony was conducted in a shrine by genuine Shinto priests, but more often the priests were imposters, using wooden trays and other paraphernalia that they had whisked away from some nearby burial ground.

There were a number of second-rate teahouses that specialised in arranging secret Shinto wedding services for the soldiers, and in those establishments it was generally the kitchen-boy who hastily donned Shinto robes over the top of his kitchen clothes and assuming the guise of a Shinto priest mumbled a few inane prayers at what was represented to be a legal and valid marriage ceremony. Those impudent impostors bargained through the medium of the teahouse servants for the type of ceremony that the bridegroom desired. An extra couple of tins of cigarettes was demanded for what was promised would be a "Number One" ceremony complete with a marriage certificate.

When we saw some of the wooden trays and other paraphernalia that had been taken from nearby cemeteries for use at those soldier weddings, we were reminded that when Commodore Perry went ashore at Kurihama nearly a century earlier to force the Japanese to open their doors, he was pleased to note the imposing chair provided for him as compared with the uncomfortable stools upon which the Japanese sat. The good commodore derived considerable satisfaction from sitting elevated there in glory, but it is doubtful that his satisfaction was as great as that of the Japanese as they watched him, perched high on his seat, because the chair had in fact been borrowed from a nearby temple and represented part of the usual equipment of a Buddhist funeral. While it may have been that the Japanese did wish him dead, the fact must also be mentioned that there were no genuine foreign chairs available at that time, and the funeral chair was the highest one obtainable.

THE
PIONEERS

*The people whom we have met so
far are the best who have as yet
been discovered, and it seems to me
that we shall never find among
heathens another race to equal the
Japanese.*

ST. FRANCIS XAVIER, Nov., 1549

About the middle of the sixth century travellers
from China began to bring to Japan news of the
teachings of Buddha, and in the years and the
centuries that followed there was a constant stream
of priests and Buddhist monks from as far west as
India who brought in teachings of the Lotus Law.
The outward glory of Buddhism, the inspiring
rituals, the prayers and chantings of the priestly
choirs, the bells, the gongs, and the incense, appealed
to the masses. The richly brocaded clothes of the
priests, and the gorgeous canonical processions, set
among the magnificent temples, added much to the
simple life of the people, a life that had previously
been so drab and monotonous. The promise of better
existences in times to come had a popular appeal.
Buddhism prospered and the curved roof of the
temples grew higher and more immense. The statues
of the deities became more elaborate and ornate.
Then nearly a thousand years after the first word
of Buddha was brought to Japan, competition arrived
when the famed Jesuit priest Francis Xavier and

several others, including some Japanese converts, landed in Kyushu. Francis Xavier preached in the streets, and although his poverty at first made him contemptible in the eyes of the Japanese, nevertheless within two years, he and his followers had made nearly a thousand converts, and before many years, it was said, there were three hundred thousand Christians in Japan, although some historians have put the figure much higher.

For the Japanese of those times, the change over was not as great as might at first be thought. The Jesuit preacher promised paradise no less than the Buddhist priest. The temple altars, the flowers, the bells, the holy water, the candles, rosaries, and incense were already there. The Jesuit missionaries were able to offer the people images no less majestic, processions more gorgeous, and services even of greater solemnity than the rites of the Buddhist priesthood. The statues of Buddha were easily changed to that of Christ, the shrines of Kwannon to those of Mary, and the images of the Buddhist saints to those of the Disciples.

Unfortunately the Christians were over militant and took sides in the political struggles of the times. They were branded as enemies of the State, and then within less than a century persecutions almost snuffed them out. They were buried alive, burned at the stake, and cast over cliffs—all except a few faithful communities who secretly persisted in their faith for over two centuries, during which time the doors of Japan were tightly shut to the Western world.

During those two centuries or so, the Buddhist

priesthood had lived a life of comparative ease, of
quiet contentment, free from worldly matters and
always with sufficient to eat and drink. The earlier
energy of the priesthood had largely spent itself.
Their days opened with the chanting of prayers at
daybreak, followed by light household duties, then
merged into long hours of meditation, and in chanting the vespers at sunset, followed by a long night
of sleep.

They pursued no scientific studies, made no inven-
tions, no agricultural improvements; they added little
or nothing to the literature of the nation. Their
lives were almost perfect blanks.

When the doors of Japan were re-opened nearly a
century ago, the Christian missionaries again came
in, and it needed just that new competition to revi-
talize the Buddhist priesthood.

The Japanese populace, no less than the Buddhist
priests, were greatly impressed with the zeal of the
first Christian missionaries, mostly from America,
who came in, even if the methods adopted by some
of the more zealous do appear to-day to have been
at times, rather startling.

For example, one of the earliest described his
method of approach in the following words:

*When the missionary reaches the village he puts
up at a hotel. He then informs the landlord that
he wishes to preach in his lower room. Permission
is generally easily obtained. The shojees (sic)
are then removed, thus throwing all the rooms into
one. The talking then begins in a conversational
way and the crowd begins to gather until the streets*

and yards are packed with listeners. The exhorter then steps on to the verandah and preaches to a respectful gathering for a couple of hours at a time.

One well-known missionary related how in 1873 he entered into a religious argument with some *mikoshi* processionists (those carrying the portable shrine at a religious festival) and endeavoured to convert them to Christianity. Certainly the times have changed. Even Japanese policemen during the last fifty years have always thought twice before entering into any form of argument with such processionists.

On another occasion the same missionary strode up to the entrance of the main hall of a temple and by his eloquence and fluency in Japanese turned the Japanese congregation away from the Buddhist temple, and persuaded them to attend instead a Christian meeting.

In a book published in 1878 by the American Tract Society, another missionary describes how upon visiting the "Dai Butz" at Kamakura, he "climbed up into his capacious lap and sat upon one of his thumbs, which were placed together in a devout attitude." Whilst recognising the devoutness, the good missionary apparently did not consider he should respect it, because he then relates how from that place of vantage he thereupon began to sing the Christian doxology. A year later he again visited the Daibutsu, where he and six friends scrambled up onto Buddha's lap, formed a choir, and sang Christian hymns to the astonishment of the priests.

This particular missionary had come to Japan in

the service of the Japanese Government as a teacher of chemistry and physics with the hope that he could at the same time spread the Gospel. He proceeded by *kago* (sedan chair), and rickshaw, and on foot over the Hakone range to Shizuoka, where he was provided with quarters in a Buddhist temple. There he found a "very atmosphere of sacred solitude." The priests were polite to him upon his arrival and sent him presents of fresh tea raised in their own garden, boxes of eggs and sponge cake, after which he conceived the idea of conducting a Bible class within the monastery and inviting the priests to attend:

In fact I had a Bible class, even in this stronghold of heathenism with nothing to interrupt except the noise of the gongs and the pagan worship in the adjoining temple.

I hope I may be pardoned for harbouring the suspicion that some of these old books and the happenings of three quarters of a century earlier, must have been read by some of General MacArthur's advisers. That at least might explain the total embargo placed on all temples and shrines during the first stages of the Occupation, when all such places were declared *Off Limits* to Occupation personnel, an order enforced by the placing of Allied sentries before them. One of the few exceptions was the Nishi Honganji Temple in Tokyo, perhaps because it was built in foreign style, or rather ancient Indian style. At any rate that came to be one of the most photographed buildings in Tokyo, and almost any day one could find Occupation soldiers sitting quietly and reverently within the temple, hoping that they might have the good fortune to witness a Buddhist religious ceremony.

If the object of the U.S. sentries first placed on guard before the temples was to protect them from souvenir hunters, then it failed to take into account that the ambitions of most of the first Occupation troops were firstly to purchase a kimono as a souvenir of Japan and then to secure discharge and a return to civilian life as quickly as possible. Curiously enough the first objective was in the early days of the Occupation as difficult to attain as the latter.

The women of Japan, acting on the urgent advice of their own Government, which had been broadcast over the radio prior to the arrival of the Occupation troops, had already cut up their kimono into *mompei* (trousers) in order to protect their virtue, only to discover when the troops did arrive, that they had destroyed their only possession which *every* Occupation soldier really coveted. Japanese swords as souvenirs had slumped. Japanese kimono had taken the place of swords as a much sought after souvenir, but few were to be seen—only unromantic trousers.

The same radio broadcast had also warned that red undergarments should be hidden, because the glimpse of that colour would inflame the passions of the troops to rape. And so it was that the red under-kimono were also cut up or otherwise disposed of. Actually that was no great loss from the souvenir angle, because red petticoats had ceased to be glamorous female undergarments in the West about the same time that European males gave up wearing red flannel chest protectors.

But let us return to the religious subject of this article.

Even before Japan had re-opened her doors, the zeal of the missionaries was very great, and many were planning to come to Japan as soon as a treaty could be concluded and their entry permitted. In fact, while Commodore Perry was negotiating a treaty, one of the chaplains in his squadron came ashore and distributed Christian tracts at a Buddhist temple. The Japanese authorities were quick to protest at that jumping of the gun, and Commodore Perry took appropriate disciplinary action.

When the treaty was concluded and when the first pioneer missionaries settled in Japan after the opening of Yokohama in 1859, much preparatory work had first to be done. Little wonder is it that up to the spring of 1872, during the period of twelve years after the arrival of the first Protestant missionaries, only ten Japanese had received baptism at their hands.

The missionaries had to spend much of those first twelve years in the prodigious task of making dictionaries, translating catechisms and doctrinal literature, and in learning the intricacies of the spoken language.

Quite apart from the immense language barrier which had to be overcome, the poor results in the number of Japanese converts during the early years was not due to any lack of zeal on the part of the missionaries, but rather to the continued hostility of the Government of those times to Christianity as a pestilential creed, and to the oppressive laws. One ordinance, promulgated as late as 1868, read:

*The evil sect, called Christian, is strictly prohibited.
Suspicious persons should be reported to the proper officers. Rewards will be given for such information.*

According to the old notice boards which at that
time still stood at the entrances to most towns and
villages, the reward varied from a maximum of five
hundred pieces of silver for information against a
padre, to one hundred pieces of silver against a common believer in Christianity.

Under the anti-Christian laws, even as late as ninety years ago, Japanese found professing Christianity
were still being tortured and thrown into prison,
where in fact many died as martyrs to their faith.
Families were broken up and scattered, and many
of the members were exiled to different parts of the
Empire.

When the Foreign Powers protested these "evil
sect" laws, Japan pointedly referred to European
history of two or three hundred years earlier, where
the records showed violent prejudices between people of different faiths, the religious wars, and the
tortures inflicted on those who would not recant.

The Tokugawa Shogunate had sent representatives
abroad in 1862, but they were more interested in
noting down in notebooks all that they saw, rather
than in listening to any criticism of Japan's behaviour. When, however, the first Imperial Japanese
Embassy, which was sent abroad in 1871, returned
and reported on the unfavourable impression that the
anti-Christian laws were creating, the notice boards
were soon withdrawn. The anti-Christian laws re-

mained on the statute books for some years, but breaches of that law were ignored.

Before Prince Iwakura went abroad as the head of that Embassy he had said that *"the Government would resist the propagation of the Christian religion as they resist the advance of an invading army,"* but following his return from abroad he recommended that tolerance be shown to the one-time evil sect. The law against Christianity still stood, but it was not enforced.

In a year or so it even became possible for a Japanese Christian to be buried in a Buddhist cemetery upon payment to the priests of the customary fees, or a little more.

Great progress was made by all the Christian missions in the years that followed, and especially when it became possible for translations of the Bible and other Christian literature to be exposed for sale and openly circulated without fear of penalties.

As often happens to Japan, the pendulum then swung far to the other side, and a decade later some Japanese statesmen and public leaders were even urging that Christianity be adopted as the national religion. At least one of them advocated that the Emperor receive baptism. Even in Kyoto, a stronghold of Buddhism, a Christian was elected to the first Diet.

For a brief period Christianity, or rather the profession of it, enjoyed much popularity, until the Buddhist hierarchy in Japan was so aroused to the dangers from that competition that they engaged an American theosophist to tour Japan as a lecturer and rally the Japanese back to the folds of Buddhism.

And so it was that the remarkable Colonel Olcott came to Japan. The *Dictionary of American Biography*, from which I shall quote hereafter, devotes a fair amount of space to the gallant colonel, and relates that he *"has been variously considered a fool, a knave, and a seer, and was perhaps a little of all three."*

Henry Steel Olcott was educated at the University of the City of New York, and then became a farmer. It was whilst farming in Ohio that he became interested in spiritualism. He then served in the Civil War, and, after being invalided home, had the honorary rank of colonel conferred upon him, a title which he clung to until his death. He practiced law and then in 1874 he published books on spiritualistic phenomena, which books, according to the *Dictionary of American Biography*, *"sufficiently convict their author of credulity or chicanery or both."* He then made the acquaintance of the famous (or is it infamous?) Madame Blavatsky, and *"during the ensuing winter they became very intimate. Under her tutelage he plunged into a study of occultism."*

When the Theosophical Society was formed he became its first president, but with all his efforts the Society did not, at that time, prosper, and so *"the Theosophical twins,"* as Madame Blavatsky referred to Olcott and herself, *"sailed for India to carry Hindu philosophy to the Hindus"* but *"within a short while they and the venerable Hindus were denouncing each other as humbugs."*

For a while he practiced mesmeric healing but with-

146

out much success. *"When in 1885 Madame Blavatsky was exposed by the London Society for Psychical Research, opinions differed as to whether Olcott had been her dupe or her accomplice."*

In the meantime he had become a Buddhist, and so it was that in 1889 he was engaged for a lecture tour of Japan.

He was a man of plausible manner and dignified appearance with a long sage-like beard; but one eye did not focus properly: it is said that occasionally that eye got loose and began to stray suspiciously and knavishly, and confidence vanished in a moment.

The Colonel's lecture tour in Japan was not a success. He was achieving nothing to stop the progress of Christianity, and so, as happened then, and since with many another entrepreneur, he suddenly found that his contract had been cancelled.

Around about that time the pendulum again swung the other way, and a reaction set in against the popularity of Christianity. It was no longer fashionable to be a Christian, and many who had professed to be Christians took fright at the national watchcry of *"Preserve the national spirit"* and hurriedly deserted the Christian schools and churches. At the same time they turned away from European dress, European amusements, and European cookery. One can well imagine, and applaud, the women of Japan for discarding their Victorian clothing for kimono fashions, but the adoption of some of the other preferences must surely have been accompanied with pangs of hunger, if not regret.

The Pioneers

The pendulum again swung back when the new Constitution in 1889 declared *"Japanese subjects shall, within limits, not prejudicial to peace and order and not antagonistic to their duties as subjects, enjoy freedom of religious belief."* But not always are constitutions inviolate.

In 1899 when the revised treaties were negotiated with the Western nations, and the days of extra-territoriality came to an end, the whole country was opened to foreigners for residence and travel. The zeal of the missionaries then had a still wider field in which to develop, and, as all know, immense progress was made in the years that followed.

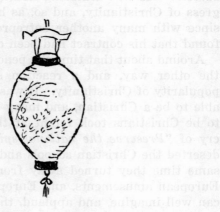

A
VISITORS
BOOK

They feed not much upon varietie.
Description of Japan by Rev.
ARTHUR HATCH, 1623

There have been times and places in Japan when passports and identification cards were deemed by the authorities even more important than in these days.

The time was about a hundred years ago and many years before that also. The places were the barriers or check points which guarded all the main approaches to Yedo, the old name for Tokyo. Such barriers were located at strategic spots where by reason of the surrounding hills, the road could be easily defended against rebels by a small force of the *Shogun's* men.

In those days even a horse required a passport before being permitted entry into Yedo; indeed it was somewhat more difficult for a horse to enter Yedo than for a woman, but it was easier for the horse to come out again than for the woman. Women could enter Yedo without great difficulty provided they really were women and not men in disguise, but before they could come out again they required a passport signed by high officials of the Shogunate.

The reason for all this was that the inspectors at the barriers were charged with keeping a sharp lookout for *de onna iri deppo*—women outward, guns inward. The escape from Yedo of the womenfolk who were held in the capital as hostages for the good behaviour of their lords, the provincial *daimyo*, and the smuggling of horses and guns into the capital would have been sure signs of an impending insurrection.

Those were the days before photography or fingerprinting were known in Japan, but the inspectors at the barriers had other means of checking the identity of travellers. The handbooks compiled for their guidance contained a mass of information concerning the various military clans, family crests and specimens of *daimyo* and other seals of authority, all of which information enabled the inspectors to detect counterfeit passports, check the bona fides of those passing through the barrier, and ensure that spies and insurgents did not slip into the capital. Particular attention was given by the inspectors to corpses, and to wounded or sick travellers who were being carried through on litters, for all of whom special passports were required to ensure that malefactors did not pass in such disguises. The plots and disguises to pass the barrier were elaborate, and despite all the precautions some succeeded in getting through.

The inspectors were generally very thorough in their work, which was carried out slowly and with elaborate dignity—except in those instances where their palms had been well greased—a fact which may have been evident to those foreigners who have attended *kabuki* drama and have noted that it has sometimes taken a pedestrian a good half-hour to get past the barrier!

Those barriers took the form of a palisade stretched across the road with a large gate in the centre somewhat after the form of a temple gate. The barriers and the whole district were guarded by trusted retainers of the Tokugawas, so that it was not an easy matter to slip around the barrier. The penalty for smuggling oneself into Yedo might be death.

The most famous of the barriers was at Hakone not far from the present Hakone Hotel on the lake shore. One side of the barrier was known as the Kanto and the other side as the Kansai. The lake is now famous for its boating, but in the days of the barrier, when it was a check point for travellers, no boats were allowed on the lake, nor was swimming permitted, in case travellers seeking to avoid examination by the inspectors might be tempted to by-pass the barrier by sailing or swimming across the lake.

An interesting, albeit moth-eaten, worm-eaten, and dust-begrimed collection of articles associated with the barrier days has long been gathered together in a building called the Hakone Museum, which stands right opposite the main entrance to the Hakone Hotel. It represents the private collection of a descendant of the proprietor of the *Honjin,* or the officially appointed inn in that district, where the *daimyo* and samurai stayed overnight on their journeyings to and from Yedo.

In addition to some timber from the old barrier,

some poor specimens of spears, pikes and helmets, there are passports of *daimyo*, samurai, farmers, artisans, horses and women.

There is a delapidated *kago*—a type of sedan chair —and a battered old palanquin both in the last stages of disrepair, and reminding us, more than anything else we have seen, of Oliver Wendell Holmes' *One Hoss Shay* on the day just prior to it falling completely to pieces:

> *How it went to pieces all at once,*
> *All at once and nothing first,*
> *Just as bubbles do when they burst.*

Then there are some maps and charts, and a medley of old Japanese account and record books which quite obviously have accommodated and still are providing a welcome place of abode for legions of bookworms.

Among these old records is one old damp-stained and tattered book which we at least found of particular interest, although it does not truly belong to the barrier era. It is a homemade book of thick coarse Japanese paper, similar to the account books that are to be seen even these days hanging on the walls of most country inns and stores in Japan.

When the Tokugawa Shogunate fell, the barrier check point likewise ceased to operate, but until the railways were developed, a decade or more later, the great inns along the Tokaido continued to accommodate the many travellers who moved along that great highway.

The book which we have described is the foreign visitors book of the Kamakura-ya, the principal inn near the Hakone Barrier. The first entry is under date of 1st September, 1871, which was a few years after the barrier days.

Over the hill from Meyonoshta, five miles an hour. Thermo 200. All troubled with consumption (of liquor) E. & O.E.

Most of the entries testify to the *"good accommodation for man and beast, the courtesy of mine host"* and the *"extremely moderate charges."* In fact on 30th September, 1871, two Scots went on record as follows:

This is to notify that during Messrs. McAfee & Sewell's stay here we received every attention requisite. Charges were extremely moderate and the undersigned may caution strangers not to be too lenient with their small change in order not to spoil a good thing.

In 1872 one visitor with some slight artistic ability made a sketch of *"Diaboots"* and on 8th August, 1874, four foreigners returning from Fuji-san wrote:—

Pilgrims returning from Fuji, and mighty glad to get back. We recommend a place at the base of Fuji on the Suyama route by name of Ichigome as a most suitable place to stay at during 4 or 5 days of wet weather provided that those who do so have an over abundant stock of patience (Job never travelled that way). Our experience we forbear relating.

In 1876 two foreigners en route overland from Kobe to Yokohama stayed there overnight. Unfortunately they make no other mention of their journey, nor do they say whether they were travelling on horseback, in a horse-drawn vehicle, in a *kago*, or

A Visitors Book

on foot. (The railway line from Kobe to Yokohama was not completed until 1889.)

An entry in July, 1876 gives an idea of costs:—

What we bought and paid for:

5 *Privileges of Hotel*	$1.25
5 *Trout fish*	.25
Potatoes for 5	.06
Dozen eggs	.12
2 *boats to head of lake*	1.62½
Very reasonable	$3.30½

The dollar was not the U.S. dollar but the Mexican or trade dollar with a value then of about fifty cents U.S. or roughly a little more than two shillings. It, however, had a purchasing power so high that Japan became the Mecca for remittance-men and those with an independent, even although small, income.

In the same year a traveller from Hongkong stayed there with his wife and three children for five weeks during August/September, and *"have been very comfortable and found the landlord and his wife to be always very obliging willing and honest."* To-day none but a reckless millionaire could afford to make such a stay at Hakone.

In March, 1877, a party of three Yokohama residents left Yokohama at 6 a.m. by carriage. as far as Odawara and thence by *kago* to Oban via Miyano-shita and Otomi Pass where there was eight to twelve inches of snow. They arrived at Hakone at 7.45 p.m., taking over twelve hours for what can be done to-day by train and bus in less than two and a half hours.

In 1879 several travellers from Australia stayed

at the inn, and in July, 1880, there is the following amazing entry:

Mr. & Mrs. Williams and Mrs. James.

Amazing that these travellers should have imagined that they possessed such uncommon names that it was unnecessary to add their initials!

In 1885 M. F. A. Fraser *"came from Swatow, China, by a roundabont route—Yokohama, Tokio, Nikko, Ikao, Kusatsu, Zenkoji, Uyeda, Kifu and Mino."*

Those certainly were the days when tourists toured Japan, and all without benefit of motorcars.

The last entry in the book is dated 1896.

Among the names of interest to be found in this visitors book are:

In 1871 Dr. & Mrs. Hepburn—the missionary doctor who devised the so-called Hepburn system for spelling of Japanese words, and so introduced order where there was chaos.

In 1872 F. Cornes the founder of Cornes & Co.

In 1873 E. H. Hunter the founder of the Osaka Iron Works, later to grow into the Hitachi Dockyard.

In 1882 Ernest F. Fenollosa, American critic and philosopher.

As fountain pens had not been invented in those days, a few entries were made with a Japanese writing brush, but the majority were in pencil. Apparently of recent years some Japanese has inked over many of the original entries and in doing so has introduced many spelling mistakes.

155

Foreigners in those days were restricted to 10 *ri* (about 25 miles) in any direction from the treaty ports, but no objection seemed to exist to their visiting Hakone or Fuji. For travel beyond the 25 mile limit, a special passport was normally required.

One of the surprising features of this visitors book is that there is no mention therein of fleas, a subject with which all visitors to Japan in those days had a scratching acquaintance, because those voracious animals were to be found everywhere even up to the ninth station on Mount Fuji. It was said that only there were conditions so rigorous that they could not multiply. That fleas were an important hazard to tourists in Japan in those early days may be judged from the following words of advice to those about to stay in Japanese inns, which are to be found in *The Yokohama Guide,* published in 1874:—

"Buy an ichibu's worth of powdered crude camphor and sprinkle abundantly upon and under the bed and on the floor of hotels for a foot or so around the bedding. Sound sleep is assured as a result."

Possibly had those early visitors to Hakone known that their entries in the visitors book would appear in print some eighty or ninety years later they might have produced something of greater literary merit. The standard throughout is not high as may be judged from the best poem in the book, with which literary work we bring this chapter to a close:

There was a young man from Yokohama,
Who essaid to climb up Fuji-yama,
But when he got back he declared by the smak,
A hell of a hill is Fujiyama. (1880)

THOSE
AUSTRALIANS

> *Zipangu (Japan) is an Iland in
> the East...the people white and
> faire, of gentle behaviour.*
> MARCO POLO, 1295

The first Australians who attempted to land in
Japan—if the mutineers of the brig "Cyprus" could
be termed Australians, which I doubt—were repelled
with shot from shore batteries. They did not succeed
in landing in Japan, nor did they ever get back to
Australia. In fact they ended up on the gallows in
England. That was in 1830.

* * * * * * *

Gold had been found in Australia as early as 1839,
but it was not until 1851 that the big nuggets and
the rich deposits at Ballarat and Bendigo in Victoria
were discovered. Then the "Roaring Days" commenced. Labourers threw down their tools; shopkeepers shut their shops; seamen deserted their ships;
soldiers slipped out of their barracks; policemen
walked off their beat; professional men left the cities
and all rushed to the goldfields.

(There were no restrictions then on entry into Australia and people were attracted from all parts of the
world, particularly from China. Japan however, had
not yet opened her doors and her people were forbidden by the Shogunate under penalty of death to
leave the country. It can therefore be said that the
Japanese were possibly the only people who did not
participate in any way in the Australian gold rush.)

Many found gold. Some made fortunes, but many also returned from the gold-fields to the cities disappointed men. Some then resolved to leave Australia and to try their luck elsewhere. With that resolution there came to Japan the first Australians, the vanguard of a great number during the following ninety-five years.

The *Japan Times Overland Mail* of 27 January, 1869, carried a sub-leader reading:—

We must not omit to mention the advent of a fine steamer, the "Albion," from Australia. She arrived in June and brought a number of passengers who had been induced to move hither by the publication in the Melbourne Argus of some excessively factual letters from a countryman here describing Japan as a new El Dorado. We did immediately what we should have done before, published a couple of articles advising intending immigrants what class of men we wanted and to what they were coming. These and the private letters of the unfortunate victims who have been seduced hither to suffer poverty seem to have checked the movement.

* * * * * * *

Australia contributed an unusually large share to the early newspaper life of Japan, among the outstanding men was J.R. Black, proprietor and editor of the *Nisshin Shinjishi*—the first newspaper (worthy of the name) ever published in Japanese—later editor of the *Japan Herald*, the *Japan Gazette*, and the *Far East*, and author of that standard work *Young Japan*.

Whether Mr. Black would have regarded himself as an Australian is, I think, most doubtful. Probably he would have insisted he was first and last a Scotsman but nevertheless he was one of a number of other early foreign residents in Japan who had come here from Australia, after trying their luck in the Australian goldfields. Although unlucky and unsuccessful as a miner he did achieve considerable distinction as a concert singer on the goldfields.

One of his sons, later known in the Japanese vaudeville world as Ishii Black, seemingly inherited some of his father's flair for entertaining, because he achieved the unusual distinction of becoming a professional reciter and storyteller in Japan. He spoke Japanese fluently and most of the time lived and dressed as a Japanese. His popularity as a storyteller stemmed from his ability to flavour the traditional Japanese stories of history, romance and mystery with some of the folklore and ideas of the West.

* * * * * * *

Among the most colourful arrivals from Australia, was Cobb & Co.'s coaching service—a name which has become famous in Australian song and story. In Japan, Cobb & Co. ran the "Yedo Mail" four-horse coach service from Yokohama to Tokyo, also services to Odawara and other places.

In 1853 four Americans who had been attracted to Victoria by the gold discoveries saw the possibilities for private enterprise in linking Melbourne with the goldfields and beyond, and founded the coaching firm of Cobb & Co. Within a few weeks the firm, which was first known as *The American Telegraph*

Line of Coaches, was running a daily service between Melbourne and the famous Bendigo goldfield.

In the early sixties when Victorian miners flocked to the newly discovered gold strikes in New Zealand, Cobb & Co. sent representatives with them. In course of time the company had spread throughout Australia and by 1870 was harnessing six thousand horses a day and covering twenty eight thousand miles of routes a week. They carried gold under the protection of mounted police escorts from the goldfields to the large cities and frequently had brushes with bushrangers, as bandits were known in Australia.

In 1862 a coach carrying a large consignment of gold was held up, the driver had a bullet through his hat and two police guards were wounded before the booty was secured. One of the persons associated with that incident subsequently found his way to Cobb & Co., in Yokohama.

* * * * * *

It is recorded in history that up to the mid-eighteen sixties the number of foreign ladies resident in Yokohama "could be counted on the fingers of both hands," and the same history then relates that on the rare occasion when a ball was held "the gentler sex had about twenty representatives all told." The apparent discrepancy in fingers is seemingly accounted for by the presence of the English military officers' wives, who presumably were reckoned as army dependents and not residents. It might surprise some of our American friends to know that there was an English military camp and that English military personnel and army dependents were stationed in Yokohama about eighty-five years before General MacArthur and the U.S. Eighth Army arrived in Japan.

The officers of the English and other regiments then quartered in Yokohama were permitted by army regulations to bring in their wives. The other ranks seem to have solaced themselves with lady friends in the grog shops down at The Swamp, along Creekside, and in Bloodtown.

In 1868 there occurred an event that considerably stirred life in Yokohama, and Australia thereby achieved another *first*.

Among the foreign ladies in Yokohama, were Lady Parkes, the British Minister's wife; Mrs. Hepburn, wife of Dr. Hepburn the American Missionary of dictionary fame; the parson's wife; the doctor's wife; the wives of several merchants; the wives of several British army officers in the Yokohama garrison; and also several ladies of divers occupations whose names for one reason or another did not appear in the Hong Lists. However, to establish the point of this article it is now necessary for us to be sufficiently ungallant as to suggest that apparently none of these ladies were young, because it is related in history that in 1868 there arrived in Yokohama from Australia the first foreign young lady—the first in fact of a great number of marriageable Australian young ladies who during the next ninety years or so arrived in Japan single, but left wedded.

Although more than one young foreigner of those days recorded the sensation of that event, our prime authority for this *first* claim on behalf of our country

is an Englishman who, in the early part of the
present century, was doyen of the upper crust of
Yokohama life and who, at the sober age of about
sixty-five years still remembered his excitement as
a young man at the arrival of Miss Gertie Brooke.

Her father, J.H. Brooke, was an unusual man. At
eighteen years of age he had been editor of a small
weekly in Lincolnshire. Then he was lecturer at the
London Polytechnic, but craving greater excitement
he went to Australia and entered the rough and
tumble of politics. It is said that he became a cabinet
minister in the State of Victoria for nearly one week.
Then, following an election defeat, he decided to
forsake Australia forever. He came to Japan, landing in Yokohama in 1862 with an amount of luggage
that set Yokohama society talking for years.

Japan in those days, and not without reason, was
considered to be a *terra incognita* and Brooke was
taking no chances. He even brought tents in case the
paper houses of which he had heard so much should
prove too "papery." He also brought hay for his
horses. What Mrs. Brooke and the lovely Miss Brooke
brought represents a list far too long for reproduction
in this account.

In those days all foreigners who could afford the
luxury—and most could—kept their own ponies, and
horse riding was one of the most popular pastimes
even with those who had lost their shape by standing too long at the bar of the Yokohama Club. Miss
Brooke brought with her a fine Australian mare,
which added to the excitement of the town, because
she was being ardently courted by young men who

possessed slower, smaller, and uninspiring looking Chinese ponies. When she set out riding, she was hotly pursued by many of the marriageable bachelors of Yokohama, except those who realised that their rotundity and weight would be too great a burden even for their sturdy but ugly tempered little Chinese ponies. In speed those ponies could not match the Australian mare, and Miss Brooke left her pursuers far behind.

J. H. Brooke subsequently abandoned commerce in Japan for journalism and became editor and proprietor of the *Japan Herald,* and was perhaps the first trained journalist to run a newspaper in Japan. Politically he was critical of Japan, but in other respects wrote the country up in such colours that many Australians were induced to come to Yokohama where they formed quite a colony.

It was, in fact to counter the severely critical Mr. Brooke, that the Japanese authorities subsidized Captain Brinkley's *Japan Mail.* Thereafter those two protagonists waged unremitting war against one another. Brinkley lived the longest and so had the last say. Indeed he had many "says" even after Brooke had passed away, and when the *Japan Herald* finally went out of existence, Brinkley wrote the bitterest of obituary notices. Said the gallant captain:

"It has been a disgrace to foreign journalism. Its methods have been the methods of the thug. The Japan Herald has been as effective and annoying as the viperist shrillings of some sideway slut."

Mention has been made of the China ponies of Mongolian breed which the early foreigners brought

163

into Japan from Shanghai and other ports in China. They were mostly evil-tempered but had a stamina almost beyond belief. There were more white than other coloured ones, probably because white ones in Mongolia had been less visible by wolves. Their hardiness was such that Sir Ernest Shackleton took a number with him on his Antarctic expedition in 1908.

Later many fast Australian racehorses and some crooked jockeys came to Japan from Australia, the former to improve the stock of the Mongolian breed, and the latter often to continue a career that had been cut short by stewards of the Australian racecourses! Curious though it may sound, one of the finest Australian thoroughbred mares brought to Japan in the early days was raced under the name of "Hitachi" while one of the fastest half-breds was known as "Young Australia." An account of the doings of some of our compatriots in the saddle and on the race tracks must, however, be reserved for another occasion.

To offset some of those dubious achievements our country scored a cultural *first*, for in 1863 an event of some importance in the social life of Yokohama occurred with the arrival from Australia of the first concert party. History describes them as "musical artists" and their names were "Miss Bailey, Mr. Marquis Chisholm, Mr. Sipp and Signor Robbio." The last mentioned gentleman hardly sounds like an Australian, but at any rate the party was formed in and came from Australia. None of these names will be found in the musical biographical dictionaries.

Apparently none achieved great fame, and possibly none topped the billboards of any concert hall in the world's large cities. Nevertheless their names are worthy of record as being the first of many hundreds of musicians and entertainers to visit Japan, pioneers among a band that eventually included the greatest international celebrities in the entertainment and musical world.

From around 1880 onwards seeds of Australian eucalyptus gum trees were brought in and planted at various places—a curious tree, known as *yukari-no-ki* in Japanese, that sheds its bark rather than its leaves. There are two giants on Awaji Island, one in the grounds of Matsu-ho Shrine near Kariya and the other a few miles further south on the edge of the coast road that runs to Sumoto. Originally there were five such trees but only two now remain. All five grew from seeds that were brought to Japan, distributed through the local village office and planted there in 1881. The two remaining trees are therefore over seventy-five years of age, although some of the local residents quite erroneously say they are over a hundred years.

There are so many other Australian gums somewhat younger and around fifty or sixty years of age to be found in the Kansai, particularly around Suma and Shioya, that one is tempted to believe that an Australian counterpart of Johnny Appleseed once lived in these parts.

* * * * * * *

Another arrival from Australia was the brilliant classical scholar, James Murdoch who, although born

165

and educated in Scotland, spent so many of his years in Australia as a teacher, a journalist, a Socialist, and later in life as a university professor as to be regarded as an Australian. He had a remarkable knowledge of Latin, Greek and Sanskrit, was proficient in French and German to which he added Spanish and Portuguese in order to study the original writings of the Jesuit and Dominican missionaries to Japan. He then learnt to read Japanese, even in its archaic forms, in order to study Japanese sources. As a result of these labours he produced his authoritative *History of Japan* in three volumes, which is still regarded by foreign scholars as the leading book in English on Japanese history, although it has been criticised for its "dreadful facetiousness."

It is of interest to recall that in 1893 Murdoch took part in a curious adventure—an idea conceived in Australia by some visionary Socialists of planting a New Australia on a grant of some twenty-five thousand acres of land in Paraguay. It was in fact an early experiment in creating a Socialist state. New Australia was a dismal failure and Murdoch was quick to withdraw from it.

* * * * * * * *

Present day Australians in Japan are engaged in a variety of callings, from diplomats to purveyors of strip tease. But the Australian always has shown a tendency to avoid the conventional and to strike out for himself along independent lines. Indeed there was once an Australian who had in turn been a school teacher, a Melbourne cable tram driver, a mariner, a black-birder, and served in World War I as commander of a "Q" ship before finally taking up residence in Japan as a marine surveyor.

Australians have played no small part in Japan since the beginning of the century, during the war, the Occupation and to date. Of all Allied troops they probably suffered numerically the most in the wartime atrocities. All too many Australian prisoners-of-war still rest here in the British Commonwealth Cemetery near Yokohama.

THE
FOREIGN
DIRECTORIES

Straight down the crooked lane,
And all round the square.

THOMAS HOOD

With the opening of each year, new foreign directories begin to appear, all of which in their own way are excellent publications, and serve a need. Apart from that need, some of us at times may flip open a directory just to see how imposing our names appear when in print, but it would have to be a very wet day and we would have to be very short of reading material before we would open any of these modern directories to while away a half hour.

The advertisements are even more dull than the rest of the contents, and are no doubt designed on the entirely erroneous assumption that everybody these days is so madly busy that he has no time to read more than headlines.

In short our modern directories are deadly dull. The only bright feature about them is the red cover. There is not a laugh in all the directories of the year.

Even twenty five years ago they were not as dull as to-day. Few foreigners who were living in Japan at that time will forget the guffaw that went up when one issue of the *Japan Chronicle Directory* came off the press and was distributed.

Details of that storm in the foreign mercantile community will be found in a later chapter, entitled

The Foreign Directories

Foreign Settlements and British Enterprises in Japan.

Fifty years ago the directories were more entertaining because they were enlivened with photographs of the firms' managing directors, each in a throat-throttling high collar. Incidentally those high collars made such an impression on the Japanese mind as the mark of a well dressed gentleman that the phrase "high collar"—transliterated as *haikara*—meaning "fashionable," found its way into colloquial Japanese.

But for good reading give me the directories of seventy or eighty years ago. The earliest foreign directories, or *Hong Lists* as they were then called, like the foreigners themselves of those days, were according to our modern standards rather queer looking. Being produced before the days of aniline dyes the covers were either black or a muddy brown, but the contents made up for all that was lacking in the colour of the covers.

The Japan Gazette Hong List and Directory for 1876 is one of my favourites. On turning its pages there is a fund of information.

The Minister at the British Legation then was that prodigy of energy and action, Sir Harry Parkes, and his staff comprised an unusual array of talent and scholarship, including such outstanding scholars on Japan as Ernest M. Satow, W. G. Aston, T.H.R. McClatchie and J. H. Gubbins. Among the other members of the staff it is interesting to note that there was a medical officer, a judge, a registrar, a court usher, an inspector, a sergeant, constables, turnkeys and a gaoler.

The Foreign Directories

In those days the Kingdom of Hawaii was represented by consuls in Yokohama, Hyogo and also in Nagasaki, but seemingly was without a representative in Tokyo.

The Imperial Government Railways were then mainly staffed with Britons. In addition to foreign engineers, draughtsmen, foremen mechanics, and clerks, the names of thirty-two foreign engine drivers and fitters are listed in the Yokohama Section. In Kobe there were a further thirty-three foreign members of the Railway Department. Many of them used to live in wooden foreign houses just above what is now Motomachi Station but which was then Sannomiya Station.

The Imperial Government Telegraphs also was largely staffed with Britons, whereas the Arsenal at Yokosuka and the War Department used French advisers.

The Naval Department on the other hand preferred British experts, and among those mentioned at the Imperial Naval College we find the names of several fine scholars, including Basil Hall Chamberlain, then a teacher, and Capt. F. Brinkley, who was then a gunnery instructor.

The Imperial Academy of Medicine and Surgery was comprised largely of German doctors and surgeons. The lighthouse keepers were mostly foreigners, as also were a number of the officials in the Imperial Japanese Customs and other Government institutions. Names of all are listed in the Directory.

It is surprising to read that as early as 1876 there were foreigners residing in most of the prefectures from as far south as Kagoshima to as far north as Aomori. They comprised telegraphists, mining engineers, silk reelers, teachers, and one who is described as a farmer. In Ikuno, where the silver mines were located, there were no less than nine foreigners. Discoveries such as this seem effectively to dispose of claims so often heard these days from newcomers, who boast that they were the first foreigners to visit some particular town or village in Japan.

In the Hakodate section there appears the name "Rev. W. Dening"—the father of Her Britannic Majesty's recent Ambassador in Tokyo.

The Mitsubishi Mail Steamship Company, which later amalgamated with a competitor and became the Nippon Yusen Kaisha, lists a fleet of twenty-eight vessels each with a European captain and chief engineer.

Turning to the advertisements there is wealth of interesting reading.

The Grand Hotel, Yokohama, goes on record as *"affording every facility for visitors, including ladies,"* and pledges itself to supply *"carriages for Odawara, Nikko and other parts of the country on shortest notice."*

Travellers who were seeking bizarre experiences must surely have been ensnared with the bait offered by the International Hotel—*"Guests accommodated with horses and carriages!"*

The Hotel du Louvre on the other hand was apparently a more conventional hostelry and the manager breathlessly announced:—

This new and magnificent hotel, situate in one of

the finest quarters of the town and in the Centre of its Business Portion, close to the Banks and Chamber of Commerce and opposite to the Catholic Church, by its Elegance and its Cuisine,—the only one of this description here—and the care bestowed on the general Superintendence, offers to Travellers unusual conveniences such as Billiards, Dinners, either private or a la carte.

All the hotels boasted of their wines and spirits, but were silent about their plumbing.

The foreign banks, some of which, such as the Oriental Bank Corporation, are now names of the past, advertised their interest rates in competition with one another. There are references to sterling, French francs, Mexican dollars, and taels, but nowhere in the book are U.S. dollars mentioned.

The foreign Insurance companies endeavoured to capture clients by holding out special inducements. One threw modesty aside and emphasized its gilt edge with the announcement:—

One of the Four Offices of the Highest Class; vide the complimentary remarks of the Chancellor of the Exchequer made in the House of Commons on 7th March, 1864.

Cobb & Co., famed coach proprietors from Australia, were then also established in Yokohama. The *Japan Gazette* sang its own praise over a space of about two inches, and then concluded with the brag that it was before the eyes of the public all the year around. The photographer boasted that he enjoyed the patronage of the Grand Duke Alexis of Russia, while the Bavarian Brewery maintained that its beer was *"the best ever brewed in the Far East, equal in quality to that of Bavaria or England."*

Dr. Collis Browne was of course a big advertiser. He recommended his Chlorodyne for dysentery, cholera, fever, ague, coup de soleil, and colds; he claimed it was *"the best remedy for consumption, bronchitis and asthma; cuts short all attacks of epilepsy, hysteria, palpitation and spasms; and is the only palliative in neuralgia, rheumatism, gout, cancer, toothache and meningitis."* And finally he boasted that *it acts like a charm in diarrhoea."*

With such a panacea on the market, one would not expect there would be much business for the local funeral undertaker. However, his address was "On the Creek, Yokohama," and his advertisement strikes a melancholy note in announcing that he had *"patent iron shells always on hand."*

The many advertisements by Chinese tradesmen and shopkeepers in Chinatown at Yokohama indicate that they also realized the importance of publicity, and it is of passing interest to note that Mr. Cock Eye was then the leading naval and military tailor and that Mr. Fat Cheong was the foremost contractor.

* * * * * * *

It is more than eighty years since Sir Harry Parkes lodged some of his scorching protests, since Capt. Brinkley taught the elements of gunnery to the first Japanese naval cadets, since British engine drivers took trains into Tokyo and Osaka stations, and since Cock Eye sewed epaulets on the uniforms of English regimental officers garrisoned in Yokohama. Earthquakes, air-raids and time have wiped out so much,

173

that we sometimes wonder whether the only links that now remain with those early days are some of the antiquated styles of bowler hats that still adorn the heads of dignified Japanese gentlemen in some country districts.

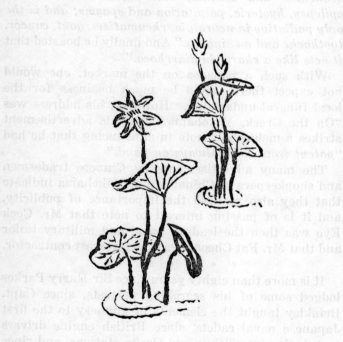

THE HONGS

*Wherefore we all agreed to goe for
Japan.*

WILL ADAMS, 1598

When the Europeans first came to the East to trade
they received a frosty reception. In China they were
referred to as *foreign devils* and in Japan as *hairy
barbarians.*

It is not surprising therefore, that in China they
should have been restricted to the one port of Canton,
and confined there to a row of buildings which the
Chinese authorities constructed for them by the river,
outside the city gates. They were forbidden entry
to the city. Those buildings contained storehouses,
offices, and living quarters, and were called *hongs.*

In the circumstances the connotation of the word
hong was not always particularly flattering, but the
foreign merchants lifted the word out of the Chinese
language and with characteristic perverseness, applied it in a complimentary sense to all important
foreign business houses in the Far East.

When Japan was opened to foreign trade about
the middle of the last century, certain places of
residence and trade were set aside for the foreigners,
which areas came to be known as the Foreign Settlements or Concessions. The business firms that established themselves in those settlements were
referred to as *hongs,* and the foreign business directories until 1879 were called *Hong Lists.*

The *hongs* in Japan were either Far Eastern

branches of large merchant houses or locally incorporated foreign firms. In the former case they were all too frequently staffed by sons of the home directors or by their protégés, with a smattering of remittance men. The percentage of failures was high. The excessive drinking of those days took its toll. Liquor was cheap and was consumed in considerable quantities.

About ninety years ago the steamship fare from London to Yokohama was one hundred and fifty five pounds sterling. Whether or not that was expensive is difficult to decide because it included drinks! That system possibly gave rise to the practice of steamship companies extending special concessions to missionaries! For the young man coming East, the voyage must have served as a training period for the short life of hard drinking and fast living that all too frequently lay ahead.

It is of interest to note that in those early days the Japanese customs officials who boarded overseas vessels took their own food on board. Apparently they did not eat foreign food and so did not expect to be "boarded" by the ships they boarded.

In the early days of Yokohama, potatoes were imported from America, onions from Bombay, and game from Shanghai. In the absence of refrigeration the spoilage was considerable, especially when the foodstuffs were brought by sailing ships. Later local beef of excellent quality was obtainable at seven sen a pound and chickens at twenty sen each. Servants received five to six yen per month.

The most important of the *hongs* in Yokohama,

PLATE I

Nagasaki about 1865. *(Courtesy of F.D. Burrows, Esq.)*

PLATE II

Yokohama from Kanagawa Bluff, looking across the Swamp (in middle) to Yokohama Bluff in right background, about 1864. (*Courtesy of F.D. Burrows, Esq.*)

PLATE III

Yokohama Settlement as seen from lower portion of Bluff, about 1863, looking across the Creek to the Bund, showing Water Street in Centre. The British Legation, and later Consulate, occupied lot no. 20 on the right corner of the Bund. (*Courtesy of F.D. Burrows, Esq.*)

PLATE IV

The Bund, Kobe, 1876, from a water colour by C.B. Bernard. (Original is in possession of Miss Diana James.)

PLATE V

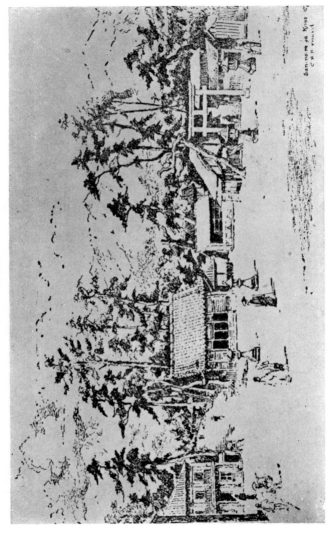

View of Sannomiya Shrine, Kobe, looking up Tor Road. (By C.B. Bernard, about 1875)

PLATE VI

Kyo-machi, Kobe, in eighteen-seventies, showing Masonic Hall in centre of picture, with Oriental Hotel on left, followed by International Club, later known as Kobe Club. In left background is the smokestack of the British-owned Kobe Paper Mill. In the right background are the trees along the banks of the Ikuta River where the new Kobe City Hall was completed in 1957.

PLATE VII

Premises of International Club (later to be known as Kobe Club) at 79 Kyo-machi, Kobe, until about 1875, when the club moved into premises near Recreation Ground. In 1879 the Club Concordia (German Club) occupied the premises at 79 Kyo-machi. (*Courtesy of J. T. Helm, Esq.*)

PLATE VIII

The Foreign Concession, Kawaguchi, Osaka, during the Meiji era, from an old woodblock print.

Nagasaki and Kobe, were located along the *Bund* or waterfront. In each port the streets behind the *Bund* were known as the back streets.

In Yokohama in the early days the private boat of each *hong* hung from davits near a flight of steps leading to the water opposite each residence. At the time of the great earthquake of 1923, many thousands of people sought shelter from the heat of the fires in the shallow water in front of the *Bund*. Later the rubble from the burnt-out city of Yokohama was dumped into the sea at this spot and the reclaimed land so formed was then converted into a park, and, in the postwar Occupation years, into a U.S. Army Dependents' Housing Area.

In Kobe, also, the *Bund* became an inland road following reclamation schemes.

* * * * * * *

On the morning of 1st January, 1868, when the foreign merchants were gathered on the decks of several vessels in Hyogo harbour awaiting the signal to go ashore for the official opening of the port, standing at the rail of one of the vessels was a young man named E. H. Hunter who had been employed in a *hong* in Yokohama, but who had decided to try his luck in Kobe on his own account.

Looking towards the shore he saw immense possibilities for the future. He saw the makings of a great port and in the background he visualized the foothills as a place of future residence for the foreign community. He founded his own company and later built an ironworks that eventually developed into the immense Hitachi Dockyard. He built a mansion

in Kobe that still stands at the entrance to a narrow
valley that runs towards Futatabi, and so the name
of Hunter's Gap was given to the path familiar to
all who know the Kobe Hills.

When he first looked towards the shore of Kobe
he noticed the *sake* breweries that were scattered
along the shore, and knowing that good water is as
essential to the making of *sake* as to the distilling of
whisky he saw other possibilities. Later he had
samples of Kobe water sent to England for analysis
and on the result was encouraged to start the first
cotton mill in Kobe, and so influenced the rise of the
cotton spinning industry in the Kansai area.

In course of time he passed on. He had lived hard
and well, as befitted a gentleman of the Victorian
era, and his Japanese friends and family decided to
take no chances on the hereafter. In what was described as a commendable spirit of practical judicious-
ness they arranged a Buddhist service elsewhere
immediately following the Christian funeral service
held in All Saints Church.

* * * * * * *

The proud *hongs* did not occupy rented rooms or
suites of rooms in somebody else's building. Each
was set in its own compound. The Japanese generally
referred to each *hong* by the land lot number rather
than by the difficult-to-pronounce foreign name.

Each comprised a main building consisting of residential quarters and offices. In the early days, at
least one of the office rooms was in Japanese style
where the *banto* interviewed the Japanese merchants.
Another room with high straight-backed chairs was

for the Chinese *compradore* staff, and another for
the *hatoba* runners who also were generally Chinese.
Near at hand were the commodious godowns and in
the rear a variety of storehouses, and outhouses
representing kitchens, washhouses, bathhouses, etc
for the use of the Chinese and Japanese servants.

Among the outbuildings there were often stables
for the racing ponies and riding horses. The *taipans*
had brought in ponies from China and race clubs
were soon formed. The juniors in the *hongs* often
held their positions, and on one or two occasions
gained the hand of the boss's daughter, by their skill
as gentlemen riders.

There was great rivalry among the *taipans* of the
hongs who were great patrons of the race clubs, and
on rare occasions when their weight and waistline
permitted them to ride they even sported "silk."
Certainly the hongs did much to plant racing in Japan. What they could not do the fast racehorses
and crooked jockeys, that were much later imported
from Australia, succeeded in doing.

There are no longer any *hongs* in Japan. That
name can hardly be applied to the businesses that
are now conducted behind frosted glass doors in
rented rooms and godowns with tightly shut doors, especially designed to keep the merchandise from being
spirited away and competitors from peeping inside.
In bygone days a Chinese godown keeper, guaranteed
by family connections or a patron, assumed full
responsibility for the contents; and, unflattering
though it may sound to the insurance companies, he
seemed to represent a more adequate cover against

theft than does the most comprehensive policy to-day.

In the early days of the *hongs,* each company was established in its own compound. The number of rickshaws at the front entrance, the number of Chinese *compradore* staff and *hatoba* runners on the premises, the number of Japanese *banto,* and Japanese merchants moving in and out of the premises, were a clear indication of the state of business. The godowns were adjoining the offices and opened on to the main streets. All people walking along the streets, including the bankers, who generally had a lien on the godown stock, were able to see whether the godowns were well stocked with merchandise or empty.

The merchandise was moved to and from the *hong* warehouses on hand-drawn carts, substituted in course of time by horse-drawn carts. In 1937 the horses, or rather their progeny, were mobilized for war service in China, went overseas and have never returned.

The aroma as one passed by the unsightly tea-firing godowns, told one how the tea market was doing. In other places the quantity of beans and chilies or silkwaste drying in the compounds outside each office told of prosperity or depression in each *hong.*

The merchandise in the godowns adjoining the office was clear evidence that the merchants in the *hongs* were in close personal contact all the time with the merchandise that they traded in, whether it was imported merchandise or export items such as the Japanese sea shells in which Samuel Samuel specialized and which contributed in some part to the

The Hongs

founding of the "Shell' fortune, as is related in a later chapter. Such quaint lines of merchandise as old porcelains, valuable bronzes, exquisite lacquerware and rare curios could be seen through the open front doors of the godowns in the leisurely process of being inspected and packed for export. The Oriental colour of that scene has long since been replaced by mass-produced lines, or the so-called "muck and truck" trade of to-day.

The shuffling or papers figured less in the *hongs* than in our modern offices. The *boy-san* press-copied all letters in tissue copy books and pasted inward mail in scrap books. The day of the file clerk had not dawned.

There were a number of clubs, but in each of the Settlements there was one outstanding club ruled over by the *taipans* of the *hongs,* whose will prevailed in the upper strata of the caste-ridden foreign settlements. In Kobe there was the Kobe Club with its unwritten laws that barred from membership master-mariners, retailers and certain other categories. The portals of the Kobe Club were originally open to those who sold liquor by the case, but not to those who retailed it by the bottle over the counter. The ban against officers of the merchant marine was later raised, but the restrictions against retailers lasted well into this century.

In the large British *hongs,* it was a custom as strict as the laws of the Medes and Persians that the respectability of all foreign employees should be established by their becoming members of the Kobe Club.

The Hongs

I personally made that discovery when, as a very junior assistant in an important *hong,* I was informed by the *taipan* that I would be proposed for membership in the Kobe Club. Dutifully I accepted my fate but without enthusiasm because I was well aware that, although receiving a remuneration that may have been commensurate with my ability, it was not large enough to enable me to move in that exalted circle.

The *hong* of which I had the privilege of being a member, and upon which I look back with respect and affection, celebrated its centenary six years later by going into voluntary liquidation, a circumstance in no way connected with my association with it.

The days of the *hongs* approached their end when the large office buildings with rooms for rent came to be built. The British Consulate in Kobe, although in no sense of the word a *hong,* was originally housed in a Japanese *mansion,* and later, after some wanderings, purchased premises on the *bund* (the site of the present day Chartered Bank) that originally had housed one of the large *hongs.* That was then the most attractive part of Kobe. A Victorian-style building with glassed-in verandahs that commanded a fine view of the sea, was set in a large garden surrounded in part by a brick wall and in part by a picket fence. In the front garden there was a tall flagstaff.

During the early nineteen-twenties when the Consulate site was offered for sale and the Consulate moved to the top floor of the then recently completed O.S.K Building, the British-owned newspaper, *The*

Japan Chronicle, saw that it marked the end of a picturesque era albeit the dawn of a more progressive one, and with a grunt of displeasure came forth with the quip that until the British Consulate secured premises of its own, the Union Jack would be flying high but not as high as the flag of the Japanese landlord.

The days of the *hongs* were the days when currencies were exchanged for their true values and not, as now, for the fictitious values that governments in their wisdom or in their power state they are worth. To effect these transactions in currencies, the bill and bullion brokers rushed about the foreign settlements to and from *hongs* and banks. At first they used pony carts, later rickshaws, and finally motorcars.

In the early days an aroma of cutch, of spices, of silk waste, and sometimes the mustiness of age hung about the *hongs.* The days of the *hongs* have passed. All has now been replaced by the smell of floor polish and the fragrant perfume of female stenographers.

Among the few things that remain to remind us of the *hong* era are some words of the jargon of those days still in common usage, such as "bund," "godown," "chow," and "tiffin."

There was no MITI in those days, and the frustrations and the mass of paper work associated with business to-day were annoyances and trials unknown to those early merchants.

The mail came in and went out once a fortnight, and while more frequently later on, the points of arrival and departure were Kobe and Yokohama,

which therefore assumed greater importance in the
export trade than did the neighbouring cities of O-
saka or Tokyo. The export trade, of necessity, became firmly entrenched in Kobe and Yokohama until
air mail in and out of Japan following World War
II changed the picture. As foreign-owned planes
were not permitted to fly over Japan in prewar days,
this was one of the last countries to enjoy the advantages of air mail.

The property owners in Kobe and Yokohama had
no inkling of the great changes that would come
about in both cities from the advent of air mail, of
how that innovation would deprive Kobe and Yokohama of the special advantages that they enjoyed in
the pursuit of export business, nor did the city
authorities realize that such a thing as air mail would
set Kobe and Yokohama—the ports of the *hongs*—
so far behind Osaka and Tokyo that they probably
will never again attain that heyday of importance
that they once enjoyed and which developed out of
the arrival of the *hongs*.

HISTORY
IN
THE
RIVER
BEDS

> *All Rivers doe in a kinde of thank-*
> *ful renumeration return their waters*
> *to the Sea.*
>
> Description of Japan by Rev.
> ARTHUR HATCH, 1623

The observant traveller, when passing between
Kobe and Osaka, whether by one of the public transportation systems or by motor car, will have noticed
that the beds of most of the rivers from Kobe to
Koshien are considerably higher than the level of the
surrounding countryside. The railway line, although
more or less on a level plane, actually passes underneath several rivers. In other places the railway
line and also the highway are constructed on long
built-up ramps so that they may pass over the raised
river beds.

The unusual geographical formations of these river
beds have of course been brought about by the circumstance that these rivers, having their sources in
the nearby mountains, are short in length and only
flow intermittently, and then for short periods after
rains. Every rainfall brings down sand and gravel
from the mountains, but so quickly does the flow
subside that much of this debris is deposited in the

river beds, which over the centuries have thus been built up to a level far above that of the surrounding countryside. As nature raised the level of the river bed, so man had to raise the height of the banks to prevent overflowing.

These rivers, generally dry, have been the scenes of disasters and terror over the centuries, even unto recent times, when torrential rains frequently have broken the banks and devastated the villages and the rice-fields on either side. From ancient times the farmers, time and again, had to set to work clearing the sand and gravel from their ruined rice fields. Building development in this area in the last two decades has obliterated most of the rice fields; but until then this region was studded all about with immense mounds, resembling ancient burial mounds, but which in fact represented flood debris cleared from the fields over the centuries at the cost of years of heartbreaking hand labour.

The Ikuta River which was on the eastern boundary of the early Foreign Settlement in Kobe, was another example of a river with a raised bed, and it also had burst its banks on many occasions in the past. A site on the eastern bank of the river near its mouth had been hastily set apart in 1868 as a burial ground for foreigners. This place known as Ono Cemetery was for various reasons looked upon by the early residents with certain misgivings. There was the constant fear that the river might again burst its banks and wash the burial ground with all its contents out to sea. Fortunately that never happened, and in 1873 when the Ikuta river was diverted to what is now known as Shin-ikuta-gawa, the danger of any such disaster was then removed. The old graves remained there until about 1952 when they were removed to the new site behind Futatabi.

Further west was the old Minatogawa, or the port river of the ancient town of Hyogo, which down through history has seen more violent happenings than any of the others. That river, which has its source in the mountains behind Futatabi and Takatori, flowed down through what is to-day known to the Japanese as Shinkaichi—the newly opened ground —or to foreigners as Theatre Street.

That river was yet another interesting example of a river bed higher than the surrounding countryside. The river bank on either side was heavily wooded with tall pine trees, and seven and half centuries ago an emperor and his court resided in a palace near the pine-lined eastern bank. In more recent times in order to make room for a growing city, the river was shifted some distance to the west, and a licenced quarter was built where was once the Emperor's palace. To-day the amusement quarter of Kobe is located where gnarled old pines formerly lined the banks of that historical old river.

Signs of the elevated river bed and of the high banks of the river are still easily discernible by movie-goers visiting the Shochikuza Theatre, and indeed that theatre is built on the elevated ground of the old river bed. The city tram that runs through the tunnel under the low arched bridge a little to the north—so familiar to motorists—is actually passing under what was once the river bed. Similarly the nearby station for the Arima-bound electric train is underground and has been excavated from underneath that river bed.

The old Minatogawa also saw the tragedy of flood, but greater still it experienced the violence of one of the most bloody and decisive battles ever fought in Japan.

About six hundred years ago Kusunoki Masashige, the great loyalist general, set out from the Imperial capital at Kyoto with a force of seven hundred horsemen to attack a rebel army of far greater strength advancing from Kyushu. At Sakurai-no-Sato near Yamazaki on the Shin-Keihan Electric Railway between Kyoto and Osaka, an old decayed pine tree marks the spot where Kusunoki said a last farewell to his son in terms so inspiring that about five hundred years later Sir Harry Parkes, the British Minister to Japan, erected there a monument which may still be seen, bearing an inscription in English, to commemorate the incident. On several railway stations between Kobe and Osaka, also on Tor Road and in several other places in Kobe, there are some interesting advertisements that depict that famous farewell scene. The advertisements are for a well-known brand of *sembei*—Japanese wafer biscuits—which are sold under Kusunoki's *kikusui*, chrysanthemum-on-water, crest as a trademark.

The *kikusui* crest has its origin in a *Changri-la* where there was a valley overgrown with chrysanthemums. It is said that when the petals fell into a nearby stream all who drank at the stream with the floating blossoms enjoyed a life well beyond a hundred years. That Chinese tradition came to be transplanted to Japan in the decorative design of chrysanthemum-on-water.

Kusunoki met and fought that vastly superior rebel force in the rocky dry bed of the Minatogawa, right where the movie fans gaze to-day at the billboards. Although performing prodigies of valour and covered with wounds (eleven in all) the brave Kusunoki had to yield to the superior force, but rather than escape he performed hara-kiri with many of his followers at a place which was probably located on or near the site of the present day Nanko Shrine compound. Several hundred years later during the Tokugawa period, the Daimyo of Mito came to Kobe to honour the brave Kusunoki, the whereabouts of whose grave was not then known. During his searches he found an unmarked grave upon which it had become the custom in later years for the members of the despised and oppressed *eta* class in Japan, to place flowers. Those unfortunates, by harsh public opinion, had been relegated to a position somewhat akin to untouchableness, and to the performance of contaminating tasks such as the slaughtering of animals, the tanning of leather, assisting at executions, the digging of graves and the like. They used to attend the graveyards, and it had become the custom for some of them who were flower vendors to place on that lonely grave any flowers that remained unsold at the end of the day. And so it was that for a long period of time those *eta* outcasts had been the only ones to tend the grave of the loyal Kusunoki.

History in the River Beds

The earliest interest of that despised class in the flower trade went back to nearly four hundred years ago when a castle, known as Hanakuma Castle, stood on the bluff just northwest of the present Motomachi railway station in Kobe, not far from where the navigation mark stands to-day. In those days every castle had an *eta* village nearby so that there would be a source of labour to attend to the sanitation and other contaminating services of the castle. When Hanakuma Castle was built, eight such *eta* families were brought in and were settled in a squalid village of shacks towards the hills somewhat to the north of the present Mitsukoshi Department Store. When Hanakuma Castle was later destroyed in battle the depressed families were then without a means of livelihood. Custom did not permit of their renting riceland or of cutting firewood, and being in dire straits they approached the local *daimyo* who gave them facilities for cultivating flowers and a monopoly of making New Year decorations in Kobe. And so to this day some of the descendants of those *tokushu buraku,* or special communities as they are sometimes referred to these days, are still the flower vendors in Kobe. Those sections of Kobe above the upper tram line which were once the outskirt villages of those depressed families are still devoted to the flower trade. Foreigners may have wondered why that part of Kobe is a distribution and wholesale centre for flowers, and why so many women and girls with baskets of flowers for sale can be seen moving in and out of that district.

The Ujikawa was another river that flowed intermittently through Kobe, along the side of the present Mitsukoshi Department Store, down to the sea. Long since it has been put underground, and to-day it is nothing more than a great underground drain. Along its banks in the years gone by were the fine flower gardens in which the members of the *eta* families raised their flowers. That was once one of the bright little spots that was ultimately swallowed up by a growing city.

But let us return for a moment to Kusunoki's grave. After the Lord of Mito discovered the grave it was honoured with a fitting monument. In the grounds in the southeast corner of the present Nanko Shrine compound in Kobe, on the right as you enter, can be seen an old monument bearing in Japanese an inscription reading *Ah! Here lies the Faithful Kusunoki!* The original grave goes back about 600 years, but Nanko Shrine is comparatively modern having been set up as late as 1871. It is worthy of a visit by foreigners.

It is always shaded—almost dark—around that monument. Outside, just over the tall wall, there is all the noise and din of a busy city street. The clatter of trams and honking of motorcars takes place there as nowhere else in Kobe. But never as I have stood in front of Kusunoki's grave have I heard that din. The raucous noise of this modern century does not seem to penetrate to such ancient spots. I have noticed the same phenomena in other hallowed places.

Certainly the entrance is cluttered up with cheap restaurants, eating stalls and a fortuneteller's booth.

But it was always so in all countries. Holy places from the beginning of time, as also the Temple of the Lord in Jerusalem, have been defiled by the hucksters and traders.

In the Minatogawa playground not far from the Shochikuza Theatre there is one of the many statues that have been erected in Japan to Kusunoki's memory. But in the Plaza in front of the Imperial Palace in Tokyo there stands the finest of all the statues of Kusunoki, in full samurai armour and mounted on a horse. That statue unquestionably was the best known and the most photographed monument in occupied Japan. Tens of thousands of Allied troops alone must have photographed it during the Occupation years.

Down through the centuries sword fights and other deeds of violence have occurred in that old Minato river bed. If any foreigner living to-day should wish to know more about those happenings, of those who fought in those battles and passed that way in the centuries gone by, he may easily see them fighting again their battles and dying in the agony of hara-kiri as they did centuries ago.

In the exact place where that famous battle was fought, similar dramas and similar acts of hara-kiri are taking place daily and may be seen by all who wish to see them. To see those things requires but little effort. It need not be a moonlight night when the wind is stirring gently in the trees. One need not visit there in the eerie hours of darkness, nor to see those things need one believe in ghosts. By a curious circumstance right where those happenings occurred centuries ago, on the actual reclaimed site of the old river bed there stands to-day the amusement centre of Kobe, and on the stages of some of those theatres can be seen almost any day, by those who are interested in old Japan, the *Kabuki* dramas of the past.

MAYA-SAN

> *The people of this Iland of Japan
> are verie superstitious in their Reli-
> going and are of divers opinions.*
> WILL ADAMS, 1611

In the early days of Kobe the temple on Maya-san was known to foreigners as Moon Temple, a purely fanciful name because the temple has no connection with the moon, but is in fact dedicated to the mother of Buddha. It probably acquired the name of Moon Temple from the annual pilgrimage made at night to the temple during the *O-bon* festival; foreigners in the early days gathered the impression that this nocturnal visit had something to do with worship of the moon. About the same time Takatori got the name of Coal Hill, because one or two shallow pits were sunk there in the early days under the advice of Kobe foreigners with a view to prospecting for coal. It is said that some coal was obtained but the quality was not good enough to repay working.

In those early days Maya-san was a favourite excursion for foreigners, partly because of the pheasants in the foothills, the troops of large monkeys in the valleys and the pleasant walk through the forests of maple, pine and cryptomeria, but mainly for the magnificent views from the summit. As with all old temples situated on lofty places, the priests had from early times planted cryptomeria trees on the sides of the mountain so that there would always be a

194

ready supply of lumber available with which to repair or rebuild the temple structures.

In April, 1872, after the foreigners had been in Kobe a little over four years they arranged a foot race from the Settlement to the temple on Maya-san and back. It was won by the local pharmacist, A.C. Sim, a Scotsman, who, incidentally, had measured by hand with a chain measure the length of the course. At that time this and other cross-country races organised by the foreigners made quite an impression on the Japanese, and planted the idea of long distance foot races which later were to become so popular in Japan. In those early days the Japanese did a great deal of running as a means of living, but not for pleasure. Official couriers, letter carriers and messengers were travelling on foot along the highways of Japan daily, and covering distances that only well-trained runners would be capable of these days.

The guide books of seventy-five years ago informed foreigners that the summit of Maya-san could be reached in about two hours walk from Kobe and that "a guide is hardly necessary." Alternatively one could travel by jinrikisha with two men, one pulling and the other pushing, to the village of Gomo and then on foot for one hour, or by *kago*, a type of sedan chair, as far as the bottom of the steps, whence there are over three hundred steps to the main temple.

In 1880 the legal fares for jinrikisha for Japanese passengers for distances measured from the Hiogo Hotel, the centre of the universe then for many Kobe foreigners, were three *sen* to anywhere in the Settlement, fourteen *sen* to Suma, eighteen *sen* to Sumiyoshi, twenty five *sen* to Akashi and eighty five *sen* to Arima. A fifty percent advance on these rates was expected from foreigners.

Before the turn of the century a walk to Moon Temple was such a popular excursion among foreigners that upon arrival at their destination it was possible to purchase at one of the several roadside teahouses located there a bottle of Bass Ale. Not infrequently in the summer time foreigners would stay overnight at the temple.

Recently whilst reading a globetrotter's account of a visit to Kobe in 1890, we came upon the following:—

A climb finally brought us to Moon Temple and in a rest house nearby we saw the red triangle of Bass Ale hanging among various emblems of the Buddhist creed. For one yen, the equivalent of two shillings, we were supplied with a quart bottle of Bass Ale, four umbrellas, and permission to help ourselves to the cherry blossom ad lib.

During the nineteen twenties funiculars and also aerial cable-cars designed by Swiss engineers became popular, and Kobe was fortunate to have a cable car to Maya-san, and both a cable car and an aerial ropeway to Rokko-san, thereby enabling golfers to reach the links on Rokko in greater comfort and with more speed than in earlier days when the journey was made up the so-called Ice Road from Sumiyoshi either on horseback, in a sedan chair, or on foot. While the modern transportation systems enable tens of thousands of people old and young to visit the mountains who would not otherwise have been able to go; they also result in both of these beautiful mountains in places being converted into unsightly trash heaps, sullied and disfigured by the litter of legions of thoughtless picnickers. The introduction of motor bus services has of recent years added to the litter, but there is ever the hope that the people can be taught the civic spirit, that these mountains are their parks, their property, their heritage, and that they who destroy the trees and shrubs and litter the mountains with trash are vandals.

Then came World War II. Japan finding herself short of metal supplies, sent missions abroad to all the occupied territories to collect and ship to Japan whatever metal they could lay their hands on, whether it was scrap from the junk heaps, bronze monuments from the public parks, or metal currency. In course of time as the Allied submarines controlled all the approaches to Japan, these supplies were cut off and word then went forth that metal should be collected within Japan proper.

As with many wartime laws in Japan, and elsewhere also, the regulations were blindly implemented and with little sense of realities. Aerial railways and funiculars were dismantled and broken up without any certainty that the scrap could then be transported to the factories. Much of it—probably most of it—was still rusting on the ground when hostilities ceased. Elevators and steam-heating systems even in the centre of Tokyo were dismantled but were never removed from the basements of buildings and after the cessation of hostilities were reconstructed again at great labour and expense.

197

Bronze name-plates from banks, buildings, and bridges; railings from parks and roadways; temple bells and images; even collections of old metal coins were gathered together in immense heaps at various places, but then for the want of transport could not be moved to the factories where the metal could be utilised. After the Occupation commenced such metal dumps became the hunting ground of Occupationaires in search of souvenirs. Anything of interest that was found could be taken away after first being weighed and paid for at the current price for scrap metal.

Among the many valuable properties that were sacrificed in the search for metal were the cableway to Maya-san and the aerial ropeway to Rokko.

* * * * * * *

These things had happened before in Japan, and elsewhere also—indeed there seems nothing new in history. The *Kinse Shiriaku*, a history of Japan of a hundred years ago, relates:

In the year 1841 the Prince of Mito was placed under house arrest at one of his secondary residences in Yedo for having melted down the bells of all the Buddhist monasteries in his domain to cast cannon with, but later he was pardoned by order of the Shogun and directed to make extensive military preparations (for resisting the threatened opening of Japan by the Western Powers).

The Tokugawa Shogunate was not concerned with the fate of Buddhism, but rather with the fate of the House of Tokugawa, reckoning that any provincial lord who could cast cannon might one day be tempted to use them against the Tokugawa forces. Road making, the building of bridges, improvement of communications, and progress generally were discouraged by the Tokugawa clan for strategic reasons, so that their enemies could not readily move against them.

In 1853 following the first visit of Commodore Perry, the construction of the artificial islands and forts in Tokyo Bay off Shinagawa was commenced and two years later the Shogun's Court gave orders that the bells and other bronze objects of all the Buddhist monasteries throughout the country should be melted down and cast into cannons and muskets. Fortunately there were many who realized that all efforts to remain cut off from the world abroad were useless, and so the measure to rob the monasteries and temples of their bronzes was opposed and soon abandoned.

* * * * * * *

That the view from the summit of Maya-san, some 2,400 feet above sea level, is one of the finest panoramas to be seen in this part of the country was a fact well known to foreigners and tourists in the early days of Kobe, but curiously enough seems to have been long since forgotten. Tourists and residents alike now frequently travel by bus and private cars sightseeing in distant places when one of the best sights is at the very doors of Kobe.

For more than ten years, following the dismantling of the funicular railway, the only approach to Maya-san from the Kobe side had been up the paths which the pilgrims and others had used from the time the temple was first built possibly thirteen hundred years ago. But at last the funicular was reconstructed and then in 1955 Kobe City added an aerial ropeway car to convey sightseers from the terminus to the summit.

Those who have not yet visited Maya-san are advised to do so preferably on the occasion of the annual festival, which falls on the eighth day of the eighth month, because it has long been said that those who make the ascent on that day acquire as much merit as if they had ascended forty-eight thousand times. It is even said by the promoters of the cable car and ropeway services that those who ride up, instead of walking as did the pilgrims in the past, likewise acquire great merit.

FOREIGN
SETTLEMENTS
AND
BRITISH
ENTERPRISES
IN
JAPAN

> Sonno Joi Sakoku—*Honour the Emperor; expel the barbarians; close the ports.*
> Political slogan in Japan about 1865–1868

In 1599, that is to say, three hundred and fifty-nine years ago, Her Britannic Majesty's illustrious namesake, Elizabeth I, Queen of England, gave to *"The Governors and Company of Merchants of London trading into the East Indies,"* later to be known as the *English East India Company,* a Charter of Incorporation whereby it was granted the exclusive right for fifteen years to trade with countries in the East Indies, including Japan. In the charter Japan was described as *"the manifold and populos sylver Islands of the Japans."* That step marked the beginning of plans for the establishment of Anglo-Japanese commercial relations.

Actually at that time no Englishman had ever visited Japan. However in the following year Will Adams, an English pilot in the service of the Dutch, became the first Englishman to reach Japan, but some years were yet to pass before trade was opened between England and *"the populos sylver Islands of the Japans."*

The governors of the East India Company were hard-headed English businessmen who were disinclined to rush into any mercantile proposition until they had carefully calculated the risks, and so it was that thirteen years were to elapse before they extended their trading activities as far east as Japan. By that time Queen Elizabeth I was dead.

The six or seven Englishmen comprising the staff of the East India Company's branch in Japan set up their headquarters in Hirado, which unfortunately was not much more than a fisher-town, and then after ten years of unsuccessful trading, during which time they lost a sum, which has been variously estimated from £1,700 to £10,000, the Governors decided to pull out of Japan.

The 22nd December, 1623, was the date set for their departure, but according to the record:

On the 22nd December many of the Japanese townsmen of Hirado came with their wives and families to take leave of the factors, some weeping at their departure. The factors then went on board intending to sail, but the Dutch merchants and many Japanese friends came on board with eatables and drinkables to have a jolly leave-taking. As there was not room on board for so large a company (over one hundred) they all went ashore to Kochiura and spent the day there, postponing their departure to the following day. At noon on

202

24th December, 1623, the vessel set sail for Batavia.
The English Factory at Hirado was a thing of the
past.

Some sixteen years later Japan adopted her policy of seclusion and then more than two centuries were to elapse before it became possible for Anglo-Japanese commercial relations to be resumed.

The resumption of trading relations took place on 1st July, 1859, when under the new treaties, Nagasaki, Yokohama, and Hakodate were opened to foreign trade. Kobe and Osaka were opened in 1868 and Tokyo in 1869.

An unusual period of forty years in Japan's history then ensued, known as the days of extra-territoriality, during which time the Foreign Settlements or Concessions, which had been set apart as places of residence and business for the incoming foreign merchants, developed into the great cities of Kobe and Yokohama. Those were the years during which Japan studied Western culture, learned the methods of international trade and industry, and emerged from a feudal nation into one of the world powers.

Mistakes were made, growing pains were encountered, and Japan was impatient for the time when extra-territoriality would come to an end, and she would administer the Foreign Concessions. That day eventually came on 17th July, 1899, but in the interval much had been learnt and Britain had made her full contribution in all phases of trade, industry, banking, insurance, education, and culture. The record of those contributions is to be found in hundreds of volumes of standard works on Japan and on all things Japanese, in scientific, cultural, and educational treatises, in the transactions of learned societies, and in the economic and industrial archives of Japan over the past ninety-eight years.

A few examples of the various contributions made by British nationals and a few names of firms and individuals will now be cited to mark the way during those years of development in Anglo-Japanese relations, rather than with any intention of writing history.

From the days when the treaty ports were first opened until now, many hundreds of British firms and institutions have opened up in Japan, and as conditions or fortunes have changed so some have disappeared from the scene. Of all the British individuals and firms who came to Japan in a trading capacity during the first two years of the treaty port days, probably not even half a dozen names could be found to-day in the pages of Trade Directories. *Jardine Matheson & Co.*, came in at the beginning both in Nagasaki and in Yokohama and are still in Japan.

R. Holme and F. Ringer were both in Nagasaki in those very early days and in 1863 merged their businesses to form the firm of *Holme Ringer & Co.*, still operating in Moji. It was customary for the partners of Holme Ringer & Co., on anniversary occasions to invite the foreign members of their staff to a formal dinner. In Nagasaki's heyday, which corresponded to the Russo-Japanese war period, more than twenty Britishers, all males, used to sit down to dinner at one immense dining table—such was the size of the firm in those days.

In Yokohama, F. Cornes and W. Aspinall amalgamated in 1861 to form Aspinall, Cornes & Co., later
changed to *Cornes & Co.* And thus, after Jardine
Matheson & Co., they rank as the oldest foreign
trading firm in Japan.

Among the most active of all the foreign firms
trading in Japan, the name of *Dodwell & Co., Ltd.,*
has always stood out prominently. Originally known
as W. R. Adamson & Co., the name was changed in
1891 to Dodwell, Carlill & Co., and in 1898 to Dodwell
& Co., Ltd. W.R. Adamson & Co., was first established in China in 1858, and by 1865 they had offices in
Hongkong, Shanghai, Hankow and Foochow, but in
later years they extended to many other ports.

Those in the tea trade still talk about those fabulous
days, when A. J. Carlill, director of Dodwell & Co.,
Ltd., until his death at the age of ninety, made a
fortune for himself and the firm by buying China
tea when all the world was bent on selling. Carlill,
his fortune and his reputation were made for life.

Among a number of the other great British hongs
in China, W. R. Adamson & Co., came to Yokohama
soon after that port was opened in 1859. The exact
date is unknown. Their name appears in the directory of 1865. On the shipping list, giving arrivals
of foreign vessels in Yokohama in 1864, there is
mention of the British vessel "Elgin" of 396 tons,
from Shanghai, as being consigned to them.

Their name does not appear in directories issued
in later years, and it is likely that during the depression years of about that period they withdrew
from Japan, as did a number of the other important

hongs. Thereafter they seem to have maintained touch with Japan through agents, Adamson Bell & Co., Ltd., until in the latter part of the last century they re-established themselves here as the firm known to-day as Dodwell & Co., Ltd.

Before the Pacific War Dodwells had offices in Kobe, Yokohama, Nagoya and Tokyo. Then, following the cessation of hostilities, immediately it became possible for what were known as "commercial entrants," or "traders" as SCAP officially dubbed them, to return to Japan, Dodwells sent in a representative. Thereafter their postwar organization developed until at one period they had over fifty-eight foreigners on their staff throughout Japan. Although the number has since fallen to around thirty-two, their Japanese staff has reached a total of 475, a number far greater than at any other time during the Company's existence in Japan, thereby indicating a policy, also to be found in other British firms, of making greater use of Japanese personnel, as they can be found and trained.

At first the banks were represented by agents. Then as trade developed they opened branches in Yokohama, and by 1864 four British banks, The Chartered Mercantile Bank of India, London & China, The Central Bank of Western India, The Commercial Bank Corporation of India & the East, and The Oriental Bank Corporation had all established their own offices. The Oriental Bank was the most famous and the most successful of all the Eastern exchange banks at that time.

Few of the banks which were then trading in Japan,

however, survived the economic panic of 1866, with its terrible Black Friday, or the terrific falls in the price of silver a few years later. When The Oriental Bank finally failed, it took with it the accumulated savings of many of the early foreign families in Kobe.

The Hongkong & Shanghai Banking Corporation was the first foreign bank to establish a branch in Kobe, that was in 1869, but it had opened in Yokohama in 1866. In Kobe it was located for some years in Kyo-machi, until it acquired its present site at No. 2 Bund. The present banking premises are the third to be built on that site.

The early success of The Oriental Bank had encouraged the investing public in the United Kingdom to support the prospectus of the promoters of The Chartered Bank of India, Australia & China. Queen Victoria was thereupon petitioned for a Royal Charter, which was granted in 1853.

The Chartered Bank of India, Australia & China, now known as *The Chartered Bank,* opened its first branch in Japan at Yokohama in 1880, and its second at Kobe in 1895, where it also was first located in Kyo-machi, in what were then magnificent premises. The building had the distinction of a large and impressive dome, but after thirty years, when the dome showed signs of weakening and falling in upon the heads of the staff and customers, the Bank acquired the Bund site of the British Consulate and built there the present premises with the British Consulate occupying a portion as tenants.

In 1877 there was also an establishment in Yokohama, known as The Bank Exchange. It was located next door to Cobb & Co., a branch of the famous Australia coaching firm of the bushranger and gold-digging days. Research has, however, shown that The Bank Exchange was the name of a billiard and bowling saloon!

In addition to the exchange banks there were also several banks specialising in loans on real estate, of which the Trust and Loan Agency Company in Kobe, represented by Jardine Matheson & Co., was an example. The name of that private bank reminded some of the young wags of the Kobe Club so much of a London pawnshop, that in 1890 they laid their plans carefully and set out late one night bent on fun. In those days the foreign community lived within the Settlement, and when they awoke the following morning they saw hanging outside Jardine Matheson & Co.'s front door, three brass balls—the sign of a pawnbroker's establishment—and an announcement that loans were granted on any reasonable security. To make the meaning clearer, a battered bowler hat, and an old pair of trousers were on display! I am the proud owner of a faded photograph which records the doings of those pranksters of sixty-seven years ago.

The Mercantile Bank of India, Ltd., now known as *Mercantile Bank Ltd.*, although the last British bank to open in Japan, has the distinction of being the first to build premises of its own in Osaka.

The British insurance companies commenced business in Japan through agents right from the time the treaty ports were first opened. The need of them was great in those clapboard towns. Fires were frequent and rates were correspondingly high—premia of five percent and more were in force at one time.

In the great Yokohama fire of 1866 when most of the Foreign Settlement and the Japanese town were destroyed, The Oriental Bank Corporation and some of the British trading firms hastily packed their books and sent them aboard a British man-of-war in the harbour for safety. Fortunately the British-owned *Japan Herald* took similar precautions regarding their type, with the result that the type was saved from destruction and, when the fire was finally extinguished, an English newspaper soon was again available.

During the midst of the conflagration the English troops then stationed in Yokohama were called out and in the hope of preventing the fire from spreading, they began blowing up a number of buildings. This action led to some furious international incidents where non-British buildings were concerned, with foreign consuls and owners protesting the action of the English soldiers amid the roar of gunpowder. But in the end it mattered not at all, because practically all the foreign-owned buildings and all the foreign consulates and legations were destroyed.

Indeed the diplomatic corps suffered so badly that on the day following the fire the Governor of Kanagawa sent two roosters to Sir Harry Parkes, the British Minister, *"to assuage his hunger!"*

The Yokohama Club miraculously escaped destruction, although it narrowly missed being blown skyward when the English soldiers used an excessive quantity of gunpowder to blow up a neighbouring building.

The damage was immense and there was considerable loss of life, but much good came out of the happening. The Yokohama Foreign Concession, previously a clapboard town resembling some Western mining town, was rebuilt in grander style. The odoriferous Swamp was filled in with debris from the town, *"thus removing a source of rheumatic and febrile complaints then very common,"* a recreation ground was created and the Yokohama Cricket Club came into being; but, most important of all, many wide roads were then created which have been a feature of Yokohama city since those early times.

The bulk of the insurance business was in the hands of British companies and in the years that followed many opened their own branches in Japan. It was not until after World War II that the idea of operating as a group was developed.

The *Peninsular & Oriental Steam Navigation Company,* was the first British shipping company to establish a regular line of steamers to Japan, and the first to open its own offices here.

In the summer of 1859, that is to say within a few weeks of Japan being opened, Thomas Sutherland of the Company's Hongkong staff (later to be knighted and to become chairman of the P. & O.) made a hurried trip to Japan on the only conveyance then available, an opium clipper, and as a result of his report the P. & O. established a service. Their first sailing to Japan was the steamer "Azof" which arrived in Nagasaki on 3 September, 1859. And so it is that almost a century has passed since the house flag of that great British steamship company was first raised in Japan. It can of course still be seen flying outside the offices of their agents, *Mackinnon Mackenzie & Co., of Japan, Ltd.*

There are not many foreign shipping companies which can claim that one of their vessels, after giving years of sterling service, had ended her days as a ship of the line in the Japanese navy. So far as I am aware the P. & O. have never claimed that unusual distinction. However, it is a fact that the first *Chusan,* a veritable baby of 699 tons as compared with the present great *Chusan* of 24,215 gross tons, did in fact become one of the most important ships in the Japanese Navy of those early days.

That first *Chusan,* a stout little barque-rigged, iron-hulled vessel, sail and steam of 80 horse power, was built in 1852. After serving on the Australian run she was transferred to the Calcutta/China service. In 1856 she was transporting British troops to trouble spots in the East in engagements and expeditions which now are almost forgotten by all except historians. Then from 1859 she was on the Shanghai/Japan run. Indeed it was aboard her that many of the first merchants to Nagasaki and Yokohama arrived together with their stocks, and their office and household furniture. On one occasion she brought 300 Indian troops of the 2nd Baluchi Regiment and 80 Tommies for the English garrison in Yokohama.

In 1861 she was sold and eventually passed into the hands of the Matsuyama clan in Japan, and was later absorbed into the Japanese navy.

In 1867, *Butterfield & Swire,* who had previously been represented by agents, came to Yokohama, and in 1887 they opened in Kobe. Their name has been in the forefront among British steamship companies in Japan since those early days.

In the early 80's they were appointed "Financial Agents of the Russian Government" in Japan in connection with Russian shipping. In those times the Russian Far Eastern Fleet, or a goodly portion of it, wintered in Japanese ports, particularly in Nagasaki, where shop signs and notices in Russian were a common feature of the Nagasaki Settlement.

Butterfield & Swire were also important insurance agents but in the early years of this century they handed over their insurance agencies to Findlay Richardson & Co., Ltd., later to be carried on by the great silk piecegoods firm of *Cooper Findlay & Co., Ltd.* In the postwar period, after an absence from the insurance field in Japan of more than forty years, Butterfield & Swire returned to insurance business in a more important way than ever before.

In speaking of the proud British hongs I cannot help but remark that they did not occupy rented rooms or suites of rooms in somebody else's building. Each was set in its own compound. The Chinese and Japanese clerks dressed in their native costumes, and the foreign staff wore bowler hats or headgear of an earlier era. Generally the only mechanical equipment in the office consisted of a massive press used for press-copying handwritten letters and invoices into copy books. The ability to make such copies without smudging the original letter was the mark of a well-trained office boy. Around the hongs there hung an aroma of cutch and spices, the smell of tea firing, or of silk cocoons, and sometimes the mustiness of age hung about them also. Those days have passed. All has now been replaced by the smell of floor polish and the fragrant perfume of stenographers!

The history of British firms in Japan can largely be found in the old foreign trade directories which were at first published in Hongkong, but which from the early eighteen seventies came to be published in Yokohama, and later in Kobe also. Unfortunately few people keep their old directories, and as each new one is issued, so the old one is generally thrown out. Directories of the last century are now rare books, and even those of pre-war years are not often seen.

Some of those directories, by reason of printers' errors or other unusual material that found their way into the pages, have even become collectors' items. There was the notorious issue of the British-owned *Japan Chronicle Directory* of about thirty years ago wherein readers were astonished to find under the name of the Vacuum Oil Company, Yokohama, (a company no longer trading on its own, but which years ago merged with others) the remark:—

Yokohama reports these people bloody impertinent. Cut the blighters out.

The Japanese compositor failing to recognise this editorial note as an instruction to him, reproduced it in type. The mistake passed the notice of the proof-readers and appeared in print to the amusement of almost everybody but the management of the company concerned. The Japan Chronicle made an effort to call in those directories that had been distributed, but generally they found the public uncooperative!

A. Cameron & Co., Ltd., was established in Kobe in 1893 by Alexander C. Cameron who had come to Japan over twenty years before. It was during the prewar years, while the late Mr. E.W. James, O.B.E., was Managing Director of A. Cameron & Co., Ltd., that he created his famous estate at Shioya, which has been a boon to the Japanese Tax Office ever since.

The premises of *J. Witkowski & Co., Ltd.*, importers and exporters, was one of the landmarks of Kobe in prewar days because of the old cannon that stood on the pavement outside the front door. It was an old-fashioned piece of the type in use in Nelson's days, and had been acquired at the break-up of an old warship in Kobe. It disappeared during the war years when it was carted away in the drive for metal scrap.

During 1944–5 Witkowski's premises were used by the Japanese Army as a prisoner of war camp, known as Kobe Camp. The office premises served as quarters for the guards and staff, and the godowns for the accommodation of the prisoners of war, who were being used for labour on the nearby wharves. After the air raids of 1945, a few battered walls, the office strong room, and the Japanese sentry box on the pavement outside the entrance to the godown were all that remained.

In 1922, when Brunner Mond & Co., Ltd., to be known in Japan after the war as *Imperial Chemical Industries (Japan) Ltd.*, or I.C.I., built their Crescent Building in Kyo-machi, Kobe, it marked the beginning of a new era in the old Foreign Concession.

For one thing, that building was the first foreign-owned reinforced concrete building to be built in Kobe, but, what was more important, it was the first of the many large modern buildings that came to be built in Kyo-machi and which soon altered the old-fashioned appearance of that road that was so reminiscent of the old Settlement days.

To antiquarians, the happening should have been of interest because Crescent Building was built on the site of the George Whymark Auction & Storage Rooms, a very old single-storied barn-like building which was cluttered up inside with dust and relics of the past. Tons of old records and early Settlement furniture went to the junk heap before that old building could be pulled down. I recall with some regret that I personally assisted in the destruction of many old directories and records of the past when the old Scottish hong of Findlay Richardson & Co., Ltd., went into voluntary liquidation in 1926. The firm had opened their first Far Eastern Branch in Manila in 1826. They came to Japan in the early eighteen-seventies but by 1926 the partners decided that, having made their money the hard way, they were not much interested in stepping aside to allow successors possibly to lose it the easy way. It thus fell to my lot, as a junior assistant, to supervise the clearing out of fifty years of records and accumulations, among which, I well recall, were innumerable banners and other decorations that had graced St. Andrew's Balls of bygone days. I should explain that with the exception of myself most of those who served in that honourable old hong were worthy Scotsmen.

I also recall that I earned a special commendation from my chief when I sold the old paper and books to a junkman for what was then the considerable sum of yen 630. My antiquarian instincts have, however, often since troubled me for the vandalism that I may have been innocently guilty of, in permitting so much of that stuff to be destroyed in the paper mills!

Among the large British firms that retired from Japan, there was one whose shipping mark can still be seen all over the world. M. Samuel & Co., later to become Samuel Samuel & Co., Ltd., in the early days of its existence in Japan shipped large quantities of so-called Japanese curios to England, including sea shells polished and painted in scenic effects, which articles were sold in vast quantities as souvenirs of Margate and other popular bathing beaches in England, and eventually found a place among the bric-a-brac that adorned many an English mantelpiece. About that time the company adopted the shell as a shipping mark.

Eventually, when the House of Samuels turned its attention to oil, their shipping mark of a shell was adopted as the trade-mark—the same "Shell" that can be seen nowadays throughout Japan and the world wherever gasoline and oil is sold.

The *Dunlop Rubber Company* originally formed in England in 1888, opened in Japan in 1908 with thirty employees, which number, before many years had passed, increased to nearly two thousand. Its advertising slogan was: "It's Dunlops. It's Dependable," and the emphasis was at first on bicycle and jinrikisha tyres that were sufficiently strong to withstand the wear and tear of Japanese roads, with motor tyres assuming a position of importance after motorcars had been invented.

It took the Japanese public some time to master the intricacies of the name, but when they did "dunropu taiya" became synonymous for motor tyres!

Dunlops have continued to advance with the times and have always maintained their position in the forefront of British manufacturing in Japan.

The oldest Australian company in Japan, *Parbury Henty & Co., Ltd.*, opened in Kobe in 1903, but its parent companies were established in Australia by James Henty in Tasmania in 1833, and by Frederick Parbury in Sydney two years later.

It is interesting to recall that James Henty's elder brother was the first settler in Victoria, Australia, and stepped ashore there at 8 a.m. on November 19th, 1834, and thereupon proceeded to unload his cargo of four working bullocks, thirteen heifers, six dogs, two turkeys, two guinea fowl, a fishing boat, a plough, plants, vines, fruit trees and seeds.

Many other names occur in the field of British pioneering enterprise in Japan, such as the great British cable companies, and interesting undertakings such as the *Clifford-Wilkinson Tansan Mineral Water Co., Ltd.*, originally established about 1880. No pretence is made of compiling a complete list of such undertakings in this short article, but rather of marking the way in the various fields of British enterprise in Japan.

In earlier days there were other British manufacturing enterprises such as Lever Bros. who sold out to Japanese interests.

Then, there have been, and are, many important British organizations that have been operating here under Japanese names or as joint British-Japanese enterprises, such for example as *Toyo Babcock K.K.*, *Teikoku Seishi K.K.*, and others too numerous to mention within the scope of this article.

And finally there is that legion of British technical men typified by *Lloyd's Register of Shipping*, the journalists, and the professional men, who have all played such a big part in the development of British-Japanese commercial relations since the very first days of extraterritoriality.

It is to all those organizations and individuals, to those foreign banks, insurance and shipping companies, merchants and manufacturers who have been carrying on business in Japan during the past ninety-eight years, that Japan owes a great debt. It was they who supplied the experience, the know-how, the cash, and the credit, which soon demonstrated to the Japanese the great possibilities within their own country.

A century, all but one year, has now elapsed since Japan reopened her ports to foreign trade. British interests have taken a full share in the commercial transactions and development of that period, and in this chapter, I have stepped back into the past and have presented the names of a few of the British firms and institutions that participated in that great era of enterprise.

Foreign Settlements and British Enterprises

This chapter appeared as an article on June 13, 1957, in a commemorative issue of *The Mainichi* on the occasion of the official birthday of Queen Elizabeth II.

THE
SMITHS
OF
YOKOHAMA

Those blessed with the name of Smith seem to have
been more prominent in the early days of Yokohama
than those who bore the equally commonplace name
of Williams.

At this point I should like to mention, in paren-
thesis, that, with respect to my last chapter, which
was originally published in *The Mainichi* newspaper,
I have been the recipient of two complaints. The
first party objected that not enough mention was
made of their name, and the second that they were not
mentioned at all.

In consequence of this experience, I anticipate that
the Smiths of this world might lodge a complaint
and challenge my claim that the name of Williams
is equally as commonplace as theirs. In support of
their contention, not unlikely they will cite an analysis
of the names in the most recent issue of the *London
Telephone Directory*. However, for my part, I insist

on having the first and last word in the controversy, which this article might conceivably give rise to, by asserting right now that an examination of the Honours Lists, the gaol lists, and all the other lists, will show that the name of Williams has a commonness about it that is unequalled by any other.

I have to admit that the *Hongkong Daily Press Directory* of 1865 lists forty-one plain Smiths and one variant, as being resident in China, the Philippines, and Japan, as against only fifteen Williamses. Fifteen out of a total of 3792 seems a rather poor showing. But I do not think it really means much. Not unlikely the upper-crust out East in those days found it easier than others to gain an entree to directory listings. And, in any case, more Williamses may then have been seeking to make their fortunes by methods more questionable than trading in the Far East.

Without comment I now throw into the ring the following amazing discovery, although actually it is apropos of nothing. According to the aforementioned Hong List, not even one person with a double-barrelled name was seeking a fortune in the far Far East in 1865!

But now let us return to Yokohama, where according to Sir Rutherford Alcock, British Minister in those days, there resided much of the *"scum of the earth."* The fact can hardly be disputed, and the records prove that in Yokohama then there were both Smiths and Williamses.

Certainly, in prewar years, there were some of the latter, who had so little pride in the rugged land

of their forefathers, and who considered the leek so
vulgar a vegetable, that, after several futile attempts
to change the spelling or the pronounciation of
Williams, they sought to mask its commonness by
hyphenating it with another. There was one such
Welshman, whom some people thought a snob. But
possibly he felt there was ample justification, as he
did not wish to be confused with his own father or
myself!

Such cowardice in respect of a name, which after
all does figure most prominently in the Court lists,
the police lists, or in fact anywhere that English
names are listed, is so little to my liking that I have
no intentions of honouring the Williamses of Japan
with a chapter!

That is why I propose to tell you instead about the
Smiths of Yokohama.

There were many Smiths. At one extreme there
was "Public Spirited" Smith. At the other, "Drunken" Smith.

* * * * * * * *

W. H. Smith, better known as "Public Spirited"
Smith, because of his willingness to devote his spare
time to the benefit of the community, originally came
to Japan as an officer in the Royal Marines, one of the
several English regiments that were stationed in
Yokohama in the early days on guard duty. That
is going back well over ninety years.

"Public Spirited" Smith played quite a part in the
life of the little foreign community of Yokohama.
He had much to do with the establishment of the
Yokohama United Club, of which he was manager

for many years, and of the Grand Hotel, of which he was managing director. He introduced brick-making and several other industries to Japan. He is also given credit for the introduction of market gardening. His head gardener was an Englishman named Jarmain, who later established a nursery of his own, and whose descendants are still in Japan.

In the early eighteen sixties when fresh vegetables had largely to be imported, Smith established his first vegetable garden on the Bluff and delighted in presenting fresh vegetables to the English military hospital in Yokohama, and to the foreign community institutions. Knowing from long experience gained during his military career, what Army rations can sometimes be like, he did not fail to supply fresh vegetables to the Tommies in the English camp, or to the French soldiers at the French camp, then located near the approach to the Bluff.

In those days potatoes were imported from America, onions came from Bombay, and some greens from Shanghai. Often those importations were made by sailing ship and consequently spoilage was sometimes very great.

Even the Christmas turkey and the holly came from Shanghai or as far away as America. The Japanese had not then discovered that by wiring *nanten* berries to holly leaves, they could produce Christmas holly that would even have deceived the observant Mr. Pickwick at his Christmas festivities.

A photograph showing "Public Spirited" Smith in that early vegetable garden on the Bluff—probably the only such photograph in existence—is to be found in an album of rare photographs now in the possession of the British Embassy in Tokyo.

The public gardens on the Bluff, one of the most attractive places in the early days of Yokohama, also resulted from Mr. W. H. Smith's tireless energy and persistence in the face of indifference from so many in the community.

Said J. R. Black in his *Young Japan,* which tells us much about those early days:—

The public gardens on the Bluff, Yokohama, were opened in 1870. A thoroughly worthy undertaking most thoroughly and unaccountably neglected by the general public ever since. On one man, mainly Mr. W. H. Smith, their support for a long time depended....By his care, however, they were kept in excellent order, and they deserved better appreciation at the hands of the community.

There were other such civic-minded foreigners in Japan, but few who so left their mark on the community, as did "Public Spirited" Smith.

* * * * * * * *

"Drunken Smith" on the other hand was a remittance man, one of many who lazed their lives away in Japan. He lived for many years in Yokohama, mixing with beachcombers down Creekside, or on the fringe of respectable society, just depending upon whether at the time he was passing through one of his lapses into drink or one of his periods of sobriety. During one of the former phases he set out for South America. Somewhere en route he forsook drink for teetotalism, and returned to Yokohama with a wife and a post-chaise. Apparently he could not afford to support either. His wife soon left him. He then drove around by himself for a while, generally wearing a pink carnation. Soon the post-chaise was advertised for sale, and after the sale of that mark of Victorian respectability he drifted downwards.

Eventually when he had completely exhausted his credit, such as it was in Yokohama, and after pledging his future, such as that also was, he went to Shanghai. Often he could be seen at the Race Club meetings sporting a red carnation in his buttonhole—that colour best matching his complexion at that time.

Despite his vicissitudes in life, he outlived the estate which was supporting him. Eventually his remittance was cut off. He was then in the depths of despair, until he was offered the job of supervisor in the foreign workhouse in Shanghai. His personal experiences of half a lifetime in mixing with bums proved invaluable. He was able to handle his last job with a fair degree of success.

Up to the time that "Drunken" Smith, the former remittance man, became supervisor in the workhouse, he had been of as little use to society as the beachcombers. Indeed he had contributed less to mankind than had one of the most infamous of all the beachcombers in the Pacific.

About 1808, Charles Savage, a Swede, arrived in Fiji in a native canoe, with ambitions of becoming a "blackbirder," as soon as he could acquire, by any foul means, a vessel suitable for the purpose. The Fijians were then simple islanders still in

The Smiths of Yokohama

the cannibal state. Savage fastened himself upon them, and remained there until he had so worn out his welcome that they killed and ate him. Little was wasted. Not even his bones, which were made into needles and distributed among the islanders as souvenirs, in which form Charles Savage proved of greater use to mankind than when alive.

* * * * * * * * * *

Between "Public Spirited" Smith and "Drunken" Smith, there were many other Smiths in Yokohama who achieved great things.

On one occasion a Williams was hanged, but that was a distinction the Smiths never achieved.

A
GENTLEMAN'S
CLUB

> *Come let's now talk with delibera-*
> *tion, fair and softly.*
>
> RABELAIS

In each of the Foreign Concessions there was a
gentleman's club where, in the days of long ago, the
taipans of the *hongs* gathered in the bar often at
11 a.m., generally at 12.30 p.m., and invariably at
5 p.m. The Kobe Club was typical.

But there were other places also where men gathered to discuss the weather and other topics. Dives
had been operating in the alleyways off Moto-machi
from the days when foreign ships first arrived in
Kobe. There were also more elite establishments
further out of town, such for example as Christine's,
with foreign hostesses.

The so-called saloons in the lanes behind Moto-
machi have always been adept at making money in
ways that would have been despised by Christine.
Indeed as far back as 1613, Capt. Saris, of the English
East India Company's trading post in Hirado, recorded how the members of his crew were *"seduced
by drink, women and sailor boarding-house keepers"*
in Nagasaki. However the fault was not all on one
side. The men were Jacks ashore after months at
sea. They had money in their pockets. They ate,
drank, fought, and made love in the special houses
provided for their entertainment on Maruyama, which

227

name thereafter in course of time came to be given to many another gay quarter in Japan.

In those days of sail, the trading vessels to Japan made their way up the China Sea in summer with the southerly monsoon behind them and lay up in Japanese ports until winter when they travelled south again with the northerly behind them. During the late summer and autumn at the peak of trade, when the trading fleet was in port, there were over six or seven hundred seamen ashore. The fights, brawls, disturbances, and amount of love making that went on in the Maruyama quarter can therefore easily be imagined. When the sailors' money was gone the keepers of the houses extended them credit against the security of their clothes. Whereupon, perforce, the sailors had to make their way back to their ships in a semi-naked condition, much to the indignation of the captains of the vessels.

But let us return to the House of Christine. She certainly was a lady as compared with the *mama-sans* of Moto-machi, although, understandably enough, that assertion would never, at that time, have been accepted in Kitano-cho tea party circles.

It should not be held against Christine if in her later years she resembled the popular conception of an elderly duchess—stream-lining was unknown then, both in transportation vehicles and the female form when clothed. In one respect she acted like a school ma'am in a seminary, in that she was a great disciplinarian. For one thing she required that all her "young ladies"—a term used by her professionally and without regard to their actual ages—should dress in evening gowns. She would have despised the technique of the Moto-machi alleyways where the tarts dressed in cheap fur coats and nothing else, or in nothing else. However all that may be, Mrs. Brown-Brown, then doyen of Kitano-cho tea party circles, referred to Christine's "young ladies" as brazen hussies, and with good reason. Without going into other details, I must admit that they all used rouge and most of them smoked—things which no nice women, and certainly none in Kitano-cho, would then have done.

Christine was somewhat of a Victorian—definitely so when she made her debut. Perhaps considering her calling, it would be more correct to say an Edwardian, in that she was pledged to pleasure but at the same time renowned for her dignity and plain business honesty. Her discretion was only equalled by that of the hall porter of the Kobe Club, who was a master at dealing with enquiries from irate wives as to whether or not their husbands were still on the club premises, or rather, still in the club bar.

Christine, as already remarked, was very much an Edwardian and could always be depended upon to display the utmost tact on and off her premises, and to protect the good name of those who patronized her house. Never would she have grasped at fame, as did the London newspaper *The Pink'Un* when it defended a prince, against its own allegations that he had been carrying on with an actress, with the slam: *"We are now able to confirm that there was nothing between the Prince and Miss Lily Langtry. Absolutely nothing. Not even a chemise!"*

Christine was not the only one in those parts with a sense of plain decent honesty in money matters. There was a saloon keeper in Moto-machi, Charlie Prop by name. "Prop" was not his real name, but was the word that had been painted prominently on the front of his saloon by the Japanese signwriter, and was intended as the abreviation for "proprietor." His surname was not generally known, and most people, outside the family circle, imagined it to be Prop. Over the decades, foreign sailors had come to know his bar as one of the few in all Kobe where they could be assured of a square deal.

Pledges for debts, or articles for safe-keeping, were left with him in complete confidence that they could be picked up on the next voyage. His financial credit with the banks was probably nil, but his personal credit with his clientele—the seamen—stood as high as that of the Rockefellers. Banzai Bill the beach-comber and other such foreign derelicts who infested the port in those days were not welcomed in his saloon and were liable to be thrown out without ceremony. He had no time for bums, but no prejudice against drunks. Albeit he never short-changed or over-charged anyone, drunk or sober, who patronized his saloon. Charlie Prop had been a seafaring man in his young days. He had been a sailor before the mast, and had been victimised by the crooks and the tarts who prey on sailors in all ports of the world. He decided to keep his own saloon shipshape. Charlie Prop, like Christine, was old-fashioned. Both had their own simple ideas that an obligation was something to be met, not side-stepped.

A Gentleman's Club

Christine's house from the outside resembled a *hong*, and therefore had the appearance of eminent respectability. In fact it rather created the impression that it was a *hong* that had painted its face lightly, tucked up its skirts and with mock modesty discretely stepped out of town to one of the quiet streets. In that house two new ideas, calculated to shock, were introduced into the conservative life of Kobe; both were then considered rather immoral, but later became fashionable among many women. I refer to the wearing of flesh coloured stockings instead of black and tans; the other, and the more daring, was the rolling down of stockings below the knee. It was not long then before some women went the whole hog and peeled off their stockings altogether —and then their corsets also. About two decades later men tried to even the score by discarding their hats.

In course of time, severe local competition and a change in tastes had to be met and Christine moved to new quarters in the centre of the city, where the enigmatic legend "IMPORT-EXPORT" on her front door was the guiding beacon, as it were, to her place of business.

Eventually a day dawned when there were whisperings in the Kitano-cho tea parties and word was passed down the bar at the Kobe Club that the House of Christine had closed its doors. The bank manager, who was known on an occasional morning to have sent a bunch of flowers to the house, was one of the few who knew that Christine had at last put her son through school in England.

A Gentleman's Club

But let us take our departure from these places, one of which after all may have been just a common bawdy house and the other certainly was no more than just a drinking saloon, and let us move to a more exalted plane. Let us enter the majestic portals of the Kobe Club of prewar days.

The doors were closed tight to females. It was as difficult for any of the female sex to pass through the front door as through the eye of a needle, because there was always a conscientious hall porter on duty to guard the front door. He became one of the oldest and most popular of the Club's servants, but as his duties called for tact rather than physical exertion, he became rather adipose.

Except for the murmur of voices from the bar, one could generally enjoy the quietness of a morgue within those walls. The halls and corridors were wide and allowed members plenty of steering room. The reading room was so long that the snoring of those dozing at one end over *The Economist* was barely audible at the other end by those reading *La Vie Parisienne*. The library covered an immense range of the best books including sixteen volumes of the unexpurgated edition of Sir Richard Burton's *The Thousand Nights and a Night*, but not D.H. Lawrence's *Lady Chatterly's Lover*. (Men had to go to the K.R. & A.C. across the way and enter their names on the waiting list for that book. However the female members of the K.R. & A.C. never played fair over it. They circulated it by hand, one to the other, without returning it to the library. Eventually it disappeared, apparently worn out by piercing eyes.)

But let us return to the Kobe Club.

There was a bowling alley well patronized by those who sought to reduce their weight by methods more agreeable than dieting. And there was an immense billiard room housing nine full-sized billiard tables, the area of the room being more than twice that of any local church, but less than half that of the largest Buddhist temple. And finally a spacious and stately dining room where, as in the bar, the juniors, according to an unwritten law, occupied positions near the entrance, whilst the *taipans* and old-timers dined in glory at the far end. I recall that it took several years for me to advance the length of that dining room.

The bar, which the members boasted was the longest in Japan, was impressive in length and for the solemnity with which the old-timers drank steadily, and held court with due ceremony, to the accompaniment of the rattling of dice. The *taipans* gathered at the far end, whilst the juniors of the *hongs* took up a position more or less commensurate with their seniority. Only the bounders pushed their way forward.

Drinking, even in summer, had to be done with coats on. Indeed there was only one day in the year when, as it were, the skirts of decorum were lifted sufficiently to permit of anyone climbing onto the bar counter. That was on Washington's Birthday when the American members entertained other members. Commencing in the nineteen-twenties and extending into the nineteen-thirties it had been customary every year on that occasion for one of the hosts, a gifted entertainer, to make a fiery speech purporting to be by a senator upon the floor of the U.S. Senate upon the subject of Arkansas politics. In the nineteen-twenties his speech was made from floor level, a year or so later he stood on a chair, but by the nineteen-thirties he had reached a standing position on the top of the bar counter! So rich was the speech in spicy hyperbole that the Kobe Club was at that time about the only safe place to give the entertainment, for like the holiest of Buddhist temples it was a place where woman could not enter.

In short, the old Kobe Club was a magnificent mass of red brick, built to meet the comforts of those who did not want to rub elbows too closely with the other fellow, designed in the "good old days" when prices were low, a place of refuge from domestic worries or possessive wives, but alas, costly and uneconomical to maintain. Cracks began to appear in the noble edifice.

A time eventually arrived when the Club could no longer carry on and was tottering to its fall, overburdened with a bank overdraft, accumulating expenses, and repairs. Then it was that an appeal was made to members to lend money to the club by subscribing to debentures. The debentures were not floated as a public issue, with investors being invited to put down their money and take their chances in a business deal. Rather it was an effort among the members to solve their club's financial problems. It was understood they were secured against loss by the club having pledged the club assets. Many imbued with the club spirit took up the debentures and so enabled the club to carry on. At one time the debenture holders even agreed to the interest rate being reduced to further assist the club in its financial extremity.

As the years went by some of the debenture holders fell on bad times, left the port, or died. But the Club was not able even then to redeem their debentures, and so it became the task of the Club Secretary to locate some other member who was willing to carry on the burden—the debentures remained outstanding—a debt of honour.

The debenture holders did not imagine that a world war would result in the club being rubbed out of existence, and then, some six or seven years later, of new arrivals with little knowledge of the past, together with a smattering of former members, reviving the club and being in control of most valuable assets that still existed only by the grace of God and the club spirit of the debenture holders, who had come to the rescue of the club when it was tottering to its fall.

It thus came about that the post-war members were able to sell the Club property and also to recover war compensation to a total of around eighty million yen.

It was at about this stage the Committee offered on a take-it-or-leave-it basis to repay the debenture holders with inflated yen—virtually to give them almost nothing. The debenture holders after the war were mostly elderly men scattered throughout the world. Some had suffered from the vicissitudes of war. Many in their need sadly accepted the settlement offered, preferring even a small amount of inflated yen to nothing at all.

Except as a one-time member of the Kobe Club of more than twenty years standing, I am not personally involved in this affair. I never owned any debentures. I have nothing at stake.

The committee asserts that it has taken legal advice on the stand adopted. The legality of its action has not been doubted, but there are some people who are bothered with old-fashioned concepts of club ethics and who, like Christine and Charlie Prop, at the other end of the social ladder, believe that there are some debts that should be considered from levels higher than the niceties of the law.

This chapter first appeared as an article in *The Mainichi* newspaper on Sept. 2, 1955. The Kobe Club has maintained its attitude of offering the debenture holders nothing more than the face value of the debentures in current inflated yen.

THE
GRIFFITHS
COLLECTION

> *Quis talia fando*
> *Temperet a lacrimis?*—VIRGIL
> *(And who can hear this tale with-*
> *out a tear?)*

During the two and a half centuries that the Tokugawa family controlled Japan, so fearful were they of the propagation of the Christian religion, or indeed of any teachings or movements which might eventually lessen their own grip upon the country, that they discouraged the writing of history, and even destroyed many of the manuscripts and records concerning early foreign intercourse with Japan.

The result has been that, in order to learn much regarding the history, and even the economy of Japan of those early days, historians have had to delve into the records and even the ledgers of the early Portuguese, Dutch, and English trading companies then operating in Japan. The diaries of some of the sea captains and travellers of those times, and the letters written by the Jesuit, and other evangelistical priests, have also been a rich source of information.

It can be said that, if it were not for the material that has been gathered from the libraries of England and the Continent, there would be many more blank pages in Japan's history than there are now. Many famous Occidental scholars have, from time to time, studied and become proficient in Portuguese, Spanish,

237

and Dutch, in addition to Japanese, in order that they might undertake research among the original records, and so uncover some of the hidden pages of Japanese history.

From the time Japan was first opened to foreign trade there has been no lack of studiously-minded men who have interested themselves in the history of Japan and the East, and who have made collections of Orientalia. Unfortunately few of those collections have survived the devastating fires and earthquakes that have been such a feature of life in Japan.

The Yokohama and Kobe foreign newspapers of the latter half of the last century carry many reports of valuable libraries of irreplaceable books being lost by fire. The foreign newspaper offices seem to have suffered heavily, which in part accounts for the comparative rarity of files of the English language newspapers that were published here during the last century. Odd volumes are to be found in various libraries, but complete files are no longer available. The largest collection of such newspaper files is to be found in the Ueno Public Library in Tokyo—the largest public library in Japan—but they have been ill preserved and to-day are gathering dust in the cellars and are rapidly deteriorating into a mass of rubbish.

In 1899, the office of the *Hiogo News,* which journal dated back to the opening year of Kobe port, was destroyed by fire, and with it was lost the complete files of that paper. A history of the Kobe Foreign Settlement, under consular jurisdiction, had been prepared from those files, and was about to be published in a more permanent form, but unfortunately all the proofs and manuscripts were lost. There was no opportunity for the work to be rewritten, and so it is that much of the early history of the Kobe Foreign Settlement has been lost for all time.

One of the finest libraries of books on Japan in English and in other foreign languages was gathered together by that brilliant Australian, George Ernest Morrison, later in life to be known by the proud title of "Morrison of Pekin." Morrison, whose father was Principal of Geelong College, was born at Geelong, in Victoria, in 1862. In 1897 he was appointed *The Times* resident correspondent in the Chinese capital of Pekin. As there were few reference books on the Far East available to him, he decided to build up a library of his own and he began to collect systematically. To quote his own words:—

In those days, books on China were at a discount. Compared with the prices that had to be paid for them later, they cost a mere song. Only in later years after the war between Japan and Russia, did the American libraries turn their attention to China. As soon as they came into the market, prices advanced enormously.

In 1917, that famous library was sold to Baron H. Iwasaki and transferred to Tokyo.

Fortunately the Morrison Library, now a part of the Oriental Library in Tokyo, escaped the air raids of 1945.

The Morrison Library is of course an outstanding collection, but there were a few other Westerners who, on a very much more modest scale, gathered together fine collections. One was the late Mr. Harry John Griffiths.

Mr. Griffiths arrived in Japan in 1907 as a pharmacist attached to the Kobe pharmacy of J. L. Thompson & Co. Having won several awards for botany in England he commenced a study of the flora of Japan. Being by nature a student and a collector, his interests soon branched out to all phases of Japanese art and culture, and in time he became a serious scholar of Japanese history and a collector of books on Japan. Later as the senior partner of J. L. Thompson & Co., (Retail) Ltd., Kobe, he became a publisher of a series of important books on Japan, including a revised edition of Basil Hall Chamberlain's *Things Japanese,* which latter book raised the ire of some of the prewar Japanese authorities. The ultranationalists did not desire that the light of historical truth be focussed upon some of her cults, such as Bushido as preached by the militarists, or on State Shintoism. Practically all the books which his company published are now eagerly sought by collectors.

During the nineteen-thirties, Mr. Griffiths' book store in Kobe became the Mecca for literary personalities. Indeed it was from Mr. Griffiths that George Bernard Shaw first heard that a complete set of his works translated into Japanese was freely on sale in Japan and even adorned the shelves of the Diet Library. Those acquainted with the Shavian manner will be able to imagine Shaw's acid comment that he did not recall having given anyone permission to translate his works into Japanese.

Although unconventional in manner and usually

careless of dress, Mr. Griffiths became impressive in appearance when in formal Japanese dress, which he always donned when participating in *Noh* dancing and *cha-no-yu* (tea ceremony), in both of which he was keenly interested. He was a non-smoker and an absolute teetotaler, but he was greatly fond of Japanese food and entertainments and had *entree* to all the better class Japanese restaurants in Kobe, where he was affectionately and with great respect known to all the geisha, and those associated with geisha life in Kobe, as "Caramel San." He greatly admired the trained high-class geisha of prewar years, and was quite an authority on the etiquette and customs of the teahouse life which the geisha lived.

That any Westerner should be more interested in Noh dancing, in the tea ceremony, in Japanese history, art, literature and religious ceremonies, than in the pursuit of wealth, was a matter beyond the understanding of those mediocre individuals appointed by the Home Department in prewar days to watch over the thought processes and activities of foreign residents in Japan—more especially when that one happened to be a person who was critical of the trend in Japan to extreme nationalism. And so Mr. Griffiths' interest in Japanese culture had incurred their suspicion, and he was marked as a person to be watched.

It was Griffiths' misfortune, and others also, that in 1939 a member of the mercantile marine named Peters, appeared in Kobe, and lodged for awhile at The Missions to Seamen, a circumstance that eventually proved most distressing for all those persons who had come into contact with him, including Griffiths, and also the padre of the Mission, both of whom were subsequently arrested.

A White Russian who happened to be a police informer alleged that Peters, when drinking with him in a bar, boasted that he was a foreign agent. Thereafter Peters was never able to convince the authorities otherwise. He was arrested, tried, and jailed, an experience that he survived for about five years, when, broken in mind and body, he died in Sakai Jail, near Osaka, before the end of the war could secure his release.

Following his arrest, Peters admitted that he had occasionally visited J. L. Thompson's book store and browsed among the books, and not unnaturally had conversed with Griffiths, who on all occasions was a highly entertaining conversationalist. Mr. Griffiths was thereupon arrested. Despite his advanced age he was thrown into jail, and examined for nearly six months over the cold winter of 1940. At the end of that period he was released after having been found guilty of no greater offence than a technical breach of the Publications Law, over the re-publication of Chamberlain's *Things Japanese,* for which he was fined one hundred yen. The fine was no doubt to save the face of those who had unsuccessfully sought to prove that he was an international spy.

During Griffiths examination following his arrest, his interrogators endeavoured to establish that those casual meetings with Peters did in fact prove that there was close collaboration between them. At one point in his examination, the two interrogators chided Griffiths with his admission that he had conversed with Peters and yet his denial that he even knew Peters' name, whereupon Griffiths protested, "But I have been talking to you two gentlemen for nearly a week, and yet I do not know your names."

Each thereupon corrected the omission by producing a name card. Griffiths read both cards, then to the first he remarked: "Your name I may soon forget, but yours," turning to the other, "I shall never forget."

On being pressed for an explanation as to why that should be so, he blandly replied: "Because, Mr. Enomoto, your name happens to be the same as that of a rebel against the Emperor, and one who sought to set up a republic in Hokkaido!"

The interrogator had possibly been too busy extracting confessions, from the guilty and innocent alike, to delve very deeply into Japanese history, and so he attentively listened while Griffiths described to him the absorbing story of Admiral Enomoto who in 1869 fought against the Imperial Forces, was later pardoned, and subsequently rose to positions of high honour within the state.

During confinement, Griffiths' jailers and interrogators acquired a greater knowledge of Japanese history and culture than they previously had. Griffiths parted company with them on friendly terms although to their disappointment he insisted on retaining, as a mark of his imprisonment, the beard that he had grown during his unwilling confinement.

It was in February 1941, some eight months after

Griffiths had been discharged from jail, that he arranged to take one of his former jailers, a man who was devoutly interested in Buddhism, to an old but little known Temple in Hyogo, Eifukuji by name, although described in some records as Seifukuji.

It was dark and the temple had been closed for the night when Griffiths and the jailer arrived. The priest was roused with some difficulty:

"Were any services held to-day for Taki Zenzaburo?" enquired Griffiths, to which the priest grumbled, probably perversely, that he did not know.

"That is understandable," replied Griffiths, "although it does so happen that Taki Zenzaburo died in this temple precisely seventy-three years ago to this very night, and at this exact hour."

When it became evident to the priest that he was dealing with a scholar and not with a maniac, he willingly opened the storehouse containing the archives of the temple and brought forth the dusty and worm-eaten volumes of bygone days. And so after turning over many pages of the forgotten past, they came upon the original record of Taki Zenzaburo, an officer in the service of the Lord Daimyo Bizen of Okayama, condemned by a decree in the name of the Emperor to perform hara-kiri for having given the order to fire upon the Foreign Settlement of Kobe, where some of the envoys of the Foreign Powers then were.

That hot-headed officer was in charge of a party of soldiers of the Daimyo of Okayama, who when passing through Kobe, not far from where the Daimaru Department Store stands to-day, became incensed at the attitude of a few foreigners and fired upon the Foreign Settlement. Following as it did upon many previous attacks on legations and individuals, the representatives of the foreign powers naturally took a serious view of the attack and stern protests were lodged with the Imperial Government, as a result of which Taki Zenzaburo was ordered to die.

But let us return to the Eifuku-ji temple on that winter night in 1941 when Griffiths visited it with his jailer friend. The worm-eaten tomes of ancient records were closed and put away, and Mr. Griffiths, who had grown up among the cloisters of an English cathedral, then asked that he should be permitted to pay for a memorial service for the brave Taki Zenzaburo. And thus at the hour of the rat, when the lights in the neighbourhood were gradually being extinguished, the candles before the Buddha were lighted, the incense burnt, the gong struck, and the priest commenced to intone the appropriate sutras for the dead.

For Griffiths it was just another interesting excursion into the old Japan that he loved so much, but the jailer went home in a quiet and pensive mood, reflecting how curious it should have been that this elderly Englishman, who had been wrongly jailed as a suspected spy, should give a thought on that anniversary night to the anguished spirit of the brave but impetuous Taki Zenzaburo.

Now to resume my story of the task upon which Mr. Griffiths had lavished half a lifetime.

The collection of literary material alone (excluding collections of curios, woodcut prints, coins, stamps, etc.) comprised over 2,300 items. The majority were books on the Far East, including such rare volumes as letters from priests of the Society of Jesus in the Orient, published in Paris in 1572, *"Atlas Japanesis"* published in London in 1670, and many similar literary treasures of the next three centuries.

In addition there were many first editions and autographed copies of standard works on Japan, original manuscripts of some of Basil Hall Chamberlain's works, unpublished manuscripts on specialised Japanese subjects by foreign students that were awaiting the necessary funds to cover cost of publication, typescript copies of early Nagasaki Consular records, etc.

There were collections of letters from such literary authorities on the Far East as Basil Hall Chamberlain, Sir Charles Elliot, Sir George B. Sansom, M. Paske Smith, and many others. There were bound copies of early foreign newspapers, and now rare English periodicals once published in Japan. Collections of photographs and post cards of the Settlement days in Japan, and a vast number of items of Japanalia, such as early maps, grammar books, guide books, election notices, etc., all of which were catalogued with cross references.

In addition there was an immense collection of Buddhist charms and amulets, paraphernalia, and literature associated with Buddhist pilgrimages in Japan. And finally several hundred unusual Japanese books, including a great number of Japanese volumes of rare and beautifully illustrated copies of various well known *monogatari* (Japanese narratives).

In 1940, Mr. Griffiths, fearing that his collection might become lost, in the event of an outbreak of war, decided to send it out of Japan while there yet remained time. He thereupon set about the task of cataloguing, and eventually had the literary material alone packed in thirty-three export shipping cases ready for shipment to the Bristol University, where he hoped it would become available for research students of any nationality.

Unfortunately, owing to Japanese restrictions, those packing cases could not be shipped away before the war. On the outbreak of war Mr. Griffiths was again jailed and his premises ransacked by the gendarmerie and others. The cases were broken open and the contents scattered. Later his various possessions, or such as remained, were taken over by an official custodian and sold.

Much of the collection has never been accounted for. The most generous assumption one can make is that perhaps some portions, which had no ready sale value during wartime, were thrown out in the excitement of the times as so much junk, and had no better fate than to wither away as rubbish.

And so the unselfish labour of more than half a lifetime, in the interests of Japanese culture, for the benefit of students of the future, by a gifted and tireless collector, and without thought of personal gain, was wiped out and lost for all time by the vandalism of a few misguided and ignorant individuals.

The Griffiths Collection

Japan is poorer to-day by the loss of the fruits of labour of that unusual man.

* * * * * * * *

The final chapter in this strange story can now be told.

Mr. Griffiths died during the war in the Canadian Academy Internment Camp; and in 1949 I was appointed executor by the British Consul-General, because I happened to be Mr. Griffiths' closest friend, and also because I was familiar with his collection.

It thus became my duty to make a claim against the Japanese Government, under the Allied Powers Property Compensation Law, on behalf of the Estate for the wartime loss, but unfortunately, despite every effort, I was not able to make much progress over the next two years owing to the absence of the basic evidence upon which to formulate a claim. By great good fortune, in 1952, I came into possession of Mr. Griffiths' inventories and other papers that were found among his effects in the internment camp after his death. Within eight months from then, I had been able to complete the claim statement amounting to 144 pages of typewritten material, which had to be submitted in sextuplicate. It comprised a completely detailed inventory of every book in the library and a descriptive inventory covering every art piece with details of date and place of purchase, and cost. In addition it included copies of letters written by Mr. Griffiths during internment protesting at the prices at which his collection was being sold. The claim statement was supported by seven Consular

248

Certificates (British and Swiss), prewar fire insurance policies, and other exhibits. The amount claimed was ¥12,042,988.

A great deal of supplementary information was subsequently called for by the Authorities, who then offered a settlement of ¥4,029,820. A period of nearly three years then passed in protests and negotiations, in the course of which the amount offered was amended in steps and eventually reached ¥6,208,-232. Although I considered the latter amount far short of adequate compensation, I finally agreed to it, because there appeared to be little hope of a more reasonable settlement forthcoming. And of course in the meantime the beneficiaries were still waiting for the money.

The sum of ¥6,208,232 was thus received by me in cash on 1st July, 1957, from the Ministry of Finance, and the same day an application was lodged to remit that sum in full to the beneficiaries without deduction of any expenses, charges or fees whatsoever. The greater amount goes to the University of Bristol, and a lesser amount, in respect of certain personal items, to Mr. Griffiths' sister.

In bringing this labour of love to a conclusion I must pass a word of thanks to those five foreign bibliophiles, each of a different nationality and some internationally known, who gave me the benefit, without fee or reward, of their expert knowledge by making appraisals of various sections of Mr. Griffiths' collection, upon which independent aid disinterested appraisals I formulated the claim.

Certainly I was then involved for more than two

years in attempting, and unsuccessfully I believe, to convince the Authorities that those experts really knew what they were talking about when it came to books. The Authorities preferred to work on the appraisals given by certain unnamed second-hand booksellers.

In fairness to the investigators appointed to examine this claim, which was admittedly an unusual one, I must, however, say that I believe their difficulty in assessing the loss arose in part from their inability to divorce from their minds the substance of the original report which was drawn up by the first property custodian (he died during the war), who sold a portion of the collection to a bookseller, and most of the art pieces to a Moto-machi curio-dealer at absurdly low prices.

The Custodian's report was one of the few documents in the case that was in Japanese, and was, I fear, the only one that was completely understood by some of the official assessors.

The official report, apparently by way of explaining the low sales prices, contains the following amazing statements: "...*details of the books are unknown except that they are mostly research books and or guide books on the Orient*," and that among the art-pieces "*there was nothing worthwhile keeping*," and on the subject of clothing, "*Mr. Griffiths was quite an old man and strangely enough he remained single all his life. He had some clothes of his own, of course....*"

The dealers who had purchased the books and curios, when called upon a year or so ago by the

Finance Ministry for appraisals, of course, not unnaturally, named amounts in line with the ridiculously low prices at which they had bought those collections during war-time. Unfortunately the appraisals of those interested dealers appear to have been given more official credence than the disinterested appraisals of my five bibliophiles.

Finally, and most of all, my acknowledgments and grateful thanks for the unfailing patience, the guidance, and assistance received from certain officials in the British Embassy, through whom, according to the Japanese regulations, this claim had to be channelled.

JUN-CHAN

But when the morn came dim and sad
And chill with early showers,
Her quiet eyelids closed—she had
Another morn than ours.

THOMAS HOOD

It was a few minutes before sailing time. The new ten thousand ton Japanese liner was all bustle and confusion as the last minute farewells were being said. The last visitors were leaving the ship, and finally came the Company's representative, the last down the gangway.

Nine hundred emigrants, sixty tourist passengers, and twelve first-class passengers lined the rails, linked with a thousand paper streamers to those on the wharf. It was a great send-off enlivened with music; and then, as the vessel edged out from the wharf, the paper streamers began to break and the music turned to the familiar tune of *Auld Lang Syne,* believed by many Japanese to be a Japanese melody.

But Jun-chan saw none of this. She was probably asleep in her cabin. Jun-chan was leaving her native land, as were many of the emigrants on board, never to return, but Jun-chan was unconcerned. She did not know. Her thoughts were always just of the immediate present.

The weather freshened that night, and for several days the vessel rolled and shook from stem to stern as she pushed out into the Pacific at forced speed. Later the wind eased off but not the vibration. The rolling continued. A stowaway was forced out of

hiding through seasickness. The vibration set the
bottles and the instruments in the doctor's cabin
rattling a lively tune as each day he treated his 350
trachoma patients. The captain received daily progress reports from the doctor, and daily grew more
worried as to whether he could get the trachoma
cases past quarantine at destination. Twenty-four
hours before that time arrived the sale of beer and
sake would be stopped and the bathing arrangements
for the emigrants would be discontinued for fear that
the alcohol or the salt water would inflame their eyes.
Then half an hour before quarantine the warning
would be broadcast through the loud-speaker system
for all eye bandages to be removed.

In the meantime everyone on board had problems
and the ship's officers were harassed on all sides.
Harassed by the representative of the emigrants, who
pressed their complaints and asserted their demands
in the manner born of a knowledge of democracy in
postwar Japan. Harassed by the tourist and first-
class passengers who resented the lack of discipline
among the emigrants, who wandered throughout all
classes and on all decks at will. The captain and the
first officer, remembering the disciplined behaviour
of the Japanese masses in prewar days, and feeling
powerless in the face of such indiscipline, hid themselves as much as possible.

But none of those problems bothered Jun-chan, nor
did she worry her little head about anything.
Although she was travelling first-class, she did not
mind if the emigrants monopolised her deck. She
smiled at all. She was not one of the captain's

worries. She was not wearing an eye bandage. She was not one of the doctor's many trachoma patients.

Jun-chan spent most of the time in her cabin, or in the corridor outside her cabin door. More often than not she dined and drank in her cabin, but when she did eat in the saloon she commanded attention. She was not above shouting at the purser or the captain. She used to bang the table with her hand, or with a spoon if one were handy, and demand service.

My children loved Jun-chan. They loved her for the smile on her face, the twinkle in her eyes, and the way she held her hands outstretched to welcome all before her. The first time they met her, she was crawling along the passageway outside her cabin. The fact is she was only fifteen months old. They adopted her immediately. My son took her to his heart.

The ship travelled on south into the tropics. The trachoma cases continued to harass the doctor and worry the captain. The number of emigrants with eye bandages did not much decrease. But Jun-chan was unconcerned and happy. Her little feet were growing stronger. She crawled about with greater speed and more assurance. She was growing more lusty. One morning came when she was as rowdy as usual, her laughter as infectious as ever. She ate her breakfast and as always she smeared the egg well over her little face, and thought it great fun.

Two hours later Jun-chan was no more.

None can lay the blame. None can say for sure that her life could have been saved. The doctor fought for nearly two hours to save her, but perhaps he was battling in the wrong direction. Over-eating was his simple diagnosis. No one criticised him, and no one should, but we can extend sympathy that so much responsibility should have fallen suddenly on shoulders so young and so little experienced in the simplest of medical remedies.

Certainly it is a fact that in some of the most remote farming districts of the Western world, far from the call of a doctor, Jun-chan most probably would have lived. Children develop convulsions there, and mothers save them by the simple and proven method of a hot bath and cold compresses on the head. Jun-chan was unfortunate to have been stricken on that great modern liner, and not in some way back-country place where only the simple home-remedy could have been administered.

The ship's carpenter built a coffin—it was just a tiny coffin. Jun-chan was gently placed inside dressed in her gayest kimono. But within the coffin they were careful to put her foreign-style little dress, her dolls, her playing blocks, and most important of all her little shoes for the journeyings that were ahead. The eyes of her mother were dry most of the time, even when the tiny coffin was closed. In Japan even mothers are not expected to shed tears in public for their dead. They are taught that "the world has enough sorrow without another contribution."

The coffin was placed on two trestles, with dishes of food offerings nearby—a plate of fruit and cakes, and a dish of ice cream which soon melted. There were lighted candles, burning incense, a large choco-

late cake, and three cakes of sweet bean paste on
the altar. Fortunately a young Buddhist priest of
the Nishi Honganji Temple who was on board was
able to recite the sutras for the dead.

Various of the passengers, ship's officers, and staff
came forward and bowed before the coffin. My family
dressed in white, the Japanese colour of mourning,
knelt before Jun-chan's coffin, each saying their silent
prayer. They knew her earthly journey was over,
but they knew also that Jun-chan was journeying on
with a smile on her face, a twinkle in her eyes, and
arms outstretched to meet and embrace that which
was before her. Later on, one confided having prayed
for a miracle.

When the coffin lid was nailed down the ship's
carpenter nonchalantly used his hammer. Two
decades ago, and still to-day in many places in Japan, a stone would be used, for fear that the spirit
of the dead might cling to the hammer and cause
injury to those who used it afterwards. When the
coffin was carried to the deck it was taken by the
most direct route. It was customary once, and still
is in some parts of Japan, to carry the coffin by a
circuitous route in order to confuse any evilly-disposed
spirit that might be intent upon following. But the
old beliefs are dying out in Japan.

My family were silent, their eyes flooded with tears,
and their hearts heavy after the last farewell. The
little coffin had been pushed overboard, followed by
the food offerings, and the little dish of melted ice-
cream. Jun-chan's mother had distributed among
those present tiny artificial white flowers. Those

also had been thrown into the sea. My family twisted theirs into little crosses.

After the coffin entered the water, the ship made a wide circle, her siren sounded a long blast and she steamed on south into the tropics.

When my family came up onto the promenade deck —the place where Jun-chan had spent so many hours with them—they found that the stewards had already placed the customary little heaps of salt to purify the deck after the passing of the dead. My son's face blanched as he marched up to the chief steward:

"Why did you do that? Jun-chan is *not* an evil spirit. She is *not* evil spirit," cried he passionately.

He was hurried to his cabin. The rest of the day passed miserably. That night he quickly dozed off, but he was tossing and turning and talking in his sleep. His cabin door was carefully locked that night, and for many thereafter, for fear that in his sleep he might get up and walk out in search of his Jun-chan.

The next day, on the occasion of crossing the Equator, was sports day for the emigrants, and the speed of the vessel was slackened to reduce the roll and vibration so that all might better enjoy the games. Jun-chan's mother bravely took her seat among the spectators, holding on her lap a photograph of Jun-chan, that the child also might enjoy the fun. There were, however, mutterings and grumblings on the part of my children that although the ship had slackened speed to between seven and eight knots for the sports, the speed had barely been reduced at all for Jun-chan's funeral.

Jun-chan

The remainder of the voyage was depressing and without enjoyment.

* * * * * * * *

When the vessel arrived at Bahia, Jun-chan's father was waiting on the wharf to greet his wife and his Jun-chan. My family watched him come on board. Their hearts were full of grief, but they wanted to tell him that they had once adopted a little girl with a smile on her face, a twinkle in her eyes, who had journeyed on with arms outstretched before her.

STRANGE TALES

A
TAXATION
MYSTERY

So long as the sun warms the earth, let no Christian be so bold as to come to Japan, and let all know that if the great King Philip or even the very God of the Christians contravene this prohibition they shall pay for it with their heads.

Japanese official decree, 1825

Contrary to what may be popular belief, tax officials can be amusing in their off-duty hours, and can tell many interesting stories when they are in the mood.

One of them was in such a mood when he asked me whether I knew Tomas Arkenny. I had never heard the name, and although I later made a point of enquiring, none of my friends knew anything of him. And yet there was his name in a recent directory and his address that of a non-existent street in Shinagawa. At least the street does not exist to-day. But the district is very old and the Tokugawa records do mention a part of Shinagawa by that name.

My taxation friend discovered this when in the course of his official duties he was assigned to investigate the whereabouts of those persons listed in the directories in the postwar period who had not submitted taxation returns. On enquiry at the publishers of the directory he was still more surprised to discover that there was no record of how the name had come to be notified or included in the directory. The entry did not appear in the proof sheets, and yet there it was in the final print. Technically such a happening is impossible but it had happened.

"Where taxation matters are concerned," reasoned my taxation friend, "there is always a simple explanation of such mysteries. But this case intrigues me. I cannot think it is a case of tax evasion. There is something uncanny about it. Can you help me to search through other foreign directories?"

Instead I introduced him to a friend with more learning, leisure and imagination than myself. In that manner a search commenced. It continued on and off for a long period of time. At first it yielded no results.

The name of Tomas Arkenny did not appear in any directories immediately before or after that issue. Then suddenly it was picked up in the *Yokohama Directory* of twenty years before. The same name, but this time an address in Kanagawa— a very old address, one that had existed in feudal days when Kanagawa was a posting stage on the Tokaido. It must have ceased to exist more than four decades ago when part of the modern transportation system between Yokohama and Tokyo was expanded. A coincidence of course. And yet curiously enough the name did not appear in any former or later issues of that particular directory.

In a Kansai Directory of 1916, the name again was found with an address in the Yanagiwara district of Hyogo, but an address which had gone out of existence some years prior to that date when new thoroughfares were constructed to make way for the Kobe city tramway system. In no other issue of that Kansai Directory does the name appear.

The search continued backwards through the years, becoming more and more difficult owing to the rarity of the old directories. The next and last time that the name was picked up was in a Yokohama Directory of 1874 where one may read "Tomas Arkenny —Anjin-machi, Nihonbashi, Tokyo."

At all times the address was in a port area of an old Japanese city. Seemingly they marked the wanderings of a seafarer, but as only one of the addresses exists to-day it is impossible to say what else they may mark.

Such is the story as heard from the taxation official and from my learned friend. And such are the details, it is said, as they now appear in the official records, but as it is a Taxation record who knows whether it is fact or fiction.

Perhaps it is a pure coincidence—I venture no guess—that there was a Tomas Arkenny, described as a mulatto, who disappeared somewhere in the Eastern Seas over 125 years ago, but whose movements, wanderings and places of abode, if any, are not known and may always remain a mystery.

* * * * * * *

Japanese writings in the era of *Bunsei,* which extended from 1818 to 1830 report that a shipload of foreigners from an English whaler landed near Tanegashima, an island south of Kagoshima, to steal cattle, but all were captured.

Despite the efforts that have been made by British historians to reconcile this Japanese account with Western records, there is much doubt as to the identity of the vessel and its nationality. The whaling industry began to develop around this period and it is known that the whaling ships often sent boats to the Japanese coast in the hope of obtaining water and fresh supplies.

The raiders at Tanegashima may even have been survivors from some vessel wrecked off the coast of China who came ashore in a lifeboat and being starving slaughtered some cattle. The roll of missing ships during the decade following 1820 points to two possibilities, the "Tobey" lost in 1822 or the "Lady Adams" which vanished with all hands in 1823. Included in the crew of the latter was a mulatto who was signed on in the Moluccas under the name of Tomas Arkenny—although there is reason to believe he might have been a Malay dubbed with an English name. With the rest of the crew of the "Lady Adams" he vanished in 1823. Whether he was among those who raided Tanegashima and was captured by the Japanese, and if so what was his subsequent fate, must remain a mystery. It is possible that being a Malay and a non-Christian his life may have been spared, and he may thus have become the sole survivor of the "Lady Adams."

Certainly happenings such as this raid must have been responsible for the re-issuance in 1825 of the famous Expulsion Decree whereby the feudal lords in Japan were reminded by the Tokugawa Government that all foreign ships coming into Japanese waters, other than Dutch ships approaching Nagasaki, were to be beaten off and destroyed. Any foreigners who landed were to be arrested and executed. Dutch ships also were warned to exercise great care in shaping their course for Nagasaki *"lest they meet with misfortune."*

* * * * * * * *

It may well be wondered, as does the taxation investigator, who is this Tomas Arkenny whose name appears in the directories? Is he a forgotten man of the past—a man whom history has passed by, one who, long after death, has been seeking his niche in history and whose biography in some mysterious way has come to be scrappily recorded in the directories of this modern age? Is it all just a series of coincidences or is there some other explanation?

Some of my story can readily be verified by any student of Japanese history. Part, I have no doubt, could only be checked by someone possessing the necessary patience and records—if there be such a person.

HEARD
IN
A
DEPARTMENT
STORE

> *On shining altars of Japan they raise*
> *The silver lamp; the fiery spirits*
> *blaze.*
> ALEXANDER POPE—*Rape of the Lock,*
> **1712**

Some time ago I was standing in front of an ultra-modern futuristic painting at an international exhibition of modern art in the Sogo Department Store at Osaka. Probably amazement was registered on my face as I gazed at a great canvas, seeking to discover some meaning in the maze of black lines.

"Do you understand it?"

I awoke from my reveries to find that I had been addressed by an earnest looking middle-aged Japanese gentleman, obviously an aesthetic type. I had to confess that it meant absolutely nothing to me. He seemed eager to carry on the conversation and continued:

"That painting has in fact been inspired by one of my photographs—I am an art photographer. The painter of that picture has sought to depict the human intellect grappling with the idea of a ghost!"

There was much more that he said as he explained the intricacies of the painting, but in the end I had to confess that both the picture and his words were quite beyond my comprehension.

"Come with me across the road to the Daimaru Department Store," he continued. "There is a photographic exhibition on the sixth floor and my photograph—the one that inspired this picture—is among the exhibits."

When we arrived there was a small crowd of people lingering near the semi-nudes. There were a number looking at the trick shots.

"There is mine" he said, indicating a very fine photograph of some pilgrims praying near an immense bronze incense burner in front of a temple. We were the only ones who stopped to admire it.

"Do you see *it*? There *it* is above the incense burner," he said excitedly, indicating what I had thought to be a beam of light amongst the incense smoke.

"I have taken that picture scores of times but *it* is always there in some form."

I left him do the talking, and he added:

"Let us have coffee together and I shall tell you more about it."

His story was of a temple near the border of Yamato Province, a well-known place and one where a saint is buried. Consequently it is the hope of many devout Buddhists that when they die some portion of their remains may rest close to those of the saint. For those whose relatives are able to pay the cost, there are small urns into which the ashes of the deceased are placed, and then for evermore and a day the urn may remain in the temple. For the convenience of the devout but poor, who cannot pay the fee to remain within the temple, there is an ossuary outside—a grim and grisly charnel pit—into which a bone, a wisp of hair or a tooth may be dropped. That small portion of the mortal shell serves for the poor the same purpose as the urn of ashes does for the wealthy.

One morning many years ago, the priests at that temple discovered that a number of the urns were empty and the contents had apparently been thrown among the ashes of the great incense burner together with some bones and other grisly remains from the ossuary. Although many explanations were offered for this remarkable happening, most of which ascribed it to supernatural forces, the acolytes are known to have whispered that it was an act of revenge on the part of a dissolute priest who was later defrocked. He had hoped to discredit the temple.

However that may be, the explanation which has been handed down among the priesthood and the faithful is that it was a divine act calculated to show that the paupers, whose corporeal remnants are in the grisly pit outside the temple, can equally well attain Nirvana as can the wealthy whose ashes repose within the temple. The devout have for a very long time accepted that explanation of divine intervention.

Whatever might be the true explanation, it is a fact that ever since that happening a tradition has existed at this temple that the ashes in the incense burner must never be disturbed. And it is said that they never need be disturbed, because although myriads of incense sticks have been burned there during the passing years, the mineral ash never accumulates. In some unexplained way the ash from the burning incense sticks disappears into thin air just as does the smoke from the burning incense.

Such was the story the art photographer related to me. Finishing his coffee he concluded:

"That is the explanation which has been given for centuries. The devout believe it. The skeptics disbelieve. But don't you see what my photographs now prove? In my photographs the ghosts of the dead can be seen rising from the incense burner, and thus no doubt it is they who carry away the new ash. This explains why the ash does not accumulate and why it is that the ashes within the burner need never more be disturbed by the living."

After that we said "Good-bye," and I hastened away. As we parted I noticed that a throng was still lingering near the semi-nudes and that the trick shots were still drawing attention, but no one was looking at the temple photograph.

Thereafter my curiosity was aroused. I visited that temple in Yamato many times in order to photograph that incense burner. I photographed it under all manner of conditions. Some days the smoke was rising in profusion from the burning incense. Some days there were only a few smouldering sticks of incense. Some days were bright days. Some days were dull. But always the photographs showed the same results.

It was clear to me that...

But No! I shall not tell what was clear to me. I

am not willing to tell the truth, nor am I prepared to invent an untruth.

Either way—the believers or the disbelievers, the faithful or the skeptics—one of them—would point a finger at me and laugh in disbelief.

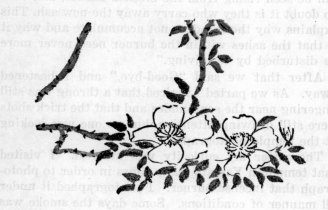

EMPTY
COFFINS

'Tis now the very witching time of night:
When churchyards yawn, and hell itself breathes out
Contagion to this world.

SHAKESPEARE—*"Hamlet"*

The recent newspaper reports of the finding of mummified corpses of great age in certain ancient burial grounds in and around arid limestone areas of Gumma Prefecture, recall to mind certain weird happenings of well over half a century ago that are still talked about in a mountain village in that prefecture. First I must emphasize that the ancient system of burial was legally permissible and was customarily adopted in those parts at that time. Cremation of the dead had not then extended to that distant village.

Because of the interpretation which I have myself placed on those strange happenings, I am prompted to withhold the true names of the persons and places even though there would be little risk at this late date of any libel action being brought against me. Otherwise the details are as told by some of the villagers.

The members of the Ando family—a fictitious name that I shall use in this chapter—were comparatively new arrivals in the village, but they were respected well enough, even though they were progressive. Being the last to build a house in the village their home was set somewhat apart from the others and was on the edge of the village.

The father had died and his various business activities had been taken over by his elder son, who had added that of an insurance agency to his other enterprises. Certainly he was the most active insurance canvasser for miles around. The second son was the only really popular member of the family, but to everybody's regret he developed consumption and eventually died in the village after a protracted illness.

In accordance with local custom all the villagers gathered at the burial service to bid the last farewell, after which the coffin lid was firmly fixed in position in their presence. As already mentioned, burial, not cremation, was the customary method of disposal of the dead in those parts at that time. As usual in that district the coffin was of stout mountain timber. The ceremony and the burial of the coffin ended at about four o'clock in the afternoon, after which the villagers dispersed to their various homes and the life of the village settled down once again to its accustomed ways and quietness. As usual the villagers retired early. No one then had any inkling of the horrors that were in store for them.

At about the hour of the rat—which is an hour before midnight—when all were deep in slumber, the sleeping animals first and later the humans were awakened by a low moaning of the wind rustling through the trees. Gradually it rose to a loud whine as it eddied among the eaves of the thatched roofs. The wind increased in intensity and came rushing in from the northeast—the direction from which the angry and disquiet spirits always come. It rattled every shutter in the village as if someone was outside seeking admission.

At the same time a flash of sheet lightning brightened up the sky, only to be followed by the most utter darkness that the villagers had ever experienced. The fire bell was heard to fall clattering to the ground and the great temple bell boomed, although all knew that the beam by which it was tolled had long since fallen in decay from its supports. The rats began scampering madly and squealing in the attics. Even the bats were heard crashing against the walls of the barns as they lost their way in frenzied flight. Owls hooted and the dogs howled all through the night. The horses shivered with fright and pranced excitedly in their stalls.

All lights were mysteriously extinguished and the people shuddered in the darkness. Later it was found that the lanterns had been snuffed out, not blown out by the wind. The murmur of the silkworms chewing on the mulberry leaves in the racks was suddenly stilled, and in the morning many were found to have sickened with disease. The frogs in the pools stopped croaking and dived deeper under the water. The toads abandoned their courting calls. Milk dried up in the breasts of nursing mothers. Broody hens left their nests and all the eggs were subsequently found to be addled. When dawn came it was seen that the paper in many *shoji* in the houses was fluttering loose or torn as if something had passed through in great haste.

None will forget that terrible night. At the hour of the tiger, which comes a few hours before dawn, a fierce fire was found to have broken out in the Ando home. Nothing could be done to extinguish the blaze. The elder son was missing and it was feared that he may have been trapped in the burning home. Some hours after daylight, when the ruins had cooled, his heavily-charred body was found among the ashes of the home.

The remaining members of the Ando family were distraught at the double tragedy that had come upon them and at the loss of their home. Fortunately they were well provided for, because the elder brother had prudently insured the property against fire and also there was a substantial life insurance policy on his life. However the family, feeling that the village had proved to be an unlucky place of residence, consulted the fortunetellers who advised that they should travel southeast as soon as possible. Shortly afterwards they moved to Tokyo and became swallowed up in the great metropolis. None in the village ever heard of them again. That is all that is known of the Ando family. It all occurred considerably more than half a century ago.

The happenings of that night were, however, never forgotten in the village, and are still talked of, although with some embellishments. Of late there has been much more talk. The old graves in the cemetery were recently opened up with a view to removing some of them to a new site, when it was noted with astonishment that the contents of some coffins were still in a remarkable degree of preservation, this apparently on account of the arid nature of those limestone hills—a circumstance that was recently reported in the press. It was then discovered, merely by chance, that in the coffin of the second son of the Ando family—the one who had died of consumption—there were no signs whatever of a mummified cadaver or of bones or of any other human remains. Indeed, beyond some burial raiment still in an astonishingly well-preserved condition and some personal belongings that were buried with him, there was nothing.

The villagers recalled to mind the happenings on that night long ago, and found the explanation of the empty coffin in a belief that the spirit of the second son, in escaping from the coffin had done so in such haste that it had taken with it in some mystical way its mortal shell. While this explanation may sound fantastic to some, I can only state that it is not thought unrealistic by others.

For my own part the happening seems to me to be one of those unusual events which, while appearing supernatural, only confirms that there is little new under the sun in the annals of crime. It appears to have a singular parallel in a ghoulish case that is to be found in the records of the Criminal Court in New Zealand.

During the mid-nineteen-thirties a fire broke out in a lonely week-end lodge in the mountains in the North Island of New Zealand and in the morning the charred remains of a man were found—obviously those of the owner of the lodge, who was known to be living there at the time. Subsequently the relatives of the unfortunate man filed a claim under a substantial life insurance policy that had been taken out by the deceased a year or so before, and also a claim under a fire policy on the lodge.

There had been, however, certain circumstances about the fire which had aroused the suspicions of the insurance companies and of the police, and the latter had been quietly pursuing extensive investigations for some weeks, one line of enquiry being a careful examination of the burial records of all cemeteries within a radius of one hundred miles of the fire. Finally the police applied to the Court for permission to open up the grave of a man who had been buried in a country cemetery forty miles away about twelve hours before the fire broke out in the cottage. On opening up the grave and lifting the coffin lid, the police found, as anticipated, that body snatchers had been there before them. The coffin was empty.

The case, which eventually ended up in the Criminal Court, was fascinating in the legal technicalities that the defence were able to intrude, but it was established that the owner of the cottage and his accomplices, seeking to defraud the insurance company, had carefully waited until a suitable death occurred. Then during the night immediately following the burial, they had opened the grave, rifled the coffin, refilled the grave, hurriedly transported the body by motor car to the cottage forty miles away, laid it out on the bed, set fire to the house at about 3 a.m. the following morning and then hurriedly left the district. The owner then went into hiding, leaving his heir and his accomplice in the crime to claim the insurance.

Empty Coffins

Unlike the body snatching committed by the elder son of the Ando family, the law caught up with the New Zealand resurrection men.

Here my story ends, but I must leave the reader to find an explanation for the weird phenomena that are reported to have occurred on that night over half a century ago, and to decide, each according to his own religious beliefs, what part the anguished and outraged spirit of the second son of the Ando family played in those strange happenings.

ECHOES
OF
THE
BATTLE
OF
ICHI-NO-TANI

*Ernest William James...died 12
Nov., 1952, public benefactor and
well beloved friend of all children.*
Memorial plaque in Shioya Country
Club, Kobe

There have been dictators since the dawn of history. Over 750 years ago, around about the time when Robin Hood and Friar Tuck were cracking heads in Sherwood Forest, Japan had a dictator, Kiyomori, the head of the Taira clan. He was sufficiently powerful to effect the removal of the Emperor and Imperial Court from Kyoto to Fukuwara, a place which in modern Kobe, about seven centuries later, became the site of a famous licensed quarters —a nightless city. Quite apart from its lecherous activities, Fukuwara was deservedly one of the tourist show places of prewar Kobe, although not officially listed as such. But that is another story.

Having secured possession of the Imperial Personage, the Taira clan found it necessary to defend the western approaches to their headquarters by constructing a fort and barrier at Ichi-no-tani, located between present day Shioya and Suma. There a

276

watch was kept for spies and for enemies of Taira attempting to infiltrate into the territory. In recent years at almost that identical spot a police checkpoint has been set up to intercept smugglers of rice. Those policemen are also constantly on the watch for the harassed and the distracted who are so sadly hopeful of bringing an end to their troubles at this picturesque place, which has the unfortunate distinction of being a notable suicide spot. Foreigners travelling daily by motorcar from Tarumi and Shioya will be familiar with the police box.

Probably only a few of the commuters who pass daily between Shioya and Suma remember or give a thought to the bloody battle that was fought there over 750 years ago. Still fewer probably turn their heads to the steep mountains and see the horsemen of Yoshitsune, of the opposing Minamoto clan, making their perilous descent down the mountain side with the object of attacking the Taira fort from the rear. Many horses stumbled and crashed with their riders. But sufficient of that intrepid band of horsemen reached the foothills to stage a desperate assault on the stronghold. After a most bloody battle which closed with Taira Atsumori having his head cut off in single combat, the Taira men were defeated and as many as possible escaped in boats from the beach, the same beach as that to which tens of thousands of Kobe residents flock every summer.

Yoshimitsu, one of the horsemen of the Minamoto clan who made the perilous descent of the mountain, was grievously wounded during the battle and blood was streaming from his forehead. He saw the red banners of Taira hauled down from the walls of the stronghold. He heard the shouts of victory. Then his horse, tortured with the pain of many wounds, bolted westward along the coast road and finally collapsed at a point near what is to-day the railway crossing west of Shioya Station.

With difficulty Yoshimitsu made his way up the nearby valley in search of water. His face was smeared with dried blood and with the sweat and grime of battle. He came to a small spring, but he fainted before he could assuage his thirst. It was dark when he recovered consciousness and the moon had risen low on the horizon. Racked with the torment of pain and fever he plunged his face into the spring water. The wound in his forehead opened. The blood came streaming into his eyes and in his delirium, looking towards the light of the moon, he saw fluttering about him what he imagined to be the red banners of Taira's men. Drawing his sword he struck two mighty blows which severed the tops off two sturdy firs nearby. Then he fell dead beside the spring.

The body of Yoshimitsu was found next day and removed. No one now seems to know where or whether any tombstone was ever erected to his memory. If so the stone has no doubt long since crumbled away with age. But the spring has not ceased to flow. As the centuries passed, erosion changed the contour of the valley and of the surrounding hills, but the spring continued to sparkle as it does to this day.

Over twenty years ago when the late Mr. E. W.

James decided to change those barren hills into a place of beauty, he cut away the mountain tops and filled in the valleys, but preserved the spring. He sensed the atmosphere that seems to linger about places where unusual events have occurred, seemingly the effect of mysterious forces that will not permit the past to die. Without knowing the story of Yoshimitsu, Mr. James marked the spring with two stone lanterns and an image of Fudo, the Buddhist deity who in his divine wrath, it is said, can foil and capture the powers of evil.

By a curious coincidence the tops of those lanterns are, in shape, not unlike the samurai helmets of 750 years ago. Within a year the tops of the lanterns had become broken off, and, although replaced, were again broken off by the time another year had passed. The story of Yoshimitsu, I am told, is known by very few, and it is only they who say that it was he who severed the tops of those two lanterns with his sword —just as he had cut down the two fir trees over seven centuries before.

It is a fact that right now the sword marks can be seen plainly where the heads of the lanterns were severed from the columns. The heads now generally rest loosely on the columns, except on those occasions when they are found lying on the ground. It is however, equally evident that any sword which cut that stone must have been of far tougher steel than any forged nowadays, and must have been wielded by a force greater than that possessed by mortal man.

The skeptics assure me that a carelessly driven motorcar must have been responsible for breaking off the heads of the lanterns. Others say that typhoons topple them off whenever they are replaced. Some lay the blame on mischievous boys. I do not know who was responsible. I have given the story as I have heard it from a rather credulous old person, but one who is more worldly wise than I in some matters.

Maybe there are scholars or historians who, after making allowances for calendar changes during the past 750 years, have reckoned out the exact anniversary day in our modern calendar of that famous battle of Ichi-no-tani. Possibly some may have been sufficiently curious and wakeful as to have kept watch on that anniversary night, and actually know whether Yoshimitsu is still crazed with the torment of his wounds, whether the blood from his forehead still flows into his eyes, and whether he still wields his sword each anniversary night as he did over 750 years ago.

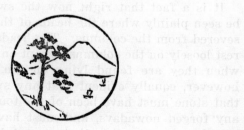

THE
CAPTAIN'S
GIRL-FRIEND

*Not only the great and small inns
but the tea-booths and cook shops
in the villages and hamlets of the
great island are abundantly and at
all times furnished with numberless
wenches....*

Dr. ENGELBERT KAEMPFER, 1694

We know from the tombstone in Fulham Church-
yard in England that Captain Saris was married.
History seems to have little to say on that score
because Saris himself did not labour that point in
his writings. But it was said that he had quite an
eye and an open heart for pretty women. East and
west he looked for them, and he found them.

*"East is East and West is West, and never the
twain shall meet,"* had not been written then. Even
if it had, Captain Saris by his behaviour would probably have disagreed with Kipling, or at least he would
not have permitted Kipling's poetry to interfere with
his own whims or pleasures.

It may be remembered that in 1613 Captain Saris
was in command of the "Clove," the first English merchant ship to come to Japan, and he came to establish a branch of the English East India Company.
He visited Tokyo, or Yedo as it was then called, and
stayed at a place not far from the present-day Ginza.
He described it as follows:—

The Captain's Girl-friend

...We arrived at Edoo, a Citie much greater than Surunga, farre fairer buildings, and made a very glorious appearance unto us: the ridge-tiles and the corner-tiles richly gilded, the posts of their doores gilded and varnished: Glass-windowes they have none, but great windowes of board, opening in leaves....There is a Cawsey which goeth thorow the chiefe streete of the Towne: underneath this Cawsey runneth a River, at every fiftie paces there is a Well-head with buckets for the neighbours to fetch water and for danger of fire. This street is as broad as any of our streets in England.

Elsewhere he relates how others did "frollicke" with certain women of the "towne," but that he personally spent his time most agreeably walking in a Japanese garden.

It may also be recalled that as the result of a "great scandal" associated with his trip he was not given another command, and, what is more, some of his souvenirs that he had brought back from Japan were burned in public in front of the Royal Exchange in London, or to quote from the Court Minutes of the East India Company *"the wicked spectacles"* were *"thereupon in open presence put into the fire, where they continued till they were burnt and turned into smoke."*

* * * * * * * *

The above notes were written at a coffee shop in Tokyo. There are scores, indeed hundreds, of coffee shops in Tokyo, but there is only one that I really know. It is between the Ginza and Nishi Ginza. I always patronise this one place because there the emphasis is on classical music. They play the music loudly. The lights are dim and there is no disturbing buzz of voices. The patrons of that place have no interest in idle conversation. Some sway slightly with the music, as if on uncertain foundations, but most sit immobile with a glassy look in their eyes. Some seem to be asleep, but the occasional movement of their hands betrays that they are following every note in the score, just as if they were conducting a symphony orchestra. Others are holding their heads seemingly in pain, but actually in an ecstasy of deep musical appreciation. It is an unusual place. One night each month they have a special performance of classical music, commencing at midnight and terminating at 6 a.m. For those, one must reserve a table in advance.

Whenever I am in Tokyo I invariably spend my evenings in that coffee shop. I have noted that many others also are regular patrons. Some seem rather queer and I should like to know more about them. But at that place you do not thoughtlessly break in upon the reveries of those who spend their evenings listening to the musicians of the past.

Among the regular visitors I have noticed several artists, and also some who are forever scribbling in note books. I have assumed the latter are poets. Rarely do I stay for less than two hours. Later I often wonder how I passed the time, or what I did during those two hours, whilst the music reverberated through the many corners of that dimly illuminated place. I rarely remember much of what was going on about me, and in this I do not believe I am unusual. I always carry there a note book and pencil. Sometimes the pencil has not been used. But there is no rule, nor any set purpose in my visits. I am moved by the spirit of the moment, or by any shades of the past there might be thereabouts.

I endeavour to take a seat in the gallery where I can command a view of those around and below me. And so it was that I saw the artist sitting in a corner. His sketch book was open in front of him. But his head was buried in his hands. He was slumped across the table. Later when I looked—it may have been seconds later, perhaps minutes later, time counts for nothing in that place—he was busily sketching. Every few seconds he raised his eyes from his sketch to study his subject. Now and again he lifted his pencil to measure distances and gauge proportions. His subject must have been opposite him, because that was where he was repeatedly looking. And yet the seat opposite to him was vacant, nor was there anyone nearby. I was amazed, but I was not mistaken. As the sketch approached completion, he gave more attention to his subject, although I could not see it. He studied it attentively before filling in the final details on the sketch. Finally he set down his pencil. A stirring symphony had commenced. Again he was slumped across the table, his head buried in his arms. The sketchbook was open in front of him. I moved over and glanced across his shoulder. The sketch bore no resemblance to anything or to anyone in that coffee shop, then or at any other time. It was more lifelike than any sketch I had ever seen before. Striding right out of the paper was a tall broad-shouldered European dressed in clothes of three and half centuries ago. A long coat heavily embroidered with gold thread, a lace cravat and frilled shirt cuffs, short breeches gathered in at the knee and white hose. His hair was long and hung in curls upon his shoulders. He carried an elaborate stick.

It was Captain Saris. He was walking in a Japanese garden, just as he related in his diary it was his custom to do, and just as I had been thinking of him some minutes before.

It is always difficult to keep our skeletons locked securely in our cupboards. Truth will out. And so there was but one difference—the only difference—between what Captain Saris wrote in his diary, and what was depicted in the sketch: his arm encircled the waist of a pretty Japanese young lady of that period, and he was planting a kiss on her lips.

IN A FOREIGN GRAVEYARD

> *Let's talk of graves, of worms, and epitaphs.*
>
> SHAKESPEARE—*Richard II*

Some months ago I had the opportunity of browsing through several bound volumes of the *Kobe Chronicle* of 1899 and 1900—the name of that newspaper was later changed to the *Japan Chronicle*. The cablegrams largely dealt with the Dreyfus case, the Transvaal War which became in history the Boer War, and also the China War which later was referred to as the Boxer Rebellion.

Among the local news there were three items that caught my attention. The first was under date of 6th September, 1899, and reported that the Japanese Authorities proposed moving the old foreign cemetery at Osaka from Minato-ku to Abeno, but that the French Consul was strongly opposed as he considered the new site unsuitable.

The second item was under date of 11th July, 1900, and reported that the new site at Abeno had been decided upon, and although only about half the size of the foreign cemetery at Kobe it would probably be ample in that there had only been four interments in Osaka in thirty years. The *Kobe Chronicle* then de-

scribed the new site as *"so very charming and home-*
like in appearance that few people will be able to
resist the inclination to go into residence right away
...and there is certain to be a large demand for
space." I thereupon made a mental note to look
at this place, and see how it had developed in the
intervening fifty-five years.

The third item in the *Kobe Chronicle* referred to
the reported finding many years before by a hunter
of squirrels and stoats, of a foreigner's body on
Nakanoshima. Actually the report had never been
accepted by the foreign community as correct because no foreigner was known to be missing just at
that time, and what was more important when the
police arrived on the scene, there was no body to
be found.

A day or so after reading through those old newspaper files I made a telephone enquiry to the Osaka
City Office for the full address of the Abeno Foreign
Cemetery. My enquiry was courteously and immediately attended to. I wrote the address in my
pocket book and then forgot all about the matter
until one day when lunching by myself at a restaurant opposite Nakanoshima, I suddenly felt the urge
to visit the Abeno cemetery. It was a cold, damp and
misty day and I knew I had a busy afternoon before
me at the office. Nevertheless as I sat gazing at the
people walking on Nakanoshima I felt impelled to
do that which I had postponed doing for so long. I
left the restaurant and crossed the bridge, but finding
nothing to interest me on Nakanoshima, I hailed a
taxi, opened the door and stepped in.

In a Foreign Graveyard

"Gaikoku-jin Rei-en, Asahi-machi, San-chome, Abe-no-ku."

The driver had his back to me and was all ready to drive off, but when he heard the address I saw him suddenly stiffen, then he slowly turned around and looked me squarely in the face.

"What did you say?"

I repeated the address. I may of course have been mistaken, but all the colour then seemed to go out of his face. He was staring at me hard as he replied:

"I have been driving taxis in Osaka for over thirty years and never until to-day have I been to that address. Now twice in the one day I pick up passengers for that place. Less than an hour ago, *right at this spot* I picked up a fare for that cemetery. And what is more, when we reached the destination he disappeared and I have not received payment. Do you intend to pay your fare?"

I showed him my money. The car started off, but he was still muttering to himself as we turned into Mido-suji towards Namba. I noticed the car was gathering speed and we were much above the limit. Nevertheless in spite of the speed and traffic he turned his head and stared at me.

"Fushigi-ya-na"—"It is strange,"—he muttered.

I was fearful of an accident, and much relieved when a motor traffic policeman drove alongside and motioned the driver into the curb. The policeman stopped in front of the taxi; the driver immediately alighted and approached him. A long conversation ensued during which they stared in my direction several times, but from my position in the taxi I could not hear a word of their conversation. Suddenly the policeman came to the taxi, roughly opened the door and gazed inside. It seemed to me he was staring through me or behind me rather than at me. I noticed his grip on the door suddenly tighten as if to support himself. His nostrils quivered. Then he gently closed the door, and motioned to the driver to proceed.

I was amazed at these happenings. The driver had been speeding and yet the policeman had not even asked to see his license. While I was puzzling over this the taxi was racing towards Namba faster than before. It then turned towards Tennoji and after bumping over a maze of narrow streets suddenly jerked to a stop in a squalid quarter outside a tumble-down wall. There was no sign or legend to mark the identity of the place, but the driver motioned me to get out. He did not speak. He did not even thank me when I paid the fare. Instead he slammed the door and sped away. Obviously he was glad to be rid of me.

The entrance to the cemetery is marked by an old iron gate which, after more than half a century, no longer moves on its hinges and now hangs permanently open. As I passed through the gate a dog rushed out, hair bristling and howling louder and more piteously than any I had heard before. It ran down the road, still howling, pursued by naught that I could see.

The cemetery, in area about that of a large football field, is not enclosed by any wall or fence, except in the front. A Japanese city presses in upon it on all sides and thus this consecrated ground serves as public ground much as does any rubbish-tip or vacant lot elsewhere. Two ragpickers are squatting on the eastern boundary in a makeshift hovel with their stock in trade on hand. The city children in the neighbourhood having been denied a proper place to play, which surely is the right of all children, gather there in fine weather. There is nowhere else for them to go. The dead probably would not object. There is far more room in that dismal place than the dead require. Certainly some effort has been made to prevent unrestricted intrusion. Rough-hewn granite blocks have been set up in the ground irregularly throughout the area, apparently to prevent squatters moving in bag and baggage. They gave to the place on that dark misty day an eerie appearance of stark grey figures standing naked in the dim light among a few broken trunks of dead trees.

The cemetery was laid out in 1900, and a check of the City records shows that eight graves were transferred there in 1904 from the older foreign cemetery in Minato-ku. The reference in the *Kobe Chronicle* to four graves is therefore obviously a case of incorrect reporting. There have been thirty-seven later burials, making a total of forty-five burials in eighty-seven years. These graves, sensibly enough, are all gathered together in one corner irrespective of race, creed, colour or nationality. That area, about the size of a tennis court, is surrounded by a new low fence freshly painted blue and topped with a strand of barbed wire to prevent the children playing gymnastics thereon. Just within the fence a low row of hedge plants has been planted that may in time grow, although with the exception of the children, who, for the want of a better place, play among the shadows of the tombs, there is no sign of life in that dreary place. Apart from about a dozen other torn and broken shrubs struggling to live, there is nothing else in the graveyard, not a blade of grass, not a patch of lichen, not even a withered flower.

It is in all truth a place of the dead. Little wonder that the Japanese in the neighbourhood refer to those within as a pitiful company of lost souls, and prefer not to talk about the place. Rather would I have my body thrown to jackals than be buried in such a wretched spot.

The dead are soon forgotten. It cannot be otherwise. Nevertheless it would appear that all has been done to preserve this area that can reasonably be expected. The truth is, it was unsuitable from the beginning for a burial ground, as the French Consul so wisely pointed out over fifty-six years ago; it is still more unsuitable to-day. Perhaps had it been a more desirable spot, the authorities may have found reason to convert the site to a block of offices for bureaucrats, just as they have filched a portion of the very desirable public recreation ground of the old Foreign Concession of Kobe.

I stepped over the barbed wire that serves instead of a gate to the small graveyard, and wandered sadly among the graves.

There is the tombstone of a baby—*The Lord gave and the Lord hath taken away*—who died eighty years ago in the old Foreign Concession of Kawaguchi.

In a Foreign Graveyard

There are the tombstones—*Hic Requiescit Corpus* —of the missionaries, and the tombstones—*Ici repose* —of the Sisters of Mercy who left their native countries to go abroad and to die in a foreign land in the cause of Charity and their Faith.

There are the graves marked by heavy tombstones —*Rest in Peace*—that tell to a world that no longer cares the names of the worthy people who lie in that last resting place.

There are the graves, unmarked by any tombstones, of forgotten men, and some no doubt who never did anything worthy of being remembered.

And finally there are some graves marked by tombstones—*In memory of*—that it were better had never been erected, so that the world might more quickly forget those buried there under the sod.

I had stopped in front of an old grave unmarked by any cross or stone. Possibly my attention had been caught by the fact that the soil had recently been disturbed. I was wondering whether perhaps a stoat burrowing near the surface had broken the ground, and then I had a premonition that I was being watched.

"Nakanoshima made do ikimasu ka?" said a voice behind me. I was so startled and a little afraid at the sudden interruption that I could not answer immediately.

"Would you tell me how I can reach Nakanoshima?" The foreigner, for it must have been a foreigner, had now repeated his question in English. He was rather tall, and shabbily dressed in ill-fitting clothes that seemed to hang on his thin frame. Even now I

cannot describe his clothes. There was something
odd about them. I cannot now recall whether it was
that they were of an old-fashioned cut, or whether
they were just old.

"You can catch a tram car on the road down to the
right," I replied.

Without another word he turned and shambled
towards the front gate. I watched him shuffle out
and turn to the right. Then suddenly I recollected
that I had not noticed his face. Indeed I could
not now swear that he had a face. He was wearing
a battered old felt hat. So few foreigners wear
hats these days that possibly I had been watching
his hat and had failed to notice his face. I hastened
to the front gate and looked down the road. I am
convinced that he could not have walked fifty yards
by the time I reached the gate, not even if he had
run, and yet he was nowhere in sight. The road was
completely deserted.

Suddenly there flashed through my mind the story
of *The Genius*. Why, I do not know. But right there
at the cemetery gate I recalled to mind all I had heard
many years before regarding a most unusual foreigner who had appeared in Kobe.

* * * * * * * *

One day a new arrival appeared among the beachcombers and derelicts who infested the port in those
days, but it was soon evident that he was not of
their type. Nobody knew how he came to be there,
and in those days nobody much cared. Such men
came and as suddenly disappeared again.

For a while he was given food and shelter by a

293

Chinese tailor opposite the Sannomiya Shrine in return for which he did odd jobs in the workroom such as the sewing on of buttons. There it was that he learned to play Chinese chess, and soon had defeated all comers in the Chinese community. He also spoke a fair amount of Chinese, but whether he had learned it in Kobe or possibly in the Chinatowns of Yokohama or Nagasaki prior to coming to Kobe, I never heard. (The Chinatowns in the port cities of Japan were then almost tourist sights.) Later he became a *hatoba* runner with one of the stevedore companies, and lived in a room along an alleyway by Ikuta Shrine. In every sense he lived on the fringe of the foreign community, rather than as a member of it.

He taught himself typewriting in the matter of weeks and within a month was proficient in shorthand. He drifted in and out of a number of jobs showing little interest in mundane work. Within the space of six months he was speaking Japanese fluently and could read a newspaper with ease. He was known to be the best player of European chess in the port, but it was not easy to get a game with him. Having mastered a subject he quickly lost interest, but did not forget it. By some strange urge he was always impelled to exercise his brain by studying something new and the more intricate it was the more satisfied he seemed.

He was tall, thin and sickly looking, probably because he neglected himself. He never mixed much with the foreign community, and even when he was earning money he did not look or dress any better than half a tramp. Towards the end he used to sit

In a Foreign Graveyard

294

in the saloons a fair bit, often staying until closing time in the early hours of the morning. He drank very little but complained that he was too tired to sleep. He was studying the Mandarin language at that time. Few people knew his name. He was referred to simply as *The Genius*.

One morning his body was found outside the old Osaka Hotel then located on Nakanoshima in Osaka. That was many years before the New Osaka Hotel was constructed. He had apparently shot himself the night before, and during the night his face had been largely eaten away by some animal. Some people blamed the rats, others suggested stoats. Nakanoshima was very different then to what it is to-day.

Certainly he must have been buried in the Foreign Cemetery at Abeno. There was no other place where he would have been buried.

* * * * * * *

I was still gazing down the road from the cemetery gate. As already mentioned it was a misty day, but even so I realised that everything seemed blurred. I thought I was about to faint. There was nowhere to sit down except right there upon the muddy ground and so I moved unsteadily towards the sexton's hut. I opened the door. There was only one chair in the hut. I moved towards it. As I did so I heard a voice behind me:

"I have come back. The trams are too crowded."

I felt sure I was about to faint. It was then that I saw the sexton. He was rising from his seat. He was staring hard. He seemed to be staring behind me, rather than at me. He was staring just as the

In a Foreign Graveyard

taxi-driver and the policeman had stared. His eyes
widened. His face puckered up in terror. His mouth
began to open, and....

This chapter appeared first as an article in *The Mainichi*
newspaper of 19th March, 1955.

THE DREARIEST GRAVEYARD -- ABENO CEMETERY REVISITED

Perhaps in this neglected spot is laid
  Some heart once pregnant with celestial fire;
Hands, that the rod of empire might have sway'd
  Or waked to ecstasy the living lyre.
                    THOMAS GRAY'S *Elegy*

I have just come from the Abeno Foreign Cemetery. When I arrived, the front gate was open. It is always open in welcome.

The entrance has been repaired during the past year, and the dead may now enter the grounds in a hearse, instead of being carried over the crumbling stone steps as was so a year ago.

Many of the shrubs that were there this time last year, and several crosses, have disappeared. Certainly some new shrubs have been planted, but most of them will be dead or trampled down within the year. Nothing can live in that place of the dead.

I found it to be more dreary to-day than a year ago, and in a year hence it will be even more dismal than to-day. As each year passes this little plot within the city of Osaka will be so much worse off, because a great and growing city is pressing in upon it, and little is being done that can save it.

Considering that it was winter, I saw it under the most favourable conditions. It was a bright sunny day. Many children were playing happily. Some boys were jumping about on the tombstones. A young couple was walking together oblivious to all around them; another couple was sitting on a pile of stones, talking quietly. A *rumpen* was squatting contentedly in a corner, the upper part of his body exposed to the sun; his coat and his shirt were spread out before him whilst he cracked the lice in the seams. Two ragpickers were busily sorting out their pickings of past weeks. Some labourers were dumping constructional material.

I wandered over to the small enclosure within which are forty-six or maybe forty-seven graves; that is to say there is one or possibly two more graves than a year ago. It is difficult to be sure where the dead are buried, because the pattering feet of boys at play so quickly flatten down the grave mounds. A favourite game, except for baseball which is played just outside the little enclosure, is for boys to swing on the monuments and to chase one another in the graveyard, jumping from gravestone to gravestone in an effort to avoid treading on the ground.

Apart from the boys there was only one other person within the enclosure—a foreigner. He was sitting on a gravestone and staring into the ground. He seemed of uncertain age, but had one of the longest beards that I have ever seen. He was resting his chin on a walking stick, similar to those which I recall seeing on sale in the walking stick shops when I first came to Japan nearly forty years ago. People no

298

longer seem to have the time or inclination to walk,
and so the shopkeepers who once earned a livelihood
selling walking sticks have turned to other occupations, or perhaps they have all died.

The man sitting on the gravestone paid no heed
to me, even if he were aware that I was there. My
presence seemed not to disturb him. I sat down beside
him.

"What a dismal and forgotten place this is," I
remarked.

"*We* do not complain," he replied, very quietly.

"But I do! This is the saddest cemetery I have
ever seen. The most forgotten place I know," I
added.

"Aye, but maybe a time will come when you will
not complain," said he, continuing to gaze into the
ground. I noticed then, with some astonishment, that
he was wearing very old-fashioned elastic-sided boots.
I remember in my childhood days seeing men wearing
similar boots, but I had not imagined that any still
existed.

"Do you often come here?" said I, turning the
conversation.

"I am always here," he replied.

"But I visit this place frequently. I have never
seen you before."

"Perhaps not," he said, "But I have seen you. Why
did you come to-day?"

"I had little else to do. That is why I came."

"You may think so, but it is not so. You came here
exactly a year ago, on this same day and at this same
hour, for the same reason that you came to-day, but

299

you may not know it. This day last year was cold, damp and misty. I watched you wander among the graves. I saw you enter the sexton's hut. I was there when you fainted."

"Tell me," I interrupted, "Was there anyone else there then, apart from the sexton?"

"Yes. One other," he replied, "but he is a wandering and a lonely soul."

"Who are you? Where do you come from?" I exclaimed.

"I came to Osaka, back in January 1868, when it was first opened to foreign trade. I lived in the Foreign Concession at Kawaguchi facing the river. It was a well-chosen spot, in fact we thought it was the best in the whole city. I used to sit on my verandah and watch the life of the city flow past on the river. There were no railways then. The roads were narrower in those days, many not much better than bullock tracks. The trade of Osaka, indeed its existence, depended upon the rivers and canals. The junks and barges were as numerous then as mosquitoes on a summer night. The population of Osaka was less than three hundred thousand. Nowadays when I wander in Kawaguchi, there is nothing to be seen of those Concession days, nothing but a few broken bricks on some vacant lot of ground—the remains of imported bricks that were brought to Japan from overseas.

"In springtime our favourite walk on a Sunday was to the nurseries at the end of Dotonbori. When I first came to Osaka there was an execution ground near Dotonbori but the sight of the crows picking the eyes out of the heads of criminals, fixed to the tops of pikes, was too horrible for us to want to see more than once. When there were any ladies in our party they generally insisted on calling at the Mitsui Drapery Store on the way back. That was the shop which grew into the Mitsukoshi Department Store."

"I died in Kawaguchi," he continued, "The city of Osaka was expanding and in 1900 the Kawaguchi cemetery was moved to this place. Hereabouts was mostly open countryside then. A few more trees than now, and cultivated fields between here and Tennoji. You could then stand on this elevated ground and look over the roof tops to what is now Umeda and beyond. Only the roofs of temples stood higher than the tops of the houses. Across that way to the right you could see the Tennoji Pagoda the one that was blown down by the typhoon of 1933."

"I suppose you could also see Osaka Castle from here," I remarked.

"Oh, no!" he said, "The original Castle was sacked and burnt when the Emperor's forces attacked it in 1868. The present castle was built in 1931. But I could see the shades and shadows of the old castle, and of those who lived there in the days of its splendour!

He then lapsed into silence. I reopened the conversation.

"This place should be fenced in. It is hallowed ground. It is being desecrated."

"But," he said "there is far more room here than the dead will ever require. The children and the people come here because there is no better place for

301

them to go. The city is pressing in upon the city folk. It is squeezing the life out of them. Why should you fence in all this vacant lot and keep them out? In any case if a wooden fence were erected, those who are desperately in need of fuel and warmth would soon break it down. The dead do not need warmth!"

* * * * * * * *

It is not enough that the Osaka City Authorities reverently refer to this burial ground as a *rei-en*. It is not enough that the International Committee of Kobe and Osaka expend each year what funds are available on this place, and make reference to it in their annual report. It is not enough that one foreigner in a hundred knows of its existence. Nor is it enough that the Osaka City Authorities and the Foreign Community continue the pretence that there is a foreign cemetery in Abeno, unless the whole purpose of this place is one where we may bury and forget our dead. If that is the only purpose, it serves well enough.

If it be consecrated ground—and I am told it is—it is also public ground, a trysting place for lovers, and a place where amorous couples meet on balmy nights in spring, a place for rag-pickers and *rumpen*, a dumping ground for constructional material, and a playground for children!

I am not now protesting. I do not now complain against any who make use of it. At the present rate of burials it will not be more than half full in five hundred years. In the meantime the city of Osaka is growing and the need of the city people for open spaces is greater than ever.

The selection of this site was made fifty-six years ago. It stands on elevated ground, but owing to the erosion of rain water much of it has been washed and weathered away during the last half century. Indeed at one corner the erosion is within ten feet of the graves. It was not a wise choice. At that time there were a few who protested it was unsuitable. But that is no excuse for the lack of effort to remedy a past mistake, or to maintain in a fitting manner what space is needed as a burial ground.

In 1897 the *Kobe Chronicle* carried an article reading:

The present condition of the cemetery plot reflects very little credit on the community .... At the best it was considered to be the dreariest plot of ground that could have been selected for such a purpose .... it is still surrounded by a rotten fence of wooden palings, which are of no avail to keep out intruders who steal the shrubs and the marble crosses .... the building of a proper wall around this plot is essential.

The *Kobe Chronicle* was referring to the Ono Foreign Cemetery in Kobe, but every statement in that article applies to-day, nearly sixty years later, with equal force to the Abeno Cemetery in Osaka.

Later on a wall was built around the Ono Cemetery. Trees and shrubs were planted, which in the following decades grew to maturity and transformed what had been a dreary wind-swept sandy plot into an oasis of beauty and quietude among an area of godowns and factories.

Half a century later, the Kobe City Authorities with foresight and good taste, which is altogether too rare amongst municipal councillors, proposed to move the Ono Cemetery to the mountains behind Futatabi. They have since created at Shuhogahara a new cemetery amid a setting of outstanding beauty. And so, it comes about that there are to-day two foreign cemeteries, separated by a distance of about thirty miles, one in Kobe that would be a credit to any city in the world, and one in Osaka that cries out for attention.

In the interests of the citizens of Osaka it is not right that so much land at Abeno should continue to be reserved for a foreign cemetery, when it is obvious that at the present rate of burials, not half will be needed in the next few hundred years. One half of the present area could well be utilised by the city authorities for some better purpose than that to which it is being put to-day, and in exchange there should be sufficient funds available to build a stone wall around the remaining half—a wall

The Dreariest Graveyard -- Abeno

high enough to keep out marauders and others who would desecrate the place and steal the stone crosses, as they do to-day.

Trees and shrubs could then be planted, which in the course of a decade would transform this dismal place of neglect into something more fitting for a great city, such as Osaka.

This chapter appeared first as an article in *The Mainichi* newspaper of 31st March, 1956.

THE
NEGLECTED
CEMETERY

Hic Requiescit Corpus

I was born in England in the year that Queen Victoria was crowned, and I died in Japan sixty-seven years later in 1904, the same year that Japanese guns were pounding on the fortifications of Russian-held Port Arthur. In those days, sixty-seven was a ripe old age in Japan, both for foreigners and Japanese alike, as anyone can verify by a scrutiny of the tombstones in any of the old cemeteries.

I arrived in Kobe on New Year's morning, 1868, on the old Pacific Mail steamer "Hermann," just in time for the opening of Kobe and Osaka, which was to take place that day.*

All of us, that is to say the merchants, missionaries, shopkeepers and tradesmen, who had decided to settle in Kobe and Osaka, had to disembark at Kobe, because the sea approach to Osaka was then so treacherous that ocean-going vessels kept well away from that port.

We came ashore in sampans and landed at the site of the first Customs House, which was about two hundred yards west of the present U.S. Consulate-General. The Customs House was then on the beach,

---

*When the "Hermann" foundered some months later with a company of Japanese soldiers on board, it is said they stood at attention and went bravely to their death in the "Birkenhead" manner. That was the story, although I was never able to learn the details.

but, following reclamation schemes during the intervening years, the same site is now well inland.

Those of us who were bound for Osaka had to
make our way from Kobe in the best manner possible.

Some went by sea in small junks, but I, fearing for
the safety of my merchandise, decided to go overland
with eight pack-horses and about ten porters to
carry my stock and personal effects. I recall it took
us a whole day to get there. There were long delays
in fording and in being ferried across the many rivers
that we had to pass.

I will not speak about my trading adventures because they proved a sad disappointment. Osaka appeared to offer no prospects and most of those foreigners who opened there soon departed for Kobe,
where opportunities were greater and the amenities
of life in the Far East more enticing. I stubbornly
stayed in Osaka. Apart from myself, and a few like
me, most of those who remained were missionaries.

Most of my contemporaries in Kobe and Osaka
died long before me. The gourmets all too frequently
died of typhoid contracted through eating oysters,
a hazardous delicacy in those days. The clubmen
were mostly gouty or liverish, and many died of
cirrhosis brought on by the drinking of unusual
quantities of whisky, which, in addition to its known
qualities, then had the added attraction of being
cheap. Some people said the teetotalers met untimely
deaths by the drinking of water which in those days
was generally contaminated. If they took the pre-
caution of boiling their water, the dangers which
they escaped were still lurking in the salads and

other foods that they ate. Sewerage systems did not exist then; houses were not screened, and flies spread contagion straight from the open drains and cesspools. Conditions in the Foreign Concession in Osaka, where I lived, were slightly better than in Kobe because the native quarter was somewhat further off and our drains had a shorter distance to run before they spilled their contents into the nearby rivers of Ajigawa and Kidzugawa.

Mothers, if they escaped the dangers of childbirth, all too often lived to see their children die from diphtheria, which was a terrible scourge in those days of open drains and polluted wells. Suicides were frequent by those who had exhausted their hope or their credit; lacking modern drugs they usually cut their throats with razors. Violent deaths in the waterfront saloons were not rare occurrences.

I do not know from what cause I died. It must have been from some galloping disease, because I recall that almost to the end I could match drink for drink with anyone. Then apparently I suddenly went into some form of coma during the last weeks, days, or hours of my life, and so naturally I have no memory of what happened during that final period of my earthly existence.

At my funeral nobody spoke of the cause of my death, at least none so far as I heard. Of course only my friends attended my funeral, and they all seemed more interested in telling one another what a fine fellow I was. It must have been a case of *nil nisi bonum;* anyhow, I confess that at the time I felt highly gratified. After the funeral, and in the years that followed, I occasionally heard less flattering stories. And so it was that, not until I was dead, did I know much of the truth about myself.

Another reason why I am not aware of the cause of my death, is that it was never engraved on my tombstone. I well recall reading the inscription immediately after the stonemason set the stone in position—just a bare statement of my name, date of birth, and date of death. Perhaps that was as much as the little money which I left, would permit. Later when I compared that short inscription with some of the other and more elaborate ones, I would grin as I thought how little it really mattered. Few people ever visited the Abeno Foreign Cemetery then, and fewer since. In fact not many people in those days, or in these, knew of its existence, and still fewer of its whereabouts. Most of those who do know of it, prefer to forget it. It is not a place that anybody is proud of—neither the Japanese authorities nor the foreign community.

Ours is in fact a forgotten cemetery, although certainly during the past two years there have been more casual visitors than for many years previously. It is whispered that the increase in visitors has something to do with a prank which one of our number resorted to a couple of years ago. Some publicity was thereupon given to this place of ours. Since then, from time to time, some few foreigners and one or two Japanese have come out of mere curiosity. Of course, the vagrants, the couples of a summer night, and the playing children are always there. Some of the recent visitors came just to check whether in this enlightened century there really does exist such a place as the Abeno Foreign Cemetery—a place so reminiscent of the days of the alchemists, or of the fabulous times of the ghoulish body snatchers of a century ago.

Those who come when the mist is hanging on the ground, wander around uneasily among the graves. Then as the chill and damp of the place penetrates to their bones, they shiver and, drawing their overcoats close about them, they hasten away. They do not look back, and they do not usually return.

There are others who come when spring is in the air. They are misled and cheered to see a few buds opening on the broken shrubs within the little burial plot. Certainly they watch with some concern the children swinging on the monuments. But occasionally they return a few months later. It is then summer, and all life and hope has been dried out of this place. The few shrubs that have not been trampled underfoot by the children have shrivelled up. The visitors then wander dejectedly among the graves. They sigh, and leave. And they do not come back again.

Summer merges into autumn, and autumn into winter. The smoke and mist of this great industrial city settles about this place of the dead. Occasionally, but it is really quite a rare occurrence, two old grave-diggers come along, and dig a new grave.

There is one foreigner who has visited our little plot on many occasions. He has come at all seasons, and I have often seen him linger among the graves. Whenever he sees a new grave, I have observed that he enters the details in a notebook. He probably knows that the newly erected cross will have disappeared and the mound will have been trampled underfoot by the time he comes again.

I remember on one occasion he made an enquiry of the sexton, or rather that is what he preferred to think of him as. I heard him enquire regarding the grave of one of our number. The old man (he is not really a sexton but rather the occupant of a tiny hut near the front gate) directed him to the Abeno Saijo. He proceeded in the direction indicated. I followed him. He arrived at the great crematorium which is about half a mile distant. I watched him gazing at the great furnace doors. He held back when a Japanese hearse drew up, and he stood quietly in the rear while the first stages of the disposal of the dead took place. Then he made his way to the general office. He was obviously surprised when he was received by white-coated men. They listened courteously to his enquiry, and then apparently amazed that anybody should show any interest in the Abeno Foreign Cemetery, ushered him into a private office and produced the record of burials. Then they pressed upon him a blueprint of the burial plot with numbered graves.

The record of course showed the eight graves that were removed from the earlier foreign cemetery in Minato-ku. Those were the ones in which he seemed to be most interested.

He returned then to our graveyard, and attempted to trace out each grave. The gravestones of some are missing. Portions of others have been stolen.

Some are so weather-worn that no living person could now decipher the inscription. He lingered long at the little grave of our youngest member—a child who was given to parents in the old Osaka Foreign Concession in Kawaguchi more than eighty years ago, and who, so soon after, was taken away again.

He stood in front of my burial spot and was obviously puzzled that it was not marked by any gravestone. He did not of course know that the stone was stolen, and that it is now lying face downwards forming the bottom of a water trough in a fishmonger's store nearby. But I do not mind. Probably there is nobody who would be interested in reading my name, and nobody here or anywhere else who would now remember it, or, if they do, they will probably have tried to forget it.

I saw him wander further along the row. He stood for a long time in front of the grave of him whom we know as "The Genius." He was gazing so intently into the ground that even I shuddered and turned away. When I looked again, he had left. He has come often since then, and I suppose he will come again.

In 1899, when the Japanese authorities decided to close down the little foreign cemetery in Minato-ku, which had met the needs of the Osaka Foreign Concession since it was opened in 1868, they selected this new site in Abeno, then an outlying district of Osaka, a site which recommended itself to them because nobody could think of any better or any more profitable use to which to put it. Under the extraterritoriality treaties that were then coming to an

The Neglected Cemetery

end, they were bound to provide a cemetery, but the selection seemed to be such a poor choice that the French Consul-General, then doyen of the Consular Corps, strongly opposed it.

The *Kobe Chronicle,* also opposed the choice, and with somewhat heavy humour wrote:—

> *The foreign residents in Osaka, who are mostly missionaries, would have liked the new plot to be larger, as the selection is so delightful that there is certain to be a large demand for space.*

Most people agreed it was unsuitable. I was among them, but I did not trouble to attend the meeting of protest. I thought I had more important things to do that day, as most others did also. In any case I had no intention of dying in Japan, and certainly not of being buried in Abeno.

Therefore one day, a few years later, it came as quite a surprise to me to find myself being bumped about in an old-fashioned Japanese hearse which was being drawn through the streets of Osaka. It was really nothing more than a glorified handcart on which a rickety house-like structure was fitted. It was not, however, designed to accommodate long Western-type coffins, and so I noted with some amusement that my coffin protruded somewhat grotesquely from each end. The cart was pulled along by two old men in front, and pushed by two in the rear. In those days the roads in Osaka were even worse than most roads to-day and little better than quagmires. As I heard the old men grunting and complaining I felt sorry for them, and wished I could apologise for the load being so heavy. I was about to speak to them, but then held back for fear that my voice might startle them, or indeed stampede them. I realised that they might drop the handle bars of the cart and run away, leaving me and my coffin stranded in the streets of Osaka—a contretemps which I did not wish to bring about.

The cart, or rather the hearse, bumped along the roads, up and down in the potholes, and my coffin rattled so uncomfortably that I began to wonder when it would split open.

On arrival at the Abeno Foreign Cemetery I noted that there was plenty of room. It was a bare and miserable neighbourhood, but over the intervening fifty years the city of Osaka has grown to such a degree that it is now pushing in on all sides on our cemetery. Indeed it is now one of the few vacant places in the neighbourhood on which to dump building material, where vagrants can doze unmolested, where couples may wander in the springtime, and where children may play on tombstones the Japanese equivalent of knuckle-bones. In the absence of parks, which in most cities are reckoned as the birthright of those who will never have a private garden of their own, there is no other place for the city folk in that neighbourhood to go.

In all truth it is a miserable spot. In my particular case I don't suppose it much mattered where I was buried, but there are more worthy folk than I buried in Abeno, and I grieve to think that they rest in such a wretched place of neglect.

Each year the International Committee of Kobe and Osaka does what it can to preserve this burial

The Neglected Cemetery

place in some state of decency, but it is a forlorn and hopeless task. Each year that Committee at its annual general meeting offers its report, tells how many new shrubs have been planted, and looks for suggestions, but, as in my time over fifty years ago, it is on that day that most foreigners find they have more important business to attend. In any case it is of little consequence to them. They do not intend to die in Japan, and certainly not to be buried in Abeno!

Indifference and procrastination on the part of the authorities, whose responsibility it is to preserve this place, will not solve this problem, but in spite of them, time will surely find a solution. Eventually this, and other places also, will be maintained in a manner more befitting the dignity of a great city, such as Osaka.

The Abeno Foreign Cemetery is built on elevated ground. The sides of the site are gradually but surely receding. Parts have been dug away by previous squatters, and in places the soil has been stolen and carted away by those who are forced by circumstance to struggle harder for an existence than I ever had to. The rain too is steadily weathering away the soil, particularly in the northwest corner. One of our number, I believe it was "The Genius," has driven a stake into the ground, and as each year passes by without anything being done to correct the mistake of fifty years ago, it is said he watches with glee the weathering approach nearer and nearer to his stake. And so, it is said, eventually a time will come when the old graves and bones will be exposed, and that considerations of decency will at last force some attention being given by the authorities to the problem of the Abeno Foreign Cemetery.

* * * * * * *

The above chapter was the third in a series of articles that was published in *The Mainichi*. The first, entitled "In a Foreign Graveyard," appeared on March 19, 1955; the second, entitled "The Dreariest Cemetery—Abeno Cemetery Revisited," appeared on March 31, 1956; and the third "The Neglected Cemetery," appeared on March 29, 1957.

It was followed by an open letter in the *Asahi Evening News* of April 23, 1957, addressed to His Excellency, The Governor of Osaka-fu, Osaka, reading:

Your Excellency:

I have resided in the Kansai area for over thirty-eight years. During that time I have seen the capital city of your prefecture develop into one of the great cities of the world.

Magnificent buildings, a remarkable transportation system, wide boulevards, and other marvels of the modern age have been created, but while all this progress has been taking place, there exists in Abeno-ku a municipal responsibility which is surely a disgrace to this great city of Osaka. As you well know, when Osaka was first opened to foreign trade a plot of land was set apart, under the international treaties of that time, at Ikeyama Shinden, Kawanami, Minato-ku, later to be known as Sakigake-cho, Nishi-ku, which land was to be maintained as a cemetery for foreigners. In 1904, owing to the expansion of the growing city, the Japanese authorities proposed that the foreign cemetery be moved and by agreement with the

The Neglected Cemetery

Foreign Consular Corps of that time, they provided a new site at Asahi-machi, 3-chome, Abeno-ku, and contracted to maintain that place as a cemetery for foreigners.

The demands upon Your Excellency's time, must be many and great, but if Your Excellency were to visit that place, to which has been given the pretentious name of Gaikokujin Rei-en, you would surely find that the commitments of the past are not being carried out.

You would find that this place, which it was agreed should be maintained as a cemetery, is now primarily being used as a dump for municipal constructional material, secondly as a public playground, and lastly as a convenient spot where the foreign dead may be buried in the ground.

If it were possible to measure the degree of sacrilege that has taken place there during the past year, if it were possible to measure the extent of desecration, if it were possible to measure the amount of vandalism that has occurred in that cemetery during the past twelve months, it would probably be found to exceed that of the previous fifty years. Monuments that stood there for over half a century are now being overturned. Stone crosses erected within the last two years have not survived even that short period.

The place is not unlike those dismal cemeteries in the slum areas of European cities of more than a century ago in the days of the body snatchers. The world has moved on since those fabulous times, but, with great respect, I venture to believe that Your Excellency, after seeing this place, would agree with me when I say that this so-called Rei-en would now disgrace a backward town in darkest Africa.

Many people are deeply moved at this lamentable state of affairs, and articles have been appearing in the Press. Certainly it is a fact that unless urgent attention is given to this problem, and unless steps are taken suitably to wall in this cemetery and maintain it in a manner customary and befitting a cemetery, and a manner contemplated in the original contractual agreements, then it is certain that sacrilege, desecration and vandalism will in time wipe out this cemetery altogether and bring odious publicity to your great city.

H. S. Williams

The Neglected Cemetery

Following upon the aforementioned publicity the Osaka City Authorities ejected the squatters, removed the constructional material, and cleared up the graveyard. Since then they have announced their intention to move the cemetery to a more suitable location.

I
MET
A
SAMURAI
IN
UENO
PARK

> *Duty is weightier than a mountain,*
> *while death is lighter than a feather.*
> An old Samurai precept, and also
> from Emperor Meiji's Imperial
> Rescript, 1882

It was around 9.30 a.m. on a cold damp Sunday in February when I arrived at the Ueno Public Library. The doors open at 9 a.m. but it was already full, and a queue about seventy-five yards long was waiting outside. I should have arrived earlier, or I should have known better than to have gone there on such a bleak day, and especially at a time so close to university exams; I should have remembered that on such a day those within would be in no hurry to leave, despite the discomfort and lack of heat that so characterizes Japanese public libraries. At least the student is slightly warmer inside than the beggar outside.

I joined the queue, impatiently awaiting my turn to enter, because once the library is full, which is from early in the morning, the admission of anyone

else is restricted to one person in for every one
person who departs.

Finally around 1 p.m. my turn came, and I entered
stiff and cold. From the numbered slip of paper
which was handed to me, I noted that I was the 934th
person to be admitted that day. From previous experience I was acquainted with the passages that
lead to the newspaper and magazine reading room
below ground level. It was of course cold down there,
but remember the Japanese student pursues his
studies in surroundings of hardship that are not
usually met with by students in many other lands.

Certainly I was then inside, but I still had to go
through the usual formalities before I could refer
to the file I desired. After searching through the
card index system and discovering the index number
of the particular newspaper file to which I wished
to refer, which was the *Nagasaki Express* of 1872,
I filled in the application form and presented it at
the appropriate desk. It was received by a clerk who
was as cold as I was. He retired to a nearby room
and some few minutes later reappeared and stated
regretfully that the required newspaper file was not
listed. I assured him that I had previously referred
to it, and had in fact once been permitted entry to
the basements below, and knew exactly where it was
to be found. After some further minutes wait, and
my renewed assurances that I could point to the
exact shelf in the dungeons below where it was to
be found, I was kindly invited to enter behind the
counter and to accompany the messenger below.
Through winding passageways, past fireproof doors,

long since out of alignment and no longer fireproof, down two flights of steps to basements deeper down, past racks of old newspaper files of the last century, mostly dust-encrusted and falling into disrepair, I made my way to the exact shelf. Many bound volumes, representing the only remaining copies in Japan of some very early foreign newspapers, were in such a state of disrepair that they had been set aside years ago for rebinding. Anywhere else they would be treasured as valuable rarities, but they still remain there in the dungeons in careless heaps, accumulating dust and awaiting the time when there will be sufficient funds available for the work of rebinding to proceed. In comparison with the basement of any bank or mercantile building it was more like a neglected tenement quarter—so little money is available in Japan for those seeking learning, so much is spent on those in pursuit of wealth and trade. Finally after some four hours of waiting and effort I was free to begin my reading. The next few hours passed quickly, but it became steadily colder. The single brazier that was intended to heat a basement room about the size of a small townhall had long since burnt out. The warmth from human bodies was no longer able to cope with the falling temperature of nighttime; gradually my feet became stiff with the cold and my fingers no longer responded to my efforts to write. Such are the discomforts among which Japanese students commonly pursue their studies. A Japanese Rockefeller has yet to appear in the money world who would rather ransom students from discomfort than set up a geisha in luxury. It was 8.30 p.m. Closing time was not until 9 p.m. but the cold was more than I could endure. After going through the necessary procedure of returning the volume and securing corresponding seals on the piece of entrance paper, without which I could not have left the building, I was free to depart.

The approach to the Public Library through Ueno Park in the daytime is not difficult, but at night a first-comer might easily lose his way. It was pitch dark and cold outside. A heavy mist blanketed the park. At the best of times the lighting is quite inadequate. I was confident I knew the way, but my thoughts were in the past. Soon I was off the trail and wandering along unlighted paths, without sense of direction. I was lost. From time to time I came upon gleams of light coming from holes in the ground; I sensed I was wandering among the dugouts and shelters of the homeless ones of Tokyo, who since the air raids have congregated in the back corners of Ueno Park—an unsavory and evil smelling place by day. Perhaps the rain had cleansed it. It smelt sweet enough that night, and the beams of light from the fires in the dugouts below ground stabbed the darkness with reassuring light as I made my way onwards.

How ironical that this place, once the burial grounds of the proud Tokugawa family—then the most powerful people in the land—should now be taken over by the homeless and the lost. I was familiar with this place in the days of its splendour, but in September, 1945, when I returned to Japan immediately following the surrender, it was a mass of ruins. The tombs of the Tokugawas had been burnt out. It was strictly *off limits*, but in those days I knew a corner where I could easily scale the wall, and, despite the risk of penalties, I often used to climb that wall so that I could once again walk in the hallowed ground of the Tokugawa family. I used to sit among the shadows and gaze at the creepers which were beginning to climb across the granite paths and up and around the tombs of *Shoguns*. I imagine I could still climb that wall to-day; I often have the craving to do so, and once again to look inside. But I now fear the Japanese police more than I feared the American MP's then.

Ueno Park has been cleaned up to some extent since 1945. It was then dotted with temporary graves of the air-raid dead. It served even more then than now as a place of refuge for the homeless. A score or more of corpses were picked up by the police each morning. In those days the living mingled desperately with the dead. It was a place of filth and hopelessness. But I was carrying a revolver then, and I was not afraid. With the passing of the years it has become almost a permanent place of abode for the homeless and for the underworld elements who seek to hide themselves among those who are without hope. And so it was that on that cold night in February, I stumbled on in that unsavoury corner of Ueno Park, with furtive shadows flitting past me. I was lost in this park of the lost. And I was afraid. I decided that my safest course was to continue rather than to seek to retrace my steps. Should I have turned back anyone following me would then have known I was lost and that I was afraid. Suddenly through the mist I came upon a long heap of large stones, apparently piled up from some broken-down wall. When I turned a corner of that heap there *he* was standing about fifty paces away. He was silhouetted against a beam of light escaping from below ground. I could plainly see his two swords. I was not brave. I was in fear and panic when I saw his hand go to his sword hilt. He was on guard. He was about to draw his sword and to attack me. I dared not advance. I was too afraid to retreat. Then suddenly his attitude changed to one of welcome, at least I sensed that from the tone of his voice. His conversation had taken on a tone of affection. He was alluding to my long absence, and he was begging me to enter his dwelling place, but he referred to it as *my* home.

A damp snowfall had set in, and the only thing of cheer in that place was the beam of light from his cavern underground.

Perhaps it was the fear of refusing his invitation, perhaps it was because of the earnestness of his entreaty that I should enter, perhaps it was the reaction to my previous panic—I do not know—but I felt grateful for his offer of shelter. I gladly bent my body double as I crept through the opening into his underground cavern. It was bright and cheerful inside, from the crackling wood fire at the far end, although perhaps a trifle damp. The shadows from the dancing flames floated up and down the rough walls and the smoke went up a crude chimney through the roof.

I Met a Samurai in Ueno Park

The shelter had been formed by removing some of the stones of the heap, digging out part of the ground and laying a rough roof of old iron, then some torn sacking and scraps of canvas on top, all held in place by rocks, which caused the roof to sag alarmingly. It was about eight feet long and about four feet wide. He indicated a box on which I should sit. It was low but the roof also was low. I then noted with some alarm that my escape had been cut off by my host, who sat in the entrance.

His hair was long and unkempt. It was tied up in a fashion with string and gave the impression, from the rear at least, of the old-fashioned *chommage* or feudal style. He was wearing a tattered cotton garment beneath which was some padded clothing as protection against the cold. All these were tied at the waist with a piece of straw rope from which were suspended his two "swords"—one a villainous look-ing iron spike from some old iron fence, the other a short length of stout bamboo. A knight in rags and tatters, but with it all the mien and manners of an aristocrat, the speech of a *kabuki* actor, and the grace of a court chamberlain.

He expressed pleasure at my "return," and enquired of my health. Then without waiting for any reply, he apologised for not having a banquet prepared. He begged me to partake of some warm *sake*—rice wine—whereupon he gracefully poured out some stale cold tea into a cracked cup. All the while he kept up a flow of conversation, only half of which I understood. The manner of his speech was unfamiliar, but seemed to be exceedingly deferential and in old idioms. He addressed me by name, and yet I could not recognise the name.

He lapsed into silence, then suddenly broke into a flow of dramatic speech. He crept through the entrance, then drawing his "sword" he stamped about outside as if in the frenzy of a sword fight. I had the impression that he was playing the part of Benkei, a national hero of feudal days. Then his mood changed, he cautioned me to remain silent. He said that we were approaching the Hakone barrier which, as you know, in feudal days guarded one of the approaches to Yedo. He said we were in great peril, and that I should leave him to talk to the guards. Again he started upon a long and dramatic recital which reminded me of something I had heard before in a *kabuki* drama. It went on maybe for ten minutes or more, until he noticed that some children, apparently from some nearby shelter, had collected at the entrance and were laughing at the strange scene within his hovel. He drew his "sword" and sprang to his feet. I heard the children's laughter as they ran down the road, and I heard him too as he stamped about outside. Then he re-entered, showed me his "sword" and said he had killed three men. He sat down, picked up a scrap of old paper from the floor and with care and great ceremony commenced cleaning the blood from off the blade, or rather that was what he said he was doing. Then he became morose and began to shout terrible imprecations. I grew alarmed because I knew not to whom they were directed. Again his mood changed when a ragpicker came to the entrance—at least that was what I judged the visitor to be from the straw bag suspended from his shoulder. With elaborate politeness my host expressed apologies for being unable to receive him. After the ragpicker had departed he turned to me and remarked that there are times when visitors are not welcome. A moment later he ripped open the seam of his garment and began to crack some of the lice sheltering there.

A tear fell as he told me of how my favourite pine tree had withered away despite every attention he had given it. He wept as he pointed to an old broomstick in the corner of his hovel and related that the cherry tree which my father had planted when I was born had failed to bloom each spring since I had left. He fondly handled an old can while he told me that he had safeguarded all my possessions during my absence in Yedo. Then, when he saw me extract a bank note from my pocket and begin to wrap it in a piece of white paper torn from my notebook, he averted his gaze to spare me the embarassment which he knew I was suffering. He received my gift reluctantly but with grace and renewed assurances that after my departure he would guard my possessions with his life. He accompanied me outside and was weeping as we parted.

It was cold and cheerless outside his dug-out. The mist was heavier and it was still snowing. I felt lonely and sad as I bid him good-bye. He again entreated me to take good care of myself and to return again before long.

I hurried off in the direction where I hoped Ueno Station might be.

I Met a Samurai in Ueno Park

When I looked back I saw his figure silhouetted against the beam of light that came from underground. His two "swords" could be plainly seen as he stood guarding the entrance. Perhaps I also dropped a tear whilst I pondered: Was he some poor demented *kabuki* actor of bygone days? Was he some unfortunate who mentally was living on a plane of his own, amid all the grandeur and pride of the past?

* * * * * * *

On arrival back at my hotel I found three fleas in my underclothing, and two lice walking across the neck of my overcoat. I had a hot bath—a very hot bath—and soon fell into a deep slumber with agreeable thoughts of the charm and grace of the courtesies of yesteryears.

PUMPKIN VALLEY

> *O'er all there hung a shadow and a fear;*
> *A sense of mystery the spirit daunted,*
> *And said as plain as whisper in the ear,*
> *The place is haunted.*
>
> THOMAS HOOD

Within a hundred miles of the city of Osaka, in Japan, there is a place known as Kabocha-dani or Pumpkin Valley, although actually pumpkins have not been grown in that valley for many many years. It is still a tiny valley in the uplands, far removed from any highway or railway line. The nearest village is a long way off, down valleys and over ranges. On the other side of the mountain through the pass there is a Buddhist temple—very old and one of the Thirty-three Temples of Kwannon, that is to say one of thirty-three places dedicated to the Compassionate Goddess of Mercy, which came to form a pilgrim circuit.

Although Pumpkin Valley is still classified in the *chiku-jimusho*—or county office—as rice field land, it is actually a wilderness of weeds, bamboo grass and wild honeysuckle, and has not been cultivated for several hundred years.

No taxes are collected on the land, and there is in fact no record now as to who last owned it. No one has ever come forward to claim the land, and it is unlikely that anybody would want to own it.

The folk from the nearest villages never go into

328

the valley to gather firewood, nor do the charcoal-burners enter it. Some people may say that there is no brushwood worth gathering there, and some may say that the soil is sour and not fit to cultivate. But the fact is the valley is haunted.

The children say there are goblins and demons in the valley. The youths and girls say there are ghosts, and their parents say it is the abode of malignant spirits.

If the ground really is sour these days, it is nevertheless a fact it was fresh and fertile some centuries ago in the days when the great city of Osaka was known as Naniwa. In those days the largest and finest pumpkins ever eaten were grown in that valley.

The farmer who grew them was never seen. His wants were apparently so few that he did not even trouble to transport the pumpkins to the towns or to the great cities where they would have commanded the best price. He used to leave them on a rough bamboo stand by the roadside, at a point where the trail from the valley joined a country road. Actually that road was little more than a pathway, and was mainly frequented by the priests and pilgrims passing to and from the Buddhist temple on the other side of the mountain.

The passers-by would help themselves to what they required and would then drop a few *mon*—copper cash—into the wooden tray, or if they preferred to pay in kind rather than in cash, as was generally the case, they might leave a small quantity of barley, or millet or a small *mochi*—a rice cake.

From time to time the supply of pumpkins was

replenished, but none ever saw the farmer who grew them. It was imagined that being too busy during the day cultivating the soil or attending to his wants, he could not spare the daylight hours to make the journey, and so brought the pumpkins there after nightfall.

Nobody cared to visit the valley where the pumpkins grew. To do so, it would have been necessary to pass over the intervening foothills that were deemed unlucky ground.

One day, however, a young priest bound for the Kwannon temple, found himself headed for the wrong valley and although he was warned by the villagers not to pass further in that direction, he replied that he had no fear of evil spirits. Confident of his ability to cope with any powers of evil, he decided to go forward and later to cross the mountain to the temple on the other side of the range.

Ultimately he came to the pumpkin patch. At the far end stood a crude hut—apparently the abode of the farmer.

The door was ajar and he could see the farmer in his homespun clothes, crouched over the *hibachi*— or charcoal brazier. His head was completely hidden from view by the top of his farming coat that had been drawn up almost over his head, evidently to keep out the cold. He seemed to be warming his hands over the brazier, although only his back could be seen from the doorway of the hut.

A teakettle was singing over a few glowing charcoals, and the aroma of fragrant tea floated towards the door.

The priest knocked several times, but the old man did not stir. "*Konnichi-wa*—Good-day,—Excuse my troubling you, may I rest here a little while?" the priest called out. Still the old man made no response. Evidently he was quite deaf. The priest thereupon entered the hut and touched him gently on the shoulder. To his horror the crouched figure toppled over and rolled along the floor. It was without hands, without feet and without a face! It seemed to be just like a monstrous pumpkin dressed in rough home-spun clothes.

Shrieking with terror the priest rushed from the hut. Eventually, possibly some days later, he arrived at the temple over the range, exhausted and very ill. There he told his story.

That is all that is known about Kabocha-dani or Pumpkin Valley.

In conclusion, however, it might be mentioned that the young priest never recovered his health. Shortly afterwards, so it is said, he showed signs of leprosy which made rapid and horrible progress.

The acolytes when telling the story used to say—somewhat irreverently—that when the unfortunate priest died he resembled, in more ways than one, a decayed pumpkin more than a human being.

spun clothes.

There he told his story.

Pumpkin Valley.

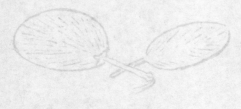

ABOUT THE AUTHOR

H. S. Williams was born in Melbourne, Australia, in 1898. He was headed for a scientific career; at first as a junior analyst in the Commonwealth Laboratory of Australia, then as a medical student at the Melbourne University. He was already seriously interested in the Japanese language and history as a hobby, and at the end of his third year in medicine he came to Japan on a holiday.

On arrival in Japan, an advertisement in the former *Japan Advertiser* caught his attention, and by replying to it he hoped to have the opportunity of seeing inside one of the *hongs* in Japan of which he had read so much. He later went for an interview, confident in the belief that he would not be engaged. To his great dismay he found that he was hired as an assistant in the old Scottish *hong* of Findlay Richardson & Co. Ltd. He thereupon temporarily postponed his return to Australia, but eventually decided to give up his career and make his future in Japan.

Later Williams became managing director of the silk firm of Cooper Findlay & Co. Ltd.

In 1941 he left Japan and enlisted in the Australian Army. He attained the rank of major and saw service in Africa, the Pacific, and Burma. He arrived back in Japan a few weeks after the surrender as a member of the Occupation Forces, and remained in the Australian Army in Japan until 1949 when he resumed his business career.

H. S. Williams is now Managing Director of A. Cameron & Co., Ltd. and sole Trustee of the famous James Estate at Shioya, near Kobe.

In 1953 he commenced writing historical articles for various publications abroad, and for *The Mainichi* newspaper in a series entitled "Shades of the Past," out of which writings this book was born.

CHRONOLOGICAL TABLE
INCIDENTAL TO ARTICLES
IN THIS BOOK

1549	St. Francis Xavier lands in Japan.
1600	Will Adams arrived in Japan, as pilot on Dutch ship "de Liefde."
1609	Dutch commenced to trade with Japan.
1613	Capt. John Saris arrived in Japan on "Clove" and opened English East India Trading post at Hirado.
1614	Proclamation issued suppressing Christianity.
1622	Great martyrdom of Christians at Nagasaki.
1623	Richard Cocks closed English trading post and left Japan.
1636	Japanese forbidden to go abroad.
1637	Shogun Iyemitsu decides to close Japan to Western World.
1638	Shimabara rebellion and massacre of Christians. Seclusion policy proclaimed in Japan.
1641	Dutch trading post confined to Deshima.
1690	Dr. Engelbert Kaempfer arrived at Deshima.
July 1853	Commodore Perry's black ships arrived in Yedo Bay.
Feb/Mar. 1854	Commodore Perry returned and signed a treaty of peace and amity with Japan.
Oct. 1854	British signed similar treaties.
Aug. 1856	Townsend Harris first U.S. Consul General landed at Shimoda.
July 1858	Townsend Harris signed treaty of amity and commerce with Japan.

Chronology

July 1858	Lord Elgin arrived in Japan.
Aug. 1858	Anglo-Japanese treaty of commerce and friendship signed.
June 1859	Rutherford Alcock arrived as Britain's first Minister to Japan.
1 July 1859	Yokohama, Nagasaki and Hakodate opened to foreign trade.
July 1861	Japanese *ronin* attack British Legation in Yedo.
25 Dec. 1867	First burials in Ono Foreign Cemetery in Kobe.
1 Jan. 1868	Hyogo and Osaka opened.
1868	Restoration of the Emperor and overthrow of Shogunate.
Jan. 1868	Admiral Bell and 11 U.S. Navy men drowned at Osaka.
Jan. 1868	Osaka Castle burnt.
4 Feb. 1868	Bizen soldiers fire on Kobe Foreign Settlement.
8 Mar. 1868	Eleven French naval men massacred at Sakai.
16 Mar. 1868	Eleven Japanese executed at Sakai.
Nov. 1868	The Emperor left Kyoto and entered Yedo, which thereafter became known as Tokyo—the eastern capital.
1 Jan. 1869	Tokyo opened to foreign trade.
3 Sept. 1870	Kobe Regatta and Athletic Club founded.
19 Aug. 1875	Agreement signed at Tokyo with Foreign Powers regarding public grounds of Kobe Foreign Settlement.
1881	The *Kimigayo*—national anthem—played for first time.
1885	Pierre Loti came to Nagasaki.
1899	Extraterritoriality came to an end.
1952	Transfer of earliest foreign cemetery in Kobe from Ono to Shuhogahara, behind Futatabi.
1955	Alienation of portion of Recreation Ground of former Kobe Foreign Settlement.

GLOSSARY
AND
BIOGRAPHICAL NOTES

A

Adams, Will English navigator. Arrived in Japan in 1600. Was later known as *Anjin Sama* (pilot). Married a Japanese lady. Died in Japan in 1620 at age of about 56 years.

Alcock, Sir Rutherford (1809–1897) Arrived in Japan as first British Consul-General. Appointed Minister in 1859. In 1865 was transferred to Pekin and succeeded by Sir Harry Parkes.

Amah Maid servant in a foreign household.

B

Banto Chief clerk, buyer, intermediary, or factor in a mercantile house.

Banzai Literally " ten thousand years." An expression of great emotion by the Japanese equivalent to "Hurrah" or in *Dai Nippon Banzai* to "Long Live Great Japan."

Bluff That section of Yokohama, overlooking the town and harbour, where most foreigners built their homes, when they ceased residing within the Concession.

Bon See *O-bon*.

Boy-san An office boy, a bartender, or a waiter in a restaurant. Stewards on board Japanese vessels resent being called *boy-san*.

Brinkley, Capt. F. Came to Japan as an instructor in gunnery to Japanese Naval Department. Later became editor of *The Japan Mail*. Author of various books on Japanese subjects. Died in 1912.

Bu A silver coin in circulation when Japan was opened to foreign trade in 1859, later equivalent to about ¼ yen. Called by foreigners *boo*.

Bund The road along the waterfront in an oriental port.

Glossary

C

Chamberlain, Basil Hall (1850–1935) Arrived in Japan in 1873 and became a teacher at the Imperial Naval School. Later became professor of Japanese philology at Tokyo Imperial University. Wrote many important books on Japanese subjects, the best known of which is *Things Japanese*. Left Japan in 1905 owing to ill health and retired to Geneva.

Cocks, Richard Chief of factory of English East India Company at Hirado from 1613 until it closed in 1621.

Compradore Senior Chinese in a foreign mercantile house or bank.

Concession See Settlement.

D

Daimyo Literally "great name." A term applied to territorial nobles, the annual income from whose lands was assessed at not less than ten thousand *koku* of rice (about 50,000 bushels).

E

Engawa Verandah of a Japanese house.

F

Foreigner The meaning of the word in Japan is a non-Japanese, but it is often used in English conversation in the sense of a Westerner.

G

Geisha Literally a "person of talents." A professional Japanese female entertainer called upon at parties and banquets to entertain the guests. They undergo rigorous training and are accomplished dancers and singers. Most of them have patrons. Lower class geisha are often little different from prostitutes.

Godown A warehouse.

H

Hakama Formal divided skirt, formerly worn by samurai.

Haori Japanese-style coat.

Hara-kiri Suicide by disembowelment. There were two forms, one voluntary, the other compulsory, the latter being imposed as a penalty for certain offences. The Japanese rarely use this word, preferring the more genteel Chinese form of the word: *Seppuku*.

338

Glossary

Harris, Townsend (1804–1875) Arrived at Shimoda 21 Aug., 1856, as first U.S. Consul-General in Japan. Appointed Minister in 1859. Resigned in 1861.

Hatoba Wharf or quay.

Hearn, Lafcadio (1850–1904) Arrived in Japan in 1890. Had various teaching appointments. Married a Japanese lady in 1891 and became a Japanese subject—Koizumi Yakumo—in 1895.

Hepburn, Dr. J. C. American physician and missionary in Japan 1859–92. Compiler of English-Japanese Dictionary, Dictionary of Bible (in Japanese) etc.

Hiogo Previously the commonly accepted Romanised form of spelling for Hyogo.

Hirado An island near the northwest coast of Kyushu where the Dutch and English trading posts were established in the 17th century.

Hong Foreign trading firm, a word rarely used nowadays in Japan.

I

Iyemitsu (1603–1651) The third Tokugawa *Shogun*. He closed the country, forbade the building of ships for oversea voyages, and attempted to stamp out Christianity. He was buried at Nikko.

Iyeyasu (1542–1616) Founder of the line of Tokugawa rulers. He became *Shogun* in 1603. He was buried at Nikko.

J

James, O. B. E., Ernest William Was born in Kobe in 1889 of English parents, and died in 1952. His father was a master mariner and an Inland Sea pilot. Mr. E. W. James was Chairman of Directors of A. Cameron & Co., Ltd., and commenced the construction of his famous estate in Shioya, near Kobe, in 1928.

Jinrikisha Literally man-power-vehicle, contracted to *rikisha*, and later Anglicised to ricksha or rickshaw.

K

Kabuki Japanese drama, generally classical or historical, where the female parts are taken by male actors.

Kaempfer, Engelbert (1651–1716) German traveller and physician. Arrived in Japan in Sept., 1690. Left in 1693. His *History of Japan* was published after his death.

Glossary

Kago A basket, slung on a pole and carried by two men, in which the commonalty travelled. In the early days, foreigners preferred *kago* to palanquins, because they were more airy. They went out of fashion, except on mountain paths, when rikisha were introduced.

Kansai (Kwansai) Literally "west of the barrier." General term applied before Restoration in 1868 to country west of the guardhouse or barrier on the Hakone Pass.

Kanto (or Kwanto) Literally "east of the barrier." General term applied before Restoration in 1868 to country east of the guardhouse or barrier on the Hakone Pass.

Kencho Prefectural office.

Kitano-cho That high section of Kobe which became the residential quarter for the elite of the *taipans*, when they ceased residing within the Concession.

Koban Large flat oval-shaped gold coins issued by various *daimyo* and other authorities in feudal days.

K. R. & A. C. Kobe Regatta & Athletic Club.

L

Loti, Pierre (1850–1923) Penname of L. M. Julien Viaud. French author. Wrote *Madame Chrysantheme* and others.

M

Mason, W. B. Came to Japan in 1875 and for over 25 years was in the service of the Japanese Government in Departments of Communications and Education. Collaborated with B. H. Chamberlain in producing *Murray's Handbook for Japan*. Killed in earthquake 1 Sept., 1923.

Meiji Era The era of the reign of Emperor Meiji (1868–1912).

Mexican Dollar Japan had no currency of a well-determined value when trade was opened in 1859, and so the foreign traders brought in Mexican $ which passed as currency in the Foreign Settlements. A reputable silver yen, also referred to as a $, of 416 grains and 900 fineness was minted in 1879.

Mikado Term once used in foreign circles to designate the sovereign of Japan. In pre-war years the Japanese normally used the expression *Tenno Heika* (Divine Emperor) when referring to their Emperor. Nowadays *Tenno* often suffices.

Mitford, A. B. (Later Lord Redesdale) 1837–1916. Attaché in Japan 1866–70.

MITI Post-war Ministry of International Trade & Industry.

Glossary

N

Nippon Same as Nihon, meaning Japan.

Norimono See palanquin.

O

Obi Ornamental sash worn by women with bow at back. When the bow was tied in the front it was the mark of a professional prostitute in the old days.

O-bon Buddhist festival in July when the ancestral souls or spirits of the dead are said to return to earth for three days.

Oiran In feudal days a high class prostitute, generally depicted with many large bamboo hairpins in her hair.

P

Palanquin A curtained box-like conveyance, suspended on a pole and carried by four men, in which a person rode in a sitting or semi-recumbent position. Used by higher classes. In Japanese—*norimono*.

Parkes, Sir Harry (1828–1885) Appointed British minister to Japan in 1865, which post he held for 18 years.

R

Rickshaw (Rikisha) See jinrikisha.

Ronin Literally "wave-men," a term applied to samurai who were not attached to any clan—one who had given up or had been dismissed from the service of his feudal master, and for the time being was his own master.

S

Sake An alcoholic beverage obtained by fermenting rice. Generally served after warming to about forty-three degrees centigrade.

Samurai A member of the military class, entitled to wear two swords, a longer and shorter one, the latter like an over-sized dirk.

Saris, John English merchant and sea captain who made first voyage to Japan (1612) on behalf of English East India Company and obtained permission for English to settle and trade in Japan.

Satow, E. M. (1843–1929) Attaché and later (1895) British Minister to Japan.

Sen One hundredth part of a yen.

Glossary

Settlement That section of land, generally waste land outside the Japanese town, that was originally set aside as the place of trade and residence for foreigners.

Shogun Literally "the general commanding an island." Term applied to the administrative or *de facto* rulers of Japan in feudal days, as distinguished from the sovereigns who were kept in seclusion in Kyoto. Also known as Taikun (Tycoon).

Shogunate The government of the Shogun.

Siebold, Dr. Philipp Franz von (1796–1866) Arrived in Nagasaki in 1823 as physician attached to Dutch East India Company. Banished from Japan in 1830 for making a map of Japan. Returned in 1860 on a semi-official mission.

T

Taipan A word borrowed from early trading days in China, meaning the manager or "big boss," as distinct from assistants, in foreign firms.

Tatami Straw floor mats, 3′×6′, found in houses, temples and other Japanese-style buildings. Two such mats represent the unit of area known as a *tsubo*.

Teahouse The word is used to denote the modest little rest-houses which are situated alongside country roads, and also the elaborate Japanese-styled restaurants in the cities, which also serve as places of entertainment, to which *geisha* may be called.

Thunberg, Charles Peter (1743–1828) Swedish physician, naturalist and traveller, appointed physician to Dutch East India Company at Deshima.

Tokaido The great highway of Eastern Japan from Yedo (Tokyo) to Kyoto.

Tokio Previously the commonly accepted Romanised form of spelling for Tokyo.

Tokugawa The family and line of Shoguns founded by Tokugawa Iyeyasu in 1603 and which controlled Japan for a period of about 250 years.

Torji Gateway to a Shinto shrine.

Townsend Harris See Harris.

Trade Dollar In 1875 the Japanese government commenced minting a silver coin stamped "Trade Dollar 420 grains 900 fine" which it was intended should take the place of the Mexican Dollar. In 1879 it was substituted by a new Silver Yen of 416 grains and 900 fineness.

Tsubo Unit of area, about 36 sq. feet, equivalent in area to two *tatami* (Japanese mats).

342

Glossary

V

Viaud, Julien See Loti.

Y

Yashiki Superior type of Japanese residence.

Yedo Old name for Tokyo; capital of Tokugawa Government.

Yen Japanese monetary unit. Originally equivalent to 50 U.S. cents at par. In pre-war 1941 the official rate of exchange was about 22 ¢ but the unofficial and open market rate was much lower. In 1958 the value of the yen is a little more than ¼ ¢, or 360 yen to US $.

Yoshiwara Licensed brothel quarter in Tokyo, but applied loosely by foreigners to any licensed quarter. Now abolished by law, April, 1958.

INDEX

Index

Index

Index

348

Index

Mexican dollars, 19, 128, 154
Miller murder case, 124
Minatogawa, 70, 187
Missionaries, 138, 306
MITI, 183
Mitsui Drapery Store, 96, 301
Moon Temple, 194
Morrison, G.E., 239
Morrison Library, 238
Murdoch, James, 165

Nagasaki 27, 204, 227; Foreign Settlement, 35; opened to foreign
  trade, 27; selection of site for Settlement, 19
Newspapers: *Hiogo News*, 72; *Hiogo & Osaka Herald*, 72; *Japan
  Herald*, 163; *Tokio Times*, 117
Nippon Yusen Kaisha, 39, 71, 171
" Number Nine," Yokohama, 41

Occupation personnel, 141
Olcott, H.S. 146
Ono Foreign Cemetery, 66, 186, 304
Oriental Bank Corporation, 172, 206
Osaka, 92; castle, 95, 301; Foreign Concession, 300; opened to
  foreign trade, 92, 300

Pacific Mail S.S. Co., 73, 305
P. & O.S.N. Co., 23, 110, 115, 210
Parbury Henty & Co., Ltd., 217
Parkes, Sir Harry, 88, 169, 173, 188, 209
Perry, Commodore, 64, 143; at Kurihama, 135
Peters, 241
Prisoners of war, Allied, 25, 167, 214
Prop., Charlie, 230
Prostitutes, 82, 228

Railways, 77, 105, 106, 112, 154, 170
Raw cotton exported from Japan, 32
Rickshaws, 96, 112, 195
Rivers in Kansai area, 97, 185
Rumpen (lumpen), 89
Russians in Japan, 35
Russian Far Eastern Fleet, 212
Russo-Japanese War, 35, 204

349

Index

Index

Other TUT BOOKS available:

TWO CENTURIES OF COSTUME IN AMERICA
by *Alice Morse Earle*

TYPHOON! TYPHOON! An Illustrated Haiku Sequence by *Lucile M. Bogue*

UNBEATEN TRACKS IN JAPAN: An Account of Travels in the Interior Including Visits to the Aborigines of Yezo and the Shrine of Nikko *by Isabella L. Bird*

ZILCH! The Marine Corps' Most Guarded Secret by *Roy Delgado*

Please order from your bookstore or write directly to:

CHARLES E. TUTTLE CO., INC.
Suido 1-chome, 2–6, Bunkyo-ku, Tokyo 112

or:

CHARLES E. TUTTLE CO., INC.
Rutland, Vermont 05701 U.S.A.